Thomas Francis Meagher and
the Irish Brigade in the Civil War

Thomas Francis Meagher and the Irish Brigade in the Civil War

DANIEL M. CALLAGHAN

McFarland & Company, Inc., Publishers
Jefferson, North Carolina, and London

The present work is a reprint of the illustrated case bound edition of Thomas Francis Meagher and the Irish Brigade in the Civil War, *first published in 2006 by McFarland.*

LIBRARY OF CONGRESS CATALOGUING-IN-PUBLICATION DATA

Callaghan, Daniel M., 1960–
Thomas Francis Meagher and the Irish Brigade in the Civil War / Daniel M. Callaghan.
      p.   cm.
Includes bibliographical references and index.

ISBN 978-0-7864-6606-1
softcover : 50# alkaline paper ∞

1. United States. Army of the Potomac. Irish Brigade.   2. United States — History — Civil War, 1861–1865 — Regimental histories.   3. United States — History — Civil War, 1861–1865 — Participation, Irish American.   4. United States — History — Civil War, 1861–1865 — Campaigns.   5. Meagher, Thomas Francis, 1823–1867.   6. Generals — United States — Biography.   7. United States. Army — Biography.   8. Irish American soldiers — History —19th century.   I. Title.
E493.5.I683C35   2011   973.7'4470899162 2 22   2006015603

BRITISH LIBRARY CATALOGUING DATA ARE AVAILABLE

© 2006 Daniel M. Callaghan. All rights reserved

No part of this book may be reproduced or transmitted in any form or by any means, electronic or mechanical, including photocopying or recording, or by any information storage and retrieval system, without permission in writing from the publisher.

On the front cover: Meagher and members of Co. K, 69th New York State Militia, the "Irish Zouaves," 1861 (collection of Michael J McAfee).

Manufactured in the United States of America

McFarland & Company, Inc., Publishers
Box 611, Jefferson, North Carolina 28640
www.mcfarlandpub.com

For Gerard and Mary. We grew up through our own Civil War.

For Billy and Margaret, and the grandchildren they never saw.

For Aisling, Shannon and DW — *God's Gifts*

Acknowledgments

I would like to express my gratitude to all the historians and enthusiasts who have contributed to keeping the memory of the Irish Brigade alive. Many will have forgotten more about the brigade than I will ever know.

I would like to thank the staff at a number of libraries who were ever helpful at various points when I was researching this work, including the National Library of Ireland, Dublin; Birkbeck College, University of London; and the Ministry of Defence Library, London.

Thanks to Jan for proofreading, again; and to Celia for the wonderful maps in the shortest possible time.

Thanks especially to my wife, Susan, after having endured the education policies of the Conservative Party for five years only to discover the rivers of the Civil War flowing through our living room.

Daniel Callaghan
May 2006

Table of Contents

Acknowledgments vii
Preface 1

1. Saved by Sumter 7
2. "You Are All Green Alike" 18
3. The Fighting 69th 27
4. Standing by the Union 35
5. Commissioning a Brigade 43
6. Frolics and Frustrations 54
7. Fort Monroe to Fair Oaks 61
8. "Column of Generous Friends" 73
9. To Malvern Hill 79
10. Rebels Resurgent 88
11. "The Longest Saddest Day" 97
12. To Fredericksburg 107
13. Visions of Hell 117
14. "Our Noble Little Brigade Has Almost Disappeared" 131
15. A Sideshow of the Big Show 147
16. Gettysburg — The "Terifick Battle" 153
17. Fire in the Rear 163
18. "What There Is Left of It" 171

Notes 181
Bibliography 197
Index 201

Preface

"This is the West, Sir. When the legend becomes fact, print the legend."
—*The Man Who Shot Liberty Valance*[1]

Only Jesus Christ and Shakespeare have had more books written about them than Abraham Lincoln. The number of volumes on the conflagration with which Lincoln will forever be associated, the American Civil War, runs at something over 50,000 and rising. The angles seem inexhaustible. Even omitting other areas such as economic, political or social studies, each year the military history of the war alone brings forth new general histories, or studies of individual campaigns, or individual battles, or individual incidents within battles, or of the individuals themselves. Within this thicket of genres and subgenres can be found the story of the individual unit, such as the regiment or the brigade. Given the polyglot nature of the Civil War armies, many of these stories take on a strongly ethnic dimension. Perhaps the most famous of these units, with the strongest ethnic dimension, was the Irish Brigade. Often referred to as Meagher's Irish Brigade, after its first commander, Thomas Francis Meagher, the brigade was part of the Army of the Potomac.

The Irish Brigade was formed in late 1861 and consisted of a number of regiments. Three regiments that were part of the brigade throughout its existence were recruited in New York — the 63rd, the 69th and the 88th New York State Volunteers. These were later joined by the 28th Massachusetts and the 116th Pennsylvania. These regiments, the New York and Massachusetts ones in particular, were primarily composed of first- or second-generation Irish, less so with the 116th Pennsylvania. The 29th Massachusetts, a thoroughly American affair, also served briefly with the brigade during the summer of 1862, as did some other New York regiments toward the end of the war.

The Irish Brigade is perhaps more fortunate than most in the amount of firsthand material that has been published describing its existence. The three most influential accounts were written by three of the brigade's veterans. David Powers Conyngham, who was a staff officer during 1863, published his general account of the brigade in 1867.[2] Father William Corby, chaplain of the 88th New York, published his *Memoirs of Chaplain Life* in 1893,[3] while the commander of the 116th Pennsylvania, Lieutenant Colonel St. Clair Mulholland, published his account of that regiment in 1903.⁴ These remain the "standard" general works on the brigade, and all modern accounts inevitably draw heavily on their wealth of detail and anecdote.⁵ Since then, other individual accounts have also surfaced. These include the letters of Color Sergeant Peter Walsh of the 28th Massachusetts, published in 1986, and more recently, the memoirs of Private William McCarter of the 116th Pennsylvania, published in 1996.⁶

As with other examples of the genre, it is hard to find a critical account of any given unit. That is not why they were written. The earlier accounts, written in the aftermath of the war, are, understandably, heroic and congratulatory with little hint of any controversy. While the later or current accounts may take a slightly more balanced view, they still remain, by and large, almost entirely laudatory, concentrating on what William Fox described as the Irish Brigade's "unusual reputation for dash and gallantry."⁷ The two exceptions to this are contained in books that are not strictly about the Irish Brigade, but nevertheless raise interesting questions about how the historiography of the brigade had developed. The first of these texts was William Burton's *Melting Pot Soldiers,* published in 1988. In his book, Burton examined the role of ethnic units, including the Irish Brigade, during the Civil War. Unlike the standard texts on the ethic regiments that emphasize the motivation of the volunteers primarily in terms of their desire to fight for the preservation of their adopted country, Burton took a more political, maybe overly cynical stance. "Like the other volunteer regiments," wrote Burton, "the ethnic regiments were a direct outgrowth of state and local politics." One of the most "significant conclusions" in his study was that "ethnicity, in the Civil War generation, as today, is a fertile field of political exploitation. There are always people ready and eager to use it for their personal advantage."⁸ The second corrective to heroic accounts can be found in Kelly O'Grady's *Clear the Confederate Way!* published in 2000.⁹ O'Grady's is the more polemical work, and his task was to reclaim the history of the many Irish who fought for the Confederacy, and whose role had been largely neglected in the postwar historiography. Agreeing with Joseph Hernon's 1968 study, *Celts, Catholics and Copperheads,* O'Grady argued that there was "a revisionist, postwar attempt to gloss over Irish sympathies for the losing side," the Confederacy. In this process of "glossing over," it was the Union Irish Brigade that became "the consummate symbol of Irish participation in the war," and as such, the history of the brigade was "the main instrument of postwar Northern and Irish revisionists who needed to provide cover for impolitic Irish sympathies in the war."¹⁰

For both Burton and O'Grady, albeit for different arguments, politics was at the core of the accounts of the Irish Brigade. What they also had in common was the identity of who was the *bête noir* in both their stories, Thomas Francis Meagher. The historian James H. Randle has written that when "popular history sings of events and makes them great, it transcends the realm of record and enters that of

Preface

myth."[11] Nowhere is this more evident than perhaps in relation to the iconic figure of Meagher. Meagher's career was colorful and controversial in equal amounts. From the heroic Young Irelander of 1848, his escape from exile in Tasmania to America, to the dashing and valiant leader of the Irish Brigade in the Civil War, the story of the fearless "Meagher of the Sword" segues effortlessly between continents. While his role with the brigade may have been prominent, it was also shrouded in controversies. These centered on what could be described as the three Cs — character, competence and courage. Although much of the evidence in the case against Meagher is circumstantial, it is, arguably, fairly persuasive. Yet, the place to find the evidence of these controversies is not in the primary or secondary accounts of Meagher and the Irish Brigade. These are areas that almost all these accounts do their best either to avoid, or tread rather delicately around.

The only substantial full-length modern biography of Meagher is that by Robert Athearn, published in 1949.[12] While Athearn does not delve too deeply into the controversies surrounding Meagher's time with the Irish Brigade, other than reporting them, he does retain a certain skepticism and critical distance between author and subject.[13] More typical was the tone set by the earlier accounts. Conyngham was unsparing in his praise of Meagher,[14] who was also the subject of two equally gushing biographical works, in 1870 by W.F. Lyons, and in 1892 by Michael Cavanagh.[15] This has continued up to the present day. Examples of this can be found in *Remember Fontenoy!* Joseph Bilby's account of the Irish Brigade, where any discussion of

"The relative calm of the Irish community in New York," wrote the historian of 69th Militia, "was shattered on May 27, 1852, when a good looking stocky stranger walked into the law office of Dillon and O'Gorman in William Street, and announced that he was Thomas Francis Meagher, lately escaped from Australia" (Library of Congress).

Preface

Meagher's possible indiscretions is confined to a brief appendix.[16] In *The History of the Irish Brigade*, a collection of historical essays published in 1997, Kevin O'Brien simply ignores any of the controversies associated with Meagher.[17] Frank Boyle, in his 1996 account of Irish regiments in the Army of the Potomac, *A Party of Mad Fellows*, does refer in the narrative to some of the questions raised about Meagher, but either makes no judgment about them or continues to bolster the accepted traditional accounts.[18]

All of these sins of omission were seized upon by Burton and O'Grady. In highlighting what was omitted from Meagher's story, and by extension the story of the Irish Brigade, they were able to make their arguments all the more plausible. In O'Grady's case, so aggressively does he argue the case against Meagher that he is guilty in reverse of the same exaggeration and imbalance that prompted his account of Irish Confederates. "The Irish Brigade's shining achievement," wrote O'Grady, "came not in its attack at Fredericksburg or Antietam but in its defense of Meagher's good name.... Indeed the Irish Brigade's popular history is mostly myth."[19] The former claim, in some respects, was true both at the time, and also carried on into modern accounts. This was not entirely for the benefit of Meagher himself. While Meagher's name became synonymous with the Brigade, it was the valor of the men who fought, and the need to preserve their gallantry, that caused doubts about their leader to be subsumed within an overall heroic, quasi-mythical narrative. The men were not to be styled lions led by donkeys, but lions one and all. Its effect, however, was to give some credence to the latter claim, a claim that was also strengthened by the tendency of historians to incorporate uncritically some of the myths or anecdotes, not just about Meagher, but about the brigade itself, into their narratives.

This was not something peculiar to the historiography of the Irish Brigade. Between 1926 and 1939, the Illinois poet Carl Sandburg published six acclaimed volumes on the life of Lincoln. In the description of one critical modern historian, Sandberg's Lincoln, "in addition to meandering dreamily in and out of Lincoln's life, also made utterly uncritical use of any and all reminiscence sources, nothing seemed too ridiculous if it allowed Sandberg to wax bard-like."[20] This continued myth-making in Civil War historiography is not confined to only the texts themselves. The frontispiece chosen for William McCarter's memoirs is a wonderful painting by Civil War artist Don Troiani, which depicts the Irish Brigade going into action. The scene depicted, however, was at the battle of Sharpsburg.[21] McCarter was a private in the 116th Pennsylvania. The 116th did not fight at Sharpsburg and was not even part of the Irish Brigade at the time. The pivotal drama of McCarter's memoirs is the battle of Fredericksburg, fought three months later. The painting was no doubt used for its stirring imagery. The memoirs themselves are an admirable addition, not just to the literature on the Irish Brigade, but to Civil

Preface

War memoirs in general. Yet there remains the underlying uneasiness in the choice of Troiani's image. In its own small way, the choice reflects the continuing historical tendency, when writing about the Irish Brigade, of always feeling the tug of wanting to print the legend.

The purpose of this study is not to print the legend, nor to provide a microhistory of the Irish Brigade, or of Meagher. Using what is known about both, and in particular the words and accounts of the men themselves, and those who observed them, this study reexamines and reinterprets existing accounts to provide a more rounded and balanced picture of the brigade and its first commander. It makes for poor history to try to honestly tell the story of one and not the other. If, in doing this, some of the luster surrounding Meagher is removed, this does not necessarily detract from the story of the brigade itself. Nor do we have to somehow embellish its role to compensate. The irony is that the story of Irish Brigade in the American Civil War needs no embellishment.

As an example, the doomed assault by the Irish Brigade on Marye's Heights outside Fredericksburg on December 13, 1862, may have become legendary. But it was not a legend. When Private William McCarter and his comrades woke up that morning, covered in frost, they would have stamped their feet, scratched themselves, gone to the toilet, blown into their cupped hands for some warmth, drunk their coffee, had their smoke, and cursed their luck at being in the army. Then, when the time came, they fell into line and got ready to carry out orders that they knew would mean death for many of them. Much of the rest is history, not legend. At Fredericksburg, except for that of the 28th Massachusetts, the battle-torn flags of the other regiments were in the process of being replaced. For that reason, the 28th took center place in the line, while Meagher also ordered that each man in the Irish Brigade was to wear a sprig of green boxwood in his cap for the assault on the heights. McCarter, an aide to Meagher, had absented himself from the safety of his position behind the lines to be with his comrades, and was wounded five times during the battle. "The piece of sprig of green that was presented to myself on the above occasion," he wrote in his memoirs over a decade later, "or rather the remains of it, I can show today preserved in a bottle."[22] If you are looking for heroism in the story of the Irish Brigade, or bathos, or humor, or humanity, there is no need to print the legend. You can simply print the facts.

CHAPTER 1

Saved by Sumter

A matter of honor

Before there was the Irish Brigade, there was the 69th Regiment of the New York State Militia. The colonel of the 69th was Michael Corcoran, from Carrowkeel, County Sligo. War or no war, the Sligo man surely must have thought to himself that it was an ill wind that doesn't blow some good. He had arrived in the States in 1849. By 1860, he had carved out a prominent niche for himself in Irish-American ethnic circles in New York. As well as being a member of the Central Council of the Fenian Brotherhood, he had also held political sinecures in the customs service and the post office. He had also taken over the management of the Hibernian Hall, a popular Irish meeting place, following his marriage to the niece of the previous owner's widow. But the prize feather in his cap was the colonelcy of the 69th. However, much to his discomfort, a cloud had recently descended on Corcoran's relatively upwardly mobile path. He was awaiting court-martial, charged with willful disobedience of orders.

The origins of this potential disgrace made it even more difficult to bear, in that the blame lay at the door of the old enemy, Great Britain. In the autumn of 1860, the Prince of Wales paid a visit to New York. The 69th, along with other New York militia units, were to parade in his honor. Three months previously the same routine had been followed to welcome the first Japanese mission to the States. Now, however, any similar show for the benefit of a member of the English royal family was bound to pose an acute sense of discomfort for any self-respecting Irish immigrant, let alone a Fenian. Corcoran's decision was to refuse to obey the order. Never, he said, would he ask men of Irish birth to pay homage to the "beardless youth" whose mother, Queen Victoria, was the oppressor of their native country. Corcoran's prominence made this a delicate situation, but such public insubordination made it difficult to arrive at any sort of arrangement with the city and state officials. So charges were brought, and the court-martial commenced.[1]

Thus the situation remained in 1861 until the start of the Civil War. At 4.30 a.m. on April 12, 1861, forces of the newly declared southern Confederacy fired on Fort Sumter, an isolated collection of bricks held by Union forces in the middle of Charleston Harbor, South Carolina.[2] The garrison at Sumter surrendered within

33 hours. On April 15, the Republican president, Abraham Lincoln, issued a proclamation calling 75,000 militiamen into national service for the term of 90 days. Many northerners felt confident that such was all that was needed to extinguish the southern rebellion, which Lincoln described as "too powerful to be suppressed by the ordinary course of judicial proceedings."[3] The response in the northern states was immediate and tumultuous. But no more than the visit of the Prince of Wales, it posed something of a dilemma for many Irish Americans.

The vast majority of even the pro-Union Irish were staunch anti-Lincoln Democrats. They despised the northern abolitionists, who many also believed were equally responsible for starting the war as the southern insurrectionists. This was further compounded by the opinion of some who saw the attempt of secession by the southern states as being on a par with any small nation seeking to assert its own freedom and independence from an overpowering neighbor, and not very different from Ireland's own struggle against Britain. Others saw the arrogance and privileges of the aristocratic land-owning slaveocracy of the south, as equally deserving of extinction as their Irish counterparts. The dilemma was partly resolved for the Union-Irish by pledging allegiance to the flag and maintenance of their adopted homeland, the United States, rather than to the Republican president. This was largely the spirit in which Irish Americans crowded into recruiting offices that April, and in which the suspended Corcoran offered his services and those of his 69th militia.

With rumors of a mighty southern war machine being ready to pounce on undefended northern cities, it was crucial that any already-organized bodies of troops, such as militias were perceived to be, were quickly mobilized. It would also be a good opportunity for Corcoran's political friends to secure his escape from the current embarrassing circumstances. "I hope you will quash at once the court martial on Col. Corcoran," read one telegram to Governor Edwin Morgan from wealthy New York businessman James Bowen. Other influential New Yorkers showered the government offices at Albany with similar messages. Thurlow Weed, the Republican politician, informed Morgan that the 69th was ready to go to war. All that was required was for the charge against Corcoran to be dropped. Allied to demands from the War Department in Washington for assistance, unsurprisingly, Morgan summarily dismissed the charges against the colonel of the 69th. Corcoran was now free to prepare his regiment for the coming decisive battle against the forces of the Confederacy.[4]

April 23 was a hot spring day as the members of the 69th made their way to Pier No. 4 on the North River to embark on the steamer *S.S. James Adger* for transporting down to the vicinity of Washington. Corcoran, who was recovering from an illness, would have to go off to war in a carriage.[5] The regiment had formed in Great Jones Street and was presented a Union flag by the wife of prominent Irish

1. Saved by Sumter

American judge Charles Patrick Daly. Through her marriage to one of New York's most prominent Irish-Americans, Maria Daly, although the daughter of wealthy and distinguished old New York families, had tempered her disdain for the lower orders, and the Irish in particular. "I thought that the poorer men should be equally cheered and encouraged," she wrote in her diary, "and so I presented the regiment with a flag."[6] Then, moving off down Broadway to "deafening cheers," the men of the 69th were led by a decorated wagon drawn by four horses, and bearing the inscription—"No North, No South, No East, No West, but the whole Union."

In 1861, excitement, patriotism and pomp characterized the march of young men to war. As one newspaper was to announce, "The supply of bunting is rapidly becoming scarce."[7] Militia regiments, not very different from the 69th, were being cheered off to war all over the country, both North and South. In Kalamazoo, the Sixth Michigan regiment was sent off in a train consisting of five baggage cars and 22 first-class passenger coaches.[8] In the South, members of the Battalion of Washington Artillery of New Orleans, effulgent in their new uniforms — allegedly made by New Orleans' best tailors at a cost of $20,000 — experienced complete strangers walking

Like other Fenians, Michael Corcoran was initially opposed to his countrymen joining the army for fear that their movement would be weakened, a fear that was well founded. He eventually relented and urged that if an Irishman had to enlist, he should enlist in an Irish regiment (Library of Congress).

along their lines "offering their pocketbooks to men whom they did not know" and southern belles "bestowed their floral offerings and kisses ungrudgingly and with equal favor among all classes of friends and suitors."[9]

For the 69th, the New York Irish had turned out en masse "to bid the gallant fellows God speed on their way." Bands escorted the regiment through crowded streets as "from an early hour in the morning immense crowds of men, women and children from all parts of the city might be seen flocking into Broadway.... They had come from Jersey City, Hoboken, Brooklyn, Williamsburg ... to witness the departure of the sturdy 69th." Marching down Broadway, one young soldier's resistance to the pressure of army life was short lived. He threw down his rifle and quit the ranks, unable to bear the cries of his wife and children, whereupon a veteran of the Mexican War of 1846–48, one Michael Cooney, stepped forward to volunteer, only to be refused. The pressure of the crowd was such, that, according to one captain, "The passage became so severe that many [of the soldiers] were almost suffocated and were carried away several yards without requiring use of their propellers in their onward march." At the wharf itself, the crowd also managed to break down the police barriers. When the soldiers were finally disentangled from friends and well-wishers, it was 7.00 p.m. before the *James Adger* cast off.[10] Amid the sound of cannon salutes, tears, cheers and songs, with "the vessels at the docks dipping their flags in recognition of the valor and self-sacrifice of the gallant fellows," the scene was described as "equally sublime and exhilarating."[11]

"Enough for a Kingdom"

> By the hush me boys, and that's to make no noise,
> And listen to poor Paddy's sad narration.
> For I was by hunger pressed and in poverty distressed,
> So I took a thought to leave this Irish nation.
> "Paddy's Lamentation"

Given the background of the Irish in America prior to the Civil War, perhaps "astounding" could also be added to the description of so many Irish being seen to support the cause of the new Republican administration so vigorously. Even the figure of 5,000 to serve in an exclusively Irish brigade, which would be suggested in the press in the autumn of 1861, would eventually prove minuscule in comparison to the overall numbers of Irish who fought for the Union during the Civil War. In 1869, the U.S. Sanitary Commission reported that 144,221 Irish-born Americans had served on the side of the Union during the Civil War, and probably three times that number of Irish descent had also taken to wearing the Union blue. While Irish could be found in regiments from most every state, it has been estimated that of the 144,000 or so, 51,700 came from New York, 17,418 from Pennsylvania, 12,041 from Illinois, 10,007 from Massachusetts, 8,129 from Ohio, 3,612 from Wisconsin, and 4,362 from Missouri.[12]

As New York was in one sense the largest Irish city in the world in 1861, it was perhaps apt that the core of the Irish Brigade would be three New York regiments — the 63rd, 69th, and 88th. At various times other regiments would also serve in the

1. Saved by Sumter

brigade — the 28th and 29th Massachusetts, the 116th Pennsylvania, and also the 4th and 7th New York Heavy Artillery. Between 1861 and 1865, including the recruitment which continued throughout the war, perhaps 7,000 men passed through the ranks. While such numbers are obviously dwarfed by the total number of Irish who served on the Union side during the Civil War — predominantly in non–Irish units — they would represent a reasonable cross section of Ireland in exile in midcentury America. The vast majority were those men whose vocation would be to exist as "the unskilled marginal workers of mid-nineteenth century America" who lived in tenements which were known as "human rookeries" and who looked askance at much of America and Americans, a view which was heartily reciprocated by their native hosts.[13]

That the Irish were a race apart is indisputable. An upper-class New Yorker, George Templeton Strong, was not far wrong when he remarked that, "Our Celtic fellow citizens are almost as remote from us in temperament and constitution as the Chinese."[14] An Irish immigrant could readily echo this sentiment when he wrote home that had he "fallen from the clouds amongst this people I could not feel more isolated. more bewildered...."[15] Much of the cause of such mutual bewilderment and suspicion was due to the nature of the most recent wave of Irish immigration to North America since the intolerable sufferings of the famines during the 1840s, and which certainly had altered the American perception of the Irish.

Prior to this, Americans could perhaps distinguish two groups: small numbers of educated and generally well-to-do newcomers who mingled easily with the native-born society, both Catholic and Protestant; and the poor small farmer, who had constituted the bulk of the migration up to 1835. While many of these remained on the Eastern seaboard, others became the traveling gangs of laborers on internal construction projects such as railroads and canals, where rations of whiskey were often part of their contract. One diarist wrote in 1846 that he rarely saw a gray-haired Irishman, inferring that they all died young, while a newspaper commented that, "there are several sorts of power working at the fabric of this republic — water-power, steampower and Irish power ... the last works hardest of all!"[16] But it was not so much these itinerant Irish laborers, whose "shanties spring up like mushrooms in the night and often vanish like mists in the morning," which were the cause of native American disquiet in the years leading up to the Civil War as it was the massive numbers of their countrymen who would follow them, the majority of whom would remain in the cities, and whose behavior and lifestyle would appear so barbarous and brutish.[17]

The immigration figures for the famine period and after tell their own tale of intolerable conditions and suffering in Ireland, with the consequence that, in the words of the census compilers, Ireland had furnished the United States with enough of her children "for a kingdom." In 1846 92,484 left, 196,224 in 1847, 173,744 in

1848, 204,771 in 1849, 206,041 in 1850. This pattern continued unabated throughout the 1850s, until, from a total Irish-American population of 961,719 in 1850, the number rose to 1,611,304 in 1860, with "solid groups of Irish of the lowest class thrown together as cohesive masses into the melting pot."[18] One Irish American journalist observed in 1850 how, "The Irish of the present day ... whom we see landing on our levees seem to be a different race of the Irish ten, 15, or 20 years since.... Dire wretchedness, appalling want and festering famine have tended to change their characters." Many were "traditionalist peasants, often Irish speakers, who might never had immigrated under normal circumstances and who carried to the new world premodern attitudes and behavior patterns diametrically opposed to those characterized as ... typically American." Many stepped off the ship "in a cape, high waisted coat, knee breeches, wool stockings protruding from a rusty pair of shoes, and a brimless caubeen on his head"; the only assets which they possessed, whether male or female, were their hands and a willingness to accept low wages which could guarantee ready employment. Almost all would begin life as unskilled laborers, and the majority would never progress further. Native-born Americans would joke about the wheelbarrow as being one of the greatest inventions of all time because it taught the Irish to walk on their hind legs. Another told of how an Irish servant girl always walked down stairs backward because she always had to use a ladder in the old country.[19]

Of course, the huge paradox in all this was why so many Irish chose to remain in the slums of the cities in the first place, given the availability of land and opportunities in midnineteenth century America. Some of the suggestions put forward by historians have an immense poignancy, even at this remove. According to one, the Irish, having just fled, "The smell of potatoes rotting in the fields ... odours of death in the cottages, by the roadsides and along the hedgerows," simply "rejected the land for the land had rejected them."[20] Even if he had the money or the actual farming skills necessary to try to settle inland, which very few would have had, this was not necessarily an entirely inviting prospect for a peasant people used to the closeness and kinship of rural Ireland. A successful Irish farmer in Missouri expressed the feelings of many when he wrote home that in spite of all the advantages America had to offer, in Ireland, "If I had there but a sore head, I would have a neighbor within every hundred yards of me that would run to see me.... But here everyone can get so much land ... that they calls them neighbors that lives two or three miles off."[21] No doubt time and distance lent a degree of enchantment to the immigrant's reminiscences, but you would look hard to find an emigrant from any age who was not similarly guilty.

Moreover, the city environment could initially have its own attractions for the newly arrived and impoverished immigrant. Their urgent needs were the most basic: to find shelter and some means of obtaining food. In New York, Boston and

1. Saved by Sumter

Philadelphia, they was a reasonable chance of "old friends and former companions or acquaintances to be met at every street corner; and there was news to give, and news to receive," while the local Democratic political machine might also provide the chance of a "start."[22] The local representative of the "boss," the block captain, would be around, slapping new arrivals on the back, and asking only a small return — the immigrant's vote — for the support provided throughout the year: jobs, coal in winter, food, and help with the government or the law. However, "traditional" or oversentimental descriptions similar to these often tend to overstate or even romanticize the forbidding environment into which the immigrant stepped, especially the appalling conditions in which they lived and worked.

The notorious slums, such as the Five Points area in New York or the so-called "Dublin rows" or "Little Dublins" in other cities, were attributed to being the product of some inherent defect in the Irish character. The commissioner of New York's Almshouse, which had more than its fair share of exiles from Ireland, remarked that "many of the famine Irish had far better been cast into the deep sea, than linger in the pangs of hunger, sickness and pain, to draw their last agonized breath in the streets of New York."[23] The journalist George Foster described the Irish Five Points neighborhood in the Sixth Ward as "the great ... ulcer of wretchedness — the very rotting skeleton of civilisation."[24] A New York City health inspector wrote in 1860 of Irish habitations: "As if human beings were but commodities on storage, the calculation seems to be, how many may be packed into a given space." In 1862 over 6,000 families, totaling 18,000 people, lived in cellars, without light, air or drainage. Not surprisingly, the death rate of adult immigrants was far above that of natives, with their children the greatest sufferers. In 1861, there were 8,339 deaths among children of foreign-born parents as compared with 1,088 among native parents. In 1863, the latter figure was to climb to 10,972. In South Boston in 1850, the Irish slums were buildings from three to six stories high, with whole families living in one room, without light or ventilation. Secret societies arose in these "shantytowns" with such names as "the Corkonians," "the Connaughtmen," and "the Far Downs," whose members engaged in bloody brawls and riots, spurred on by the ever-present catalyst of drink.[25]

In 1853, the *Chicago Tribune* demanded to know, "Why are the instigators and ringleaders of our riots and tumults, in nine cases out of ten, Irishmen?" Even normally sympathetic organs such as the New York *Irish News* acknowledged that the character of the typical famine immigrant was that of a cultural conservative, "a bundle of habits and associations, with a number of unanswerable longings, likings, and propensities which stay in his nature though he change place." Another commentator complained that the Irish "love to clan together," and "are content to live together in filth and disorder, and enjoy their balls and wakes and frolics without molestation," never being at peace except when they were fighting and "being sociable with paving bricks."[26] It is little wonder that many Americans would perceive the Irish to be poverty stricken, filthy, ignorant, drunken and disorderly when even such prominent Irish Americans as Archbishop Hughes, seeing the utter destitution of the newer Irish immigrant, described them as constituting, "the debris of a nation ... a fine stock run down and debased by three centuries of deliberate oppression," and went on to recommend that immigration be stopped for at least a decade.[27]

Hughes, privately, was expressing what many Americans came to express both publicly and violently, especially in the decade prior to the Civil War. Slums and ghettos, where violence, death and disease are a way of life, have often existed and do exist quite readily alongside more prosperous and respectable areas. It is only when the inhabitants or the lifestyle of the former appear to threaten the latter that the call goes up for "something to be done." Such was the case with the Irish and "Know-Nothingism" or "nativism."

Fears and Know-Nothings

"Can one throw mud into pure water and not disturb its clearness?" asked one native-born American in attacking the problem of immigration in 1835. This questioning and opposition to immigrants, especially Catholic immigrants, had lead to sporadic outbursts of violence since the start of the century. But largely in response to the perceived effects of the massive Irish immigration of the late 1840s and early 1850s, antiforeign parties or societies arose in New York and elsewhere which evolved into the Know-Nothing movement.[28] Its main platform was to reduce the power of foreign-born voters in politics, both through domestic curbs for those already there, and also though halting the apparent endless inward flow. It was overwhelmingly "a movement of the laboring and middle classes," who were themselves threatened by economic and political dislocation, and, in a familiar fashion, turned on the new and strange arrivals as the cause and eventual solution of their problems. During the 1850s there would be pitched battles between Irish and Know-Nothings in Philadelphia; Lawrence, Massachusetts; Newark, Baltimore; Brooklyn and St. Louis.

The charge sheet against the Irish did appear fairly incontrovertible. They had undoubtedly swelled the numbers of slums, violations of the Sabbath, drunkards, paupers, brawls and crimes. The lobbying by the Catholic hierarchy for tax support for Catholic schools as against the American public schools, which were regarded by one archbishop as wellsprings of "Socialism, Red Republicanism, Universalism, Infidelity, Deism, Atheism, and Panaetheism," and for church control over church property, which in many areas was owned by a lay board of trustees, all fanned the flames of anti-Catholicism.[29] When a papal nuncio, Cardinal Bedini, visited America in 1853 and 1854, riots broke out in several cities that he visited, and his safe departure was executed only by smuggling him on board a ship in New York Harbor to escape a mob.[30]

But perhaps the crucial focal points for recruits to Know-Nothingism were economic and political. Often offering to work for a bare pittance, which in many cases was a whole lot more than was available along the hedgerows of Ireland, the Irish could readily be blamed for forcing wages down. And most blatantly of all, they were also guilty of perverting the democratic process. Under federal law, immigrants could become American citizens only after five years in the United States, but in some cities, Democratic judges could be found to issue naturalization papers almost as soon as the immigrant stepped off the boat. Even without this benefit, by the early 1850s the waves of Irish who had begun to arrive during the mid-1840s were eligible to vote in any case and the block captain would ensure that they did, and would do so en masse for the favored candidate. During his journey to the States in 1860, William Howard Russell recorded the views of some American passengers who felt that, while "The Irish are useful for making roads," the Irish in the cities "should not be allowed to vote as they are — the men are ignorant creatures who swamp the respectable people in New York and elsewhere.... They swamp local elections & put power in the hands of the lowest order of citizens."[31]

This tactic of block voting, combined with straightforward physical intimidation, was also repeated with the roving gangs of Irish laborers in the country who could mysteriously show up in close run districts at election time. During the campaign for elections to the Senate during 1854, the Republican candidate from Illinois, one Abraham Lincoln, described how, in one town, he met "about fifteen Celtic gentlemen, with black carpet sacks in their hands." Lincoln had been told that "about four hundred of the same sort" were to arrive before the election "to work on some new railroad," but what he feared most was they would all "swear to residence" in order to swell the Democratic vote.[32]

Given the coincidence of economic disruption and apparent political impotency, it is hardly surprising that one American should ask despairingly, "Are American mechanics to be borne down, crushed, or driven to the western wilds?" or that a political "third force" such as Known-Nothingism should emerge.[33] Nor should it be surprising that its immediate effect on the Irish was to make them even more clannish and isolated in their enclaves, hardly fertile recruiting ground for a war against slavery which many of the northern New England "puritans," the most "native" of "nativists," would be advocating in 1861.

A better title to the bottom

One of the ironies associated with the relationship between the Irish and the blacks in America was that, as described by one historian, "Only blacks were more self-conscious about, or had more invested in, the relationship between wartime military service and their acceptance in the nation."[34] Yet the Irish contempt toward the blacks was implacable, even if it was heartily reciprocated. In 1850, the *New York Tribune* had also commented on the strange phenomenon of the Irish who, having escaped so recently themselves "from a galling, degrading bondage," should vote against all proposals to give greater rights to blacks and should come to the polls on election day shouting, "Down with the Nagurs! Let them go back to Africa, where they belong."[35] Frederick Douglass, the foremost colored spokesman of his day, echoed this sentiment, professing himself "at a loss to understand why a people who so nobly loved and cherished the thought of liberty at home in Ireland could become, willingly, the oppressor of another race here."[36] Oppressor was perhaps the wrong term. The number of Irish who owned slaves was negligible. And while they certainly acquiesced and supported in the oppression of the blacks, this was largely the manifestation of the underlying cause of Irish and black hostility, economic competition.

"Respectability," wrote one historian, "was appalled by the Irish precisely as the Irish were appalled by the freed Negro," or indeed, the prospect of hundreds of thousands of freed Negroes.[37] As it always is, competition at the sharp end of the social scale was fierce, something which those not at the sharp end tend not to take into account. Once they arrived in America, the immigrant Irish, particularly in the northern states, and despite much of the nativist workers' fears, were entering into the market for jobs once exclusively held by blacks. Observing the rising tide of immigrants, Douglass would admonish his people to learn skilled trades or perish: "Every hour sees the black man elbowed out of employment by some newly arrived immigrant whose hunger and whose color are thought to give him a better title to the place."[38] It is little wonder, given their economic condition, that the Irish would be opposed to the abolition of slavery if that were to mean thousands of freed blacks trekking north in search of jobs.

The economic and social standing of the Irish in the southern states was even lower than that up North, so much so that a slave could be reported as bemoaning that his master treated him "as badly as if I were a common Irishman."[39] While the tale may be apocryphal, the basic economic fact was that the black slave was a valuable commodity, while the supply of Irish was cheap to employ, and cheap to replace. The labor of digging ditches and trenches, of clearing the wastelands and the forests on the plantations, and of repairing the levees was done by Irish laborers. Accidents and fatalities were frequent features of this work. In his journey through the South in 1861, Russell again recorded how one chargehand described the process of clearing land was so dangerous for the slaves and mules, that employers "generally get it done if we can by Irishmen."[40] It was better to use the Irish, who cost nothing to the employer if they died, "than to use up good field hands in such severe employment." Another particular demonstration of this phenomenon was the task of loading a boat with cotton. Negro hands were sent to the top of the bank to roll the bales to the top of the gangway, down which they slid "with fearful velocity." Irishmen were at the foot of the gangway to move them into place, a position in which "niggers [were] worth too much to be risked ... if the Paddies are knocked overboard, or get their backs broke, nobody loses anything."[41]

Like their northern counterparts, the southern Irish were staunch supporters of the Democratic Party. The stand of the Democrats on slavery, which was essentially antiabolitionist, was one of the main reasons why the Irish were so solidly Democratic in their political allegiance, and also why they detested the Republicans as much as they did the blacks. The more radical Republicans, many from New England, appeared to be preoccupied with black slavery in the South, while oblivious to what could be seen as white wage slavery in the north. Irish American politicians, such as Mike Walsh, were quick to exploit genuine grievances of the impoverished laborers. "The great and fruitful source of crime and misery on earth," Walsh declared, "is the inequality of society — the abject dependence of honest willing industry upon idle and dishonest capitalists.... Demagogues tell you that you are freemen.... They lie; you are slaves ... bowed down by that worst form of slavery — the slavery of poverty."[42] The shedding of radical tears solely over the plight of the black underdog understandably struck many Irish as rank hypocrisy. When, in January 1860, a large cotton mill in Massachusetts collapsed and burned, and scores of Irish girls employed there died in the disaster, the *Irish American* asked indignantly: "Shall the black slave of the south monopolize all the sympathies of Massachusetts, while her own white slaves perish in hundreds without a remonstrance in order that cotton may be manufactured at a shade less cost?"[43]

CHAPTER 2

"You Are All Green Alike"

Making hay while the sun shines

Despite the patent apathy of many Irish toward the plight of the slave, the underlying cause of the war, the excitement, the pomp and the sheer sense of adventure propelled many young men, and not just Irish, into uniform that spring of 1861. By April 26, the 69th had arrived at Annapolis. The men decamped in the Naval Academy for a week, doing guard duty and railroad repair on the Baltimore line. On May 4, the 69th moved camp into the grounds of Georgetown College in Washington itself, despite complaints from its Jesuit president. A new banner had been presented to the regiment, carrying the message, "Presented to the 69th Regiment in commemoration of the 11th October, 1860," recalling the regiment's own recent legacy of rebellion in its refusal to parade for the Prince of Wales the previous autumn. Yet another flag bore the motto, "Gentle when stroked, fierce when provoked," lying between two Irish wolfhounds. However, the only provocation that the 69th was subject to during their stay at Georgetown was from the West Point cadets who were temporarily attached as drill masters, and who no doubt relished putting the green militiamen, in more ways that one, through their paces for up to seven hours daily.[1] The cadets were soon able to knock the Irishmen into some sort of shape. This was much to the delight of their commander, Colonel Corcoran, who, "with a glowing cheek and gladdening eye ... looked upon them when in martial array before him."[2]

Although the initial crisis atmosphere in Washington had passed, the Lincoln administration remained in an uncomfortable position. Great hopes were placed on the actions of Virginia, the most influential of the southern states. She had not yet seceded, and the administration was anxious to avoid any provocation that might affect the result of the state plebiscite on secession to be held on May 23. This meant that Washington itself remained in a militarily vulnerable position, overlooked as it was by Arlington Heights on the south side of the Potomac River in Virginia, and which, if occupied by Confederate artillery, could make life very uncomfortable in the capital. All this changed when another milestone was passed on May 23, as Virginians ratified the decision to secede. That night, the Federal army, including the 69th, left Georgetown and crossed the river to occupy the

2. "You Are All Green Alike"

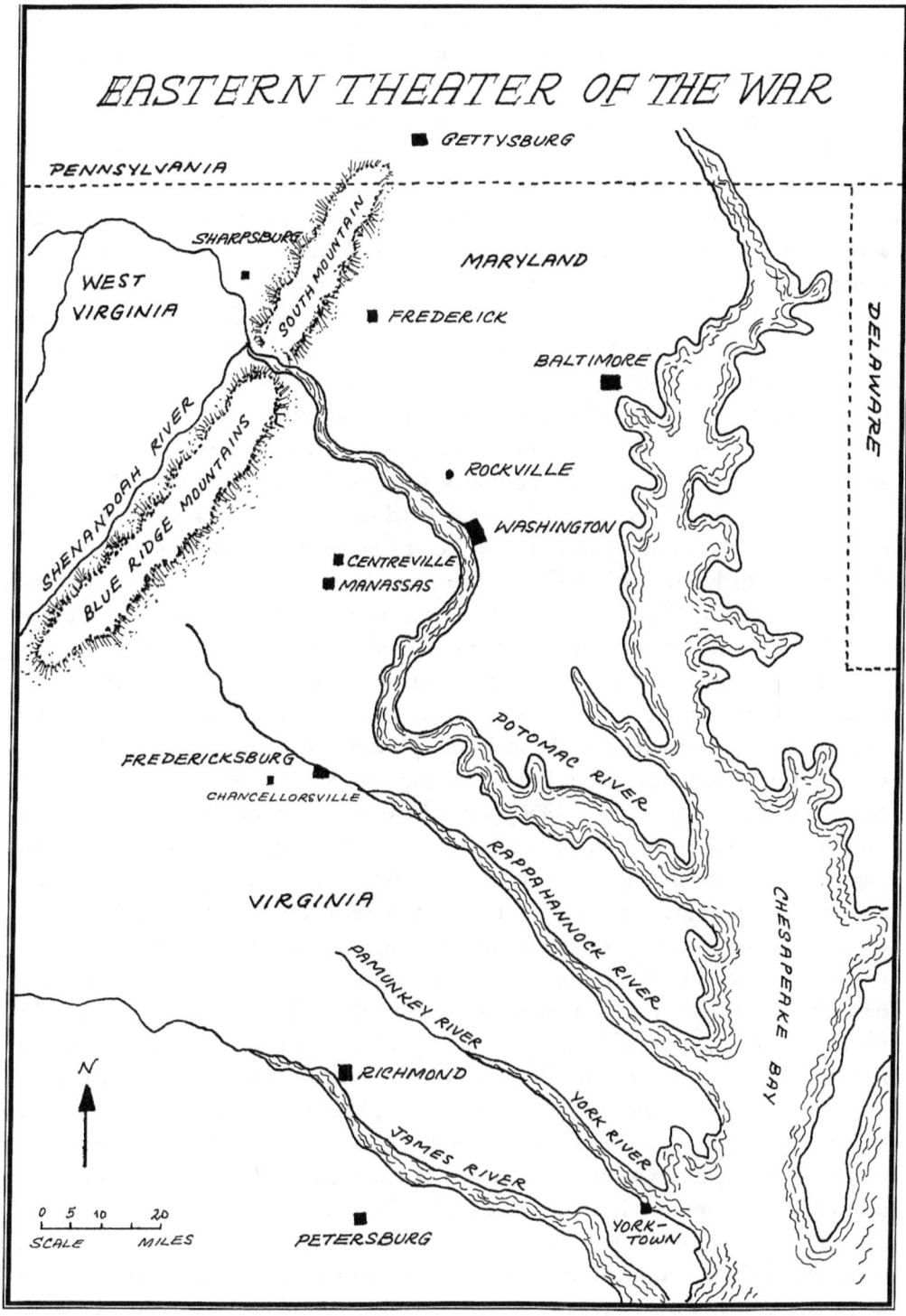

Heights. With the 69th were 300 new recruits, including a company of Irish Zouaves which had joined the regiment that very day, led by one Captain Thomas Francis Meagher.

On the same April day on which the 69th had steamed out of New York Harbor, there appeared in a New York daily the following businesslike advertisement: "YOUNG IRISHMEN TO ARMS! TO ARMS YOUNG IRISHMEN! IRISH ZOUAVES — One hundred young Irishmen — healthy, intelligent and active — are wanted at once to form a company of Irish Zouaves, under the command of THOMAS FRANCIS MEAGHER, to be attached to the 69th Regiment, N.Y.S.M. No applicants fewer than 18 or above 35 years will be enrolled in this company. Application to be made at No. 36 Beckman Street, corner of William Street, between the hours of 10 a.m. and 5 p.m."[3] While commencing to drill his new company at Captain Phelan's Billiard Saloon, Meagher was anxious for his Zouaves to join the 69th as soon as possible. It was initially hoped they could travel to Washington early in May. When this appeared unlikely, Meagher himself went to the Washington to try to exert his influence. This appeared to do the trick, as he very shortly reported that the Zouaves would soon be at the front. "It would seem that the difficulties which have hitherto intervened have been surmounted on the personal application of Mr. Meagher at the War Department," wrote the New York–based *Irish American* newspaper, with a mixture bordering on pomposity and smugness.[4]

Small as this episode was, it partly exposed the initial influence someone like Meagher could exercise with the war in its infancy, when "political" officers could hope to outmaneuver regular channels and procedures within both the army and the governmental bureaucracy. But as the war progressed, the star of the political generals would begin to wane. Many, though not all, were simply incompetent and unfit to command men in battle. This had never necessarily been a handicap. What happened was that they were simply left behind in the vastness which the demands of war would eventually make upon the country. When the war reached that stage, the faceless men behind the desks would once again have their day, and as Meagher would find out, they would once again see off the gaudy usurpers from the early days of the war. But that time was a couple of bloody years down the road. The mood was jolly and excitable on that moonlight May night as the 69th marched up to Arlington Heights. Crossing the Potomac into Virginia, the men were, in a sense, entering enemy territory for the first time. Meagher himself had a toehold on the commission ladder that could prove the stepping stone to much bigger things. He had even raised his own company, no doubt almost an independent command in part of his own mind. Glory hunting in the short term however was to prove an elusive business. The wagons following the marching men were loaded, not with extra ammunition and medical supplies, but rather with plentiful supplies of picks and shovels, as they were immediately put to work constructing a fort on the Heights.

2. "You Are All Green Alike"

Time and money

As the days of digging passed into weeks one regular officer wrote to his superiors that the new works were indeed "progressing finely.... The 69th New York is the only regiment at work on it, and they seem to be working admirably."[5] One Irishman wrote to a newspaper describing how, when Colonel Corcoran would come to observe the work in progress and compliment the men, "Well, when that came I tell you that the dirt flew."[6] It was also reported that the Irishmen in the 69th had begun to describe themselves as the "Northern shovelry by way of comparing their native industry with the reputed indolence of Southern chivalry."[7] However, while such patriotic stoicism may have been attributed to the regiment in later accounts, at the time, familiarity with the required tasks did not necessarily make the men feel any better. One man wrote home that his hands were "red as a ripe cherry from the sun, which is very intense here, my pants are rolled up to the knees, my drawers inside my stockings, and all covered with mud." The only small consolation was that the result of their labor was eventually to be named after their commander, namely Fort Corcoran.[8]

But that was insufficient to compensate for the disappointments of camp life, both in terms of excitement and, more ominously, for lack of pay. In early July, after 10 weeks in the army, the men of the 69th had still not been paid, an event that was to become a fairly regular feature of army life in general throughout the war. In New York, a civilian aid committee was reporting cases of destitution among the regiment's families. On hearing this, some companies in effect tried a sit-in, refusing to leave their quarters until they got their money. In the face of this mutiny, Corcoran took immediate action, parading the rest of the regiment under arms, and informing the strikers that unless they returned to duty at once he would open fire on them. Wisely, they believed him, and the insubordination ended forthwith.[9]

The paymaster eventually visited Fort Corcoran on July 15, but the problems of the commander did not end there. Bad feeling was further exacerbated by a bitter row over when exactly the regiment's three months' service was due to expire. Apart from taking part on a few reconnaissance patrols, the principal weapons used by 69th to date had been a pick and a shovel. Combined with the lack of pay, many of the men were quite happy to call it a day as regards this soldiering lark. By their calculations, their three months' enlistment had started the day they left New York, April 23, which would see them mustered out in July. Various Irish benevolent societies in New York had already met to plan a reception for the 69th on its return. It was not to be. Apparently, "owing to the great amount of public business at hand, the proper officer had omitted mustering it [the regiment] into service until May 9 (i.e., the day they were mustered in at Georgetown), so that it would be in all probability August 9 before they could return." Corcoran went to explain the unrest

Corcoran, left, and other officers of the 69th New York State Militia at Fort Corcoran in 1861 strike various martial poses for the photographer. Meagher, leaning across the cannon, stares directly at the camera (Library of Congress).

in the regiment to their brigade commander, Colonel Sherman, who said he would look into the matter. A Lieutenant Colonel Hamilton, secretary to General Winfield Scott, the general in chief himself, also went to the regiment with the message from Scott that "if the 69th refused to move forward, it was the first time in history that Irishmen had ever been known to turn their backs on friend or foe."[10] Whether the final resolution of this controversy would again require loaded muskets trained on the Irishmen was not immediately tested, as, on July 15, the same day they got paid, the regiment was drawn up on parade to be informed that the following day they would be marching. The digging and drilling was over; "muskets were to be in the best order — cartridge boxes full," and each man "to carry three days rations in his haversack."

Following this announcement which foreshadowed an imminent battle, men were to be seen everywhere, "some seated on kegs, others on knapsacks, others again on rude blocks and two or three on drums, writing their last letters home." Passing through the chapel within Fort Corcoran, hundreds went to confession, heard by

2. "You Are All Green Alike"

Father Bernard O'Reilly, who had been attached to the 69th. At noon on Tuesday, July 16, they set off on a march that would lead them to a sluggish brown stream known as Bull Run. Led by a company of engineers, then drummers and fifers, followed by Corcoran, with the chaplain, doctors, and Meagher, who had been detailed as a special aide, the 69th was finally going to war.[11]

"You are all green alike"

The Union army was also headed for the first of its thumping defeats by the Confederate forces. It would receive an even worse defeat in 1862 at almost the exact same spot, in a battle known as the Second Bull Run. The following year, in the summer of 1863, when the Union army found itself again heading toward this area in Virginia, the response from one Irish soldier when asked the weary question "Where's this grand army going to now Pat?" was a resigned, "O then, don't you know; we're goin' to Bull Run to get our annual batin."[12] It would take a couple of years and several hard knocks for such cynicism and fatalism to take hold among the volunteers. The mood of the men on the road to their first "annual batin" in that summer of 1861 was more eager, more naive, even if they were none too fond of their brigade commander, Colonel William Tecumseh Sherman.

It was Sherman who bore the brunt of the men's bad feeling over the enlistment fracas, an incident that did nothing to endear Sherman himself to the regiment. "Soon after I had assumed command," he wrote rather stiffly in his memoirs over a decade later, "a difficulty arose in the 69th, an Irish regiment."[13] Sherman placed himself further in the 69th's bad books by forbidding them to bring more than one ambulance on the march. Consequently, when one of their captains, James Breslin, had been accidentally wounded during the trip, they had cursed him even more, because, with no spare ambulance, the captain had to bounce along with the troops as they made their way to the battle.[14] Sherman was eventually destined to become one of those almost mythological figures the war would throw up. But in July 1861, he was just another inexperienced, highly strung colonel leading an even more inexperienced set of men toward their first major battle. And the inexperience showed all round. The term "army" was perhaps too grand a word for the patchwork of militiamen in a variety of uniforms, with some units on both sides dressed in blue and gray, who comprised the Army of Washington, as it was called, under the overall command of Brigadier General Irwin McDowell. As an example, the 69th as it marched off to battle was commanded by Corcoran, a former postal clerk; the lieutenant colonel, James Haggerty, was a house carpenter by trade, while Meagher, who would be Corcoran's special aide, had the "battle" at Widow McCormack's cabbage patch in 1848 as his only martial experience. The omens were not promising.

Indeed, if McDowell had been able to have had his own way over the politicians, this army would not have been on the march at all. On June 29, he had pleaded with Lincoln for a postponement of the offensive against the Confederates until the army was better organized and better trained, especially with many of the original three-month enlistments due to expire shortly. Lincoln would have none of it. "You are green, it is true," he said, "but they are green, also; you are all green alike."[15] Lincoln was also keenly aware that the North, having got over its initial fright after the fall of Fort Sumter, was now baying for retribution. Northern public opinion demanded action to crush the rebel army at Manassas and thenceforth to march on Richmond, capital of the new Confederacy. Horace Greeley of the *New York Tribune*, who once emboldened young men to "Go West," now ran a standing headline urging "Forward to Richmond! Forward to Richmond!" which other newspapers then picked up in a chorus of northern jingoism. But perhaps it was just possible that the deployment of Confederate forces in northern Virginia at that time did present the North with such an opportunity to put a quick end to the war.

It could be said that there were in effect four armies in northern Virginia in July 1861. McDowell had about 35,000 based in and around Washington. Their nearest target, about 30 miles away to the southwest, was the Confederate army at Manassas under Brigadier General Pierre Gustav Toutant Beauregard, numbering about 23,000. Farther off to the northwest behind the Bull Run Mountains, the Confederates had another 11,000 under Major General Joseph Johnston, who were facing 14,000 Federal troops under Major General Robert Patterson. The plan, which McDowell had reluctantly presented to Lincoln, called for Patterson to "fix" the Confederates under Johnston in position, i.e., to prevent them from reinforcing Beauregard while the latter was attacked by the superior numbers of the Army of Washington. Perhaps Lincoln's logic was not so rash, as 35,000 green troops should have been able to overwhelm less than two-thirds of their number. They might have, except that Patterson failed utterly in his task. Wrongly believing himself to be outnumbered, confused by orders from Washington as to what his exact intentions should be against Johnston, Patterson "chose the safer course of maneuver," maneuvering himself "right out of the campaign." On July 18 and 19, Johnston's army simply marched away from Patterson and headed for the railway at the town of Piedmont to entrain for the depot at Manassas Junction. It was Johnston's reinforcements, which, at the end of the day, were to make the difference between defeat and victory.[16]

McDowell's men were blissfully unaware of such political and military developments as they made their way from Washington to Manassas. Sherman's brigade, which consisted of two other regiments along with the 69th, was in a division commanded by Brigadier General Daniel Tyler, in which there were a further four

2. "You Are All Green Alike"

brigades.[17] One soldier described how no one wanted to be left behind as "Men who had been under the surgeon's care for weeks buckled on their armor and obstinately refused to be left behind while the death blow was given to the rebellion."[18] Soon, however, their initially leisurely and expectant march was to give way to confusions and frustrations in the hot July weather of 1861. At every turn of the road, troops halted to clear away trees felled by the rebels or to seek cover from masked or hidden batteries. Each delay meant that the men all down along the line had to come to a halt. They would no sooner start off again only to be halted once more. Even Sherman recalled the "standing for hours and wondering what it meant."[19] Any novelty value or initial excitement wore off quickly after the first day's hesitant advance. The weather was hot, feet began to ache, and as the historian of the campaign remarked, McDowell's army "already displayed the volunteer soldier's disinclination to pay attention to orders and restrictions ... Sherman's brigade proved particularly troublesome in this regard."[20]

Sherman had warned the men that there should be no straggling from the line and no foraging of food from the Virginian farms they might pass. But as the halts became more wearisome, little heed was passed on such admonitions. "When thirsty, the men climbed fences and grouped around wells, cisterns, streams; when hungry, they kicked aside the haversacks that they had emptied earlier and took to knocking apples, chasing chickens, shooting pigs, and occasionally killing a cow ... the blackberries hanging ripe on every hand lured men to break ranks and officers dashed about screaming useless threats." The 69th in particular already had no time for Colonel Sherman and all his works and words. On hearing such as, "'Colonel Sherman says you must keep in ranks,' 'Colonel Sherman says you must close up,' 'Colonel Sherman says you must not chase pigs and chickens,' rich brogues answered, 'Tell Colonel Sherman we'll be havin' all the water, pigs, and chickens we want! Who are ye, anyway?'"[21] Despite being on the road since dawn, on the second day, Sherman's troops had covered only seven miles. By this time they were beginning to encounter the first of the entrenched Confederate positions, who nevertheless began to fall back before the advance of the Union army, destroying property as they went. At the end of the second day, July 17, Tyler's division was the furthermost advanced when the army camped for the night, being halfway between the towns of Germantown and Centreville, just east of Bull Run.

McDowell did not want to force his way across Bull Run with the Confederates ready and waiting opposite. His original battle plan had been to swing around to the south of the Confederate line, cutting off their supply line to Richmond, and thus forcing them to retreat or to fight at a disadvantage. To maintain the impression that his army was advancing straight down the Warrenton Turnpike to Manassas, McDowell ordered Tyler to attack Centreville at first light on July 18. Until the rest of the army was in position Tyler "was not to bring on an engagement."

The following morning, McDowell discovered that the roads to the south were impassable, and changed the plan so that two of his four divisions would now swing around to the north, crossing Bull Run farther upstream at a ford called Sudley Springs. As these two divisions then attacked southward, driving the Confederates back, his remaining two divisions, including that containing the 69th, could then cross the Stone Bridge over Bull Run and join the rout of the enemy.

Tyler, meanwhile, had marched into Centreville unopposed, with some companies continuing to scout forward to the fords at Bull Run, across which the Confederates had retreated the night before. At Blackburn's Ford these men were suddenly subject to a sharp fire from several positions across the river. Tyler, who should have ordered a withdrawal in accordance with McDowell's orders, instead ordered more support forward. A substantial skirmish developed in which the Union troops were not coming off best. Sherman's men arrived at the scene double time and immediately found themselves ducking and dodging Confederate shells along with their comrades.[22] A furious McDowell soon arrived, ordering Tyler to hold his position, but not to engage further. Tyler, however, for the second time that day, ignored his orders and started bringing his brigades back to Centreville, with Corcoran's men "retrieving from the roadside overcoats, blankets, canteens, knapsacks and thousands of other articles discarded on the hasty march to Blackburn's Ford."[23]

McDowell spent the following two days making a reconnaissance of the new crossings north of the Stone Bridge, and reissuing food and ammunition to the troops, both of which had been discarded with equal measure on the hot march from Washington. As they bedded down on the night of July 20, "coughing and moaning from leg cramps," the men of the 69th probably felt they had not had much rest since they left Washington. Apart from their daytime exertions, on a previous night they had slept in a low meadow where the heavy dew had drenched them to the skin — all this of course being blamed on Sherman who had ordered them to camp there. On another night, a frightened horse had charged through their camp, scattering muskets in all directions, in response to which, "In an instant five thousand men were on their feet, ready to grapple with cavalry of the enemy."[24] Even so, it is doubtful whether sleep came easily that clear summer's night. Everyone knew it was the eve of a great battle. As much for a single regiment such as the 69th, as for the great continent itself, "There was never again such a night north or south of Bull Run," one historian has evocatively written, "It was the twilight of America's innocence."[25]

Chapter 3

The Fighting 69th

First blood at Bull Run

In the darkness of early morning on July 21, the soldiers of the Army of Washington began to form ranks. Some had not slept at all. Some had just begun to sleep. None had slept adequately. In the dark, men could not find their places in the line, and then the line could not find the road. When it did, just as on the other marches, "it was stop and go but mostly stop, except that now there was the added confusion of darkness and bone deep weariness as they stumbled over logs and roots and were stabbed at by branches in the woods." At about 9:30 a.m., already two and a half hours behind schedule, the head of the flanking column reached the designated upper crossing, Sudley Springs, and halted for a rest. Downstream, Sherman's brigade had been in position opposite the Stone Bridge across Bull Run and to the right of the Warrenton Turnpike since 6 a.m. Despite their presence, the Confederates, or at least enough of them to check the Union advance temporarily, had divined McDowell's plan. Captain Nathan G. "Shanks" Evans, commanding the troops opposite Sherman's at the Stone Bridge, dispatched the majority of his force northward to meet the anticipated threat from the left flank, while the Confederate commander, Beauregard, began to order most of his brigades, which he had positioned at the lower fords, to follow suit. As the lead regiment of one of McDowell's flanking divisions — the Second Rhode Island Regiment, commanded by Colonel Ambrose Burnside — emerged from a wood about a mile south of Sudley Springs, it was met by the fire of the Fourth South Carolina and the First Louisiana, Evans' troops. The Battle of Bull Run was under way.[1]

For the first half of the battle, the Union army met with some success. They had the advantage in that they were initially attacking against smaller numbers, with the Confederates constantly trying to shift troops from their original positions northward to stem the advance. Beauregard's men were steadily pressed back, even though successive Union brigades were joining the attack only piecemeal after making their crossing at Sudley Springs. Around noon, with the Union assault beginning to stutter, McDowell ordered Tyler's division to cross the river, even though the Stone Bridge was still held by the rebels. Sherman led his troops north of the

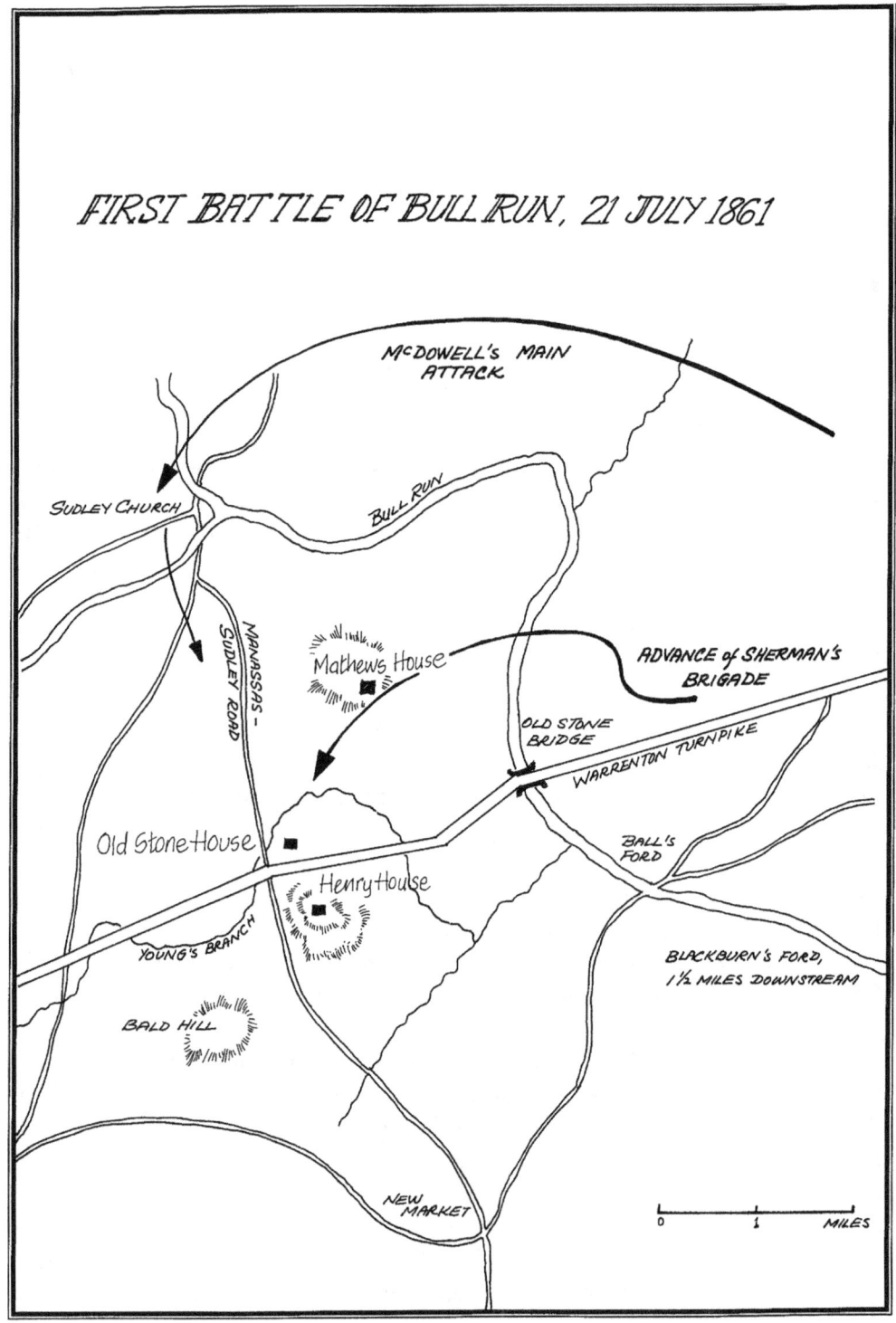

bridge to a nearby ford, where they crossed the river "eager, excited, thrilled with hot desire to bear our share in routing the enemy."[2]

Sherman's immediate concern, however, was that he might be fired on by the Union soldiers who would be advancing on his right, especially as two of the companies in the 69th were wearing gray uniforms. As it was, this worked to their advantage. They had emerged almost behind the Confederate line of defense. As the 69th cautiously made their way eastward toward the sound of the battle, they came in sight of the 4th Alabama Regiment. This regiment had moments earlier been ordered to fall back in the face of the Union advance. As described by one of their officers, they were retiring "in good order through the woods on our left" when they saw the gray uniforms approaching from their right. These "gray uniforms" were so far within the Confederate lines that they "were confidently regarded by us as friends." Suddenly Corcoran's men opened "a murderous fire" on the Alabamians, forcing them to reel back in confusion.[3] But not before the Alabamians had fired a return volley which killed acting Lieutenant Colonel Haggerty. Haggerty, according to Sherman's report, "without orders, rode over and endeavored to intercept their [the Confederate] retreat."[4] The arrival of the 69th onto the battlefield was noticed by Colonel Burnside. In his report he wrote how, "It was Sherman's brigade, with the 69th New York Militia in advance, that arrived about 12.00 o'clock and by a most deadly fire assisted in breaking the enemy's lines."[5] With the arrival of Sherman's fresh troops on the scene, who were now able to merge with the main body of Union troops advancing down the Sudley Springs Road, the Union advance appeared irresistible. With victory apparently again in his grasp, McDowell rode along the line shouting, "Victory! Victory! The Day is ours."[6]

A "damned Stonewall"?

Not quite. And certainly not if one Thomas J. Jackson had anything to do with it. In a war that threw up many eccentrics and many great generals, Jackson took pride of place in both camps. Among his many idiosyncrasies, he believed one side of him was heavier than the other; he would often ride with one hand in the air to let the blood flow downward and "lighten" that arm and by doing so improve his balance.[7] As McDowell's forces began to push his comrades back across the Warrenton Turnpike, the climax of the battle, and Jackson's part in it, took place on a rising known as Henry House Hill. It was here the initially routed Confederates were making their final stand. Jackson was sent to reinforce these men and had posted his force just behind the crest of the hill, out of the direct line of artillery fire and waiting the charge of the Federal infantry.

Off to the right front of Jackson, the Confederate brigadier general Barnard Bee was attempting to rally his wavering men. "There is Jackson standing like a stone wall!" he called out, "Rally behind the Virginians!" And a legend was born. At least one observer placed a different spin on Bee's remarks, claiming that he had been berating Jackson for standing "like a damned stone wall" and not coming to his aid. Whatever the case, and Bee being mortally wounded almost immediately afterward not being in a position to clarify the matter, Jackson would belong to the ages as "Stonewall" Jackson.[8]

With the fight for the Hill now moving toward a bloody climax, the two most forward Federal batteries, containing 11 guns, commanded by Captains Charles Griffin and James R. Ricketts, which had been inflicting severe damage to the Confederates, were lost. Similar to the incident between the 69th and the Fourth Alabama, a regiment, this time in blue, approached the batteries from some woods 70 yards to their right. Thinking it might be infantry support, the gunners held fire for a few minutes. This was just enough time to allow the blue-clad soldiers to level their muskets and deliver a volley into the ranks of the gunners, for the regiment was the 33rd Virginia of Jackson's brigade. Every cannoneer went down and the guns were taken. At almost the same moment, two regiments of Zouaves which had been posted to the right of Griffin's and Rickett's batteries broke under the charge of Confederate cavalry and fled back down the slope, dragging with them another regiment of infantry. As a consequence, when Sherman was ordered to send in his brigades to try to take the hill, although they even managed to recapture some of the recently lost artillery pieces, the absence of artillery support and the piecemeal tactics which were used in the assault were too much to overcome.[9]

The pattern of the assault on Henry House Hill was one that would recur throughout the war to deadly effect on the Federal troops and the subsequent Irish Brigade in particular. The troops were advanced piecemeal; in this case they attacked regiment by regiment, with one advancing when the other was beaten back. As one of Jackson's biographers succinctly put it, "The [Federal] infantry ... was not well handled."[10] First up on this day was the 2nd Wisconsin. They were clad in gray militia uniforms and had already been badly shot up by both comrades and enemies. As they marched to the crest of the hill and were silhouetted across the top, they were met with a withering fire, mainly from Jackson's men lying just behind the crest. The Wisconsin men kept up the fight for a while, until eventually falling back in some confusion, not stopping until they had crossed back over the Warrenton Turnpike. Next was the turn of the 79th New York, known as the Highlanders. They quickly met the same fate as the 2nd Wisconsin. Finally, it was the turn of Corcoran's men.

Described by one historian, "It was a medieval moment.... [A] strange green banner above them ... bayonets glittering like spears above their bowed heads ... Latin words rolling from the lips of Father O'Reilly, who commended every soul to God."[11] The men, in their shirtsleeves and carrying nothing but their guns and ammunition, heard Meagher call out, "Come on, boys, here's your chance at last!"

3. The Fighting 69th

As they ran up the side of the hill, they came under the fire of the rebel batteries and muskets. The Zouave company which Meagher had raised would suffer particularly badly, as would other Zouave companies, conspicuous targets in their red outfits. The scene from the charge that is most often recounted is that of the color bearer who was ordered by Corcoran to lower the flag as it was drawing too much enemy fire. "Don't ask me to do that, Colonel," the bearer protested, "I'll never lower it," upon uttering which he was then shot dead. The flag was immediately raised by another soldier who met the same fate. John Keefe, the third color bearer that day, then had it torn from his hands by a rebel. Keefe shot him and retook the colors, only to be taken prisoner by more Confederates. Keefe, obviously a resourceful man, then shot two of his captors with a concealed revolver, retrieving the flag yet again, and capturing a rebel and a captain's sword in the bargain.[12]

However many individual acts of bravery there may have been, they were never going to be sufficient to shift Jackson's men. Three times the Irishmen rallied to try to reach the crest of the hill, only to be driven back each time. "It was nothing but rally, charge and repulse," one soldier described it, "Still the boys went to their work like bricks."[13] A watching officer, Colonel Alexander Porter of the 16th U.S. Infantry, recorded how the 69th "nobly stood and returned the fire of the enemy for 15 minutes," until eventually, like the Wisconsin men and the Highlanders before, they were forced back.[14] Captain Kelly, who would write the official report after the battle following Corcoran's capture during the retreat, described how they were "finally driven off, owing principally to the panic of the regiment which preceded us."[15] While it may indeed have been "a gallant charge, gallantly led and gallantly sustained,"[16] it was certainly symptomatic of the tide turning against the Federal forces on that July day. The valiant stand of the Confederates at Henry House Hill, combined with the fact that many of the Federal forces had been fighting and marching for nearly 13 hours, now under a hot July sun, had McDowell's army near breaking point. It was at this time that Jackson led his men forward to counterattack the still advancing but increasingly demoralized Federals, telling them that, "When you charge, yell like furies."[17] Also arriving on the scene were Confederate reinforcements from the Shenandoah Valley. The Federal troops watched in consternation as the rebel line thickened and lengthened to their front. Consternation then turned to anger and along their front shouting could be heard. "Where are our reserves? ... Betrayed! We are betrayed! Sold Out!" The militia men had fought a good fight, better than probably anyone had a right to expect. But when the long gray line at their front sprang at them, "bayonets snapping and glinting in the sunlight as the shrill, unearthly quaver of the rebel yell came surging down the slope they faltered. Then they broke."[18] What was subsequently called "the great skedaddle" had begun. According to Kelly's report, "The panic was too general, and the 69th had to retreat with the great mass of Federals."[19]

Retreats and rumors

What began as a sullen retreat, as the Federal soldiers began to leave the field slowly and with scattered resistance at first, soon turned into a rout. With men separated from their companies, and officers losing control, the last shred of discipline disappeared among the ranks of the Federals. A wild scramble began for the crossings over Bull Run. Only members of Sherman's brigade, including the 69th and some regular soldiers, maintained their discipline during the withdrawal. "By the active exertions of Colonel Corcoran," wrote Sherman in his report, "we formed an irregular square against cavalry, and we began our retreat towards that ford of Bull Run by which we had approached the field of battle."[20] Slowly the hollow square of stalwarts withdrew from the field, eventually falling to pieces itself as the crossings were reached. It was at this point that Corcoran and a number of others were separated from the main body of the regiment and were captured by a contingent of Virginia cavalry.[21] One of the officers captured with Corcoran, James Rorty, later wrote in reply to Sherman's official battle report in which the brigade commander had said that the "69th fell back [from Henry House Hill] in some confusion," that it had been Sherman who initially ordered the 69th to retire. When Corcoran was then later attempting to get his men across the river, it was again Sherman who had told them "to get away as fast as they could as the enemy's cavalry were coming," and it was the disorder and straggling caused by this "license to run" which led to them being cut off.[22]

Meagher, however, escaped unharmed in one of those strange and controversial episodes that characterized his battlefield experiences during the Civil War. Even Meagher's own account is picturesque and not particularly glorious. Retreating down Henry House Hill, he claimed to have been knocked head over heels and left senseless on the field, only to be rescued by a passing trooper of the 2nd U.S. Dragoons who recognized Meagher and pulled him across his saddle to take him out of danger. He then hitched a ride on an artillery wagon until, crossing another stream, he was pitched out of the wagon into the water as the column was attacked by some marauding Confederate cavalry. After floundering about for a while, he once more joined with the melee of retreating soldiers, and did not stop again until he reached their previous campsite where he met up with some other members of the 69th. Upon hearing that most of the regiment was up ahead on the road, he took the regimental doctor's horse and caught up with it. Finally, "At three o clock in the morning of the 22nd of July, famished and naked almost, the 69th passed through the familiar gates of their old quarters" at Camp Corcoran. Other accounts were to prove less bizarre but more damning.[23]

The *London Times* correspondent, William Russell, claimed that he saw Meagher running "across country" away from the battle. As he passed Russell, Meagher was heard to exclaim that the Confederates had "established their claim to be a belligerent power," asserting that the Federal army had "been beaten handsomely,

3. The Fighting 69th

and [the Confederates] are entitled to it."²⁴ Russell's charges, allied to his scathing account of McDowell's army, aroused a storm of protest in Washington and New York newspapers, with some soldiers making threats on Russell's life. Another journalist, Henry Villiard of the *Cincinnati Commercial*, who had taken a dislike to Meagher before the war, claimed that Meagher was drunk before the battle. On the way to Bull Run, Villiard described how he had come across Meagher resting with a cocked pistol in his right hand. "Well, captain, are you ready for the fray," Villiard called out. "Yes," replied Meagher, "There is nothing like being always ready for the damned rebs." According to Villiard, Meagher's eyes and his unsteadiness in the saddle showed plainly that "he had braced himself internally for the fight."²⁵ Less easy to dismiss were the remarks of Judge Daly's wife, Maria Daly, who recorded how an officer in the 69th had told her that during the battle Meagher "was intoxicated and had just enough sense and elation to make one rush forward, and afterward fell from his horse drunk and was picked up by troopers."²⁶

Charges like these would follow Meagher throughout his participation in the war, but it was rare that the bravery of the soldiers themselves was called into question. A Confederate officer was quoted as saying that amid the melee as the retreat began, the Irish had stood "like a rock in the whirlpool rushing past them ... fought like heroes," and "did retire slowly." Even a correspondent from the generally ultra-jingoistic southern newspapers wrote that the 69th regiment, now being generally referred to as "The fighting 69th," even it had comprised of such "strolling vagabonds as they could pick up in the low groggeries ... in New York," had "fought like tigers;" while another southern journal had said, "All honor to the 69th, even in its errors," its "errors" of course entailing fighting on the "wrong" side.²⁷ Indeed the men of the 69th were still in fighting mood immediately after the battle, as the question of their three-month enlistments arose again.

Bull Run had furnished a great many young men, and not just the Irish, with all the military experience they desired, at least for the present. "We were taken to the shambles to be slaughtered," wrote one soldier, "all we saved is our honor."²⁸ As the clamor of the "three month men" rose, they became mutinous again, especially the 69th. So much so that Sherman, that "rude and envenomed martinet" as Meagher would later describe him, trained a battery of guns on the regiment, and insisted that he would give the orders to open fire if the men dared to leave camp.²⁹ He was just the man to order their use as well, especially in the immediate aftermath of the battle, as one regimental historian wrote, "The milk of human kindness was rather deficient in him at the time."³⁰

A further incident, which involved Lincoln himself, began one morning soon after the "mutiny" was put down. As Sherman was walking through camp, a captain of the 69th called to Sherman from a crowd, "Colonel, I'm going to New York today." When Sherman said that he had signed no pass, the officer answered, "I need no leave. My time is up and I'm going." Aware that others were watching the outcome, Sherman "turned on him sharply." Never one to waste words, or gestures, Sherman thrust his hand inside his coat and calmly told the officer that "the question of your terms of service has been submitted to the rightful authority and the decision has been published in orders. You are a soldier, and must submit to orders until you are properly discharged. If you attempt to leave without orders, it will be mutiny, and I will shoot you like a dog!" The captain retreated.

Later the same day Lincoln paid a surprise visit to Sherman's brigade. "We heard you'd got over the big scare," Lincoln told Sherman, "and we thought we'd come over and see the boys." Lincoln's carriage pulled up outside the entrance to Fort Corcoran and Sherman called out the 69th who gathered around the president. After Lincoln had made what Sherman described as one of the "neatest, best, and most feeling addresses I ever listened to," the disgruntled captain from that morning managed to approach Lincoln and loudly complain that Sherman had threatened to shoot him. "Mr. Lincoln looked at him," recalled Sherman, "then at me, and stooping his tall, spare form toward the officer, said to him in a loud stage whisper, easily heard from some yards around, "Well, if I were you, and he threatened to shoot, I wouldn't trust him, for I believe he would do it." The crestfallen captain retreated once more, as his comrades whooped with laughter, and Lincoln's carriage pulled off.[31]

Little did the unfortunate captain realize that the following day the regiment would finally receive its orders for sailing to New York in any case, in preparation for being mustered out at the end of their "long three months." On Saturday, July 27, the 69th landed at the Battery in New York and marched up Broadway, cheered on by "the greatest crowds ever seen in New York City," with "The crack Seventh Regiment turned out as an escort of honor from the wharf to the armory" on Essex Street. There they were drawn up and dismissed, with instructions to return on Monday and be mustered out of the service. At Bull Run, Sherman's brigade had suffered the highest numbers of casualties, with the 69th suffering the most: 38 men were killed, 59 wounded, and 95 missing, a total of 192, or about 16 percent of their strength. The men had acquitted themselves well, and a great adventure appeared to be ending. Yet before the month was out, and despite the bad feeling which the fiasco over the enlistment dates had caused, most of the 69th, after having been mustered out, decided to volunteer for another three years. On August 26, the *New York Daily Tribune* wrote how "The Irish spirit of the North is thoroughly aroused, and thousands are ready to obliterate the sad memories of the first engagement in which the green flag waved gloriously beside the Stars and Stripes." Yet such sentiments would have seemed preposterous a bare six months previously, as Irish Americans, for a variety of reasons, would have appeared to be perhaps the single-most unlikely candidates to rally round the flag. Now there was talk of organizing an entire brigade of 5,000 men composed entirely of Irish.[32]

Chapter 4

Standing by the Union

"Let the Irish then do the fighting"

Whatever the reasons men might subsequently want to fight for the Union, it was unlikely that what exactly they were fighting for greatly troubled the majority of those who were on that dusty July march through northern Virginia to that first great battle at Bull Run. The three-month enlistment period itself was a sign how many felt that the rebellion would be swiftly crushed, and signed up so they would not miss their chance at playing soldiers. The flight from Henry House Hill would change all this. New recruits were to enlist for a term of three years, and any man, whether native born or just stepped off an immigrant ship, would have to have a good reason to give his free consent to such a condition. The defeat at Bull Run had clearly demonstrated that there really was going to be a war, and as Sherman would later remark, war meant fighting and fighting meant killing.

Yet, while the 69th had taken around 1,000 men into the fight at Bull Run, the main problem for its colonel in finding this number had been one of selection rather than recruitment. Such was the rush of enthusiasm and excitement after the firing on Fort Sumter, that Corcoran could have enlisted 5,000, except that the War Department had limited the number he was able to put under arms. This was not an uncommon experience among volunteer regiments during the early stages of the war, yet the Irish American community in 1861, antiabolitionist, antinativist, and as remote from so many of their fellow citizens as Chinese, could hardly have been viewed as fertile recruiting ground for the Union army.

The subsequent attachment which the Irish displayed toward their adopted country, not unsurprisingly, surprised many Americans, not the least of which were many from the southern states. Seeing only what they wanted to see, namely the Irish antipathy toward blacks, many believed that they hated "the nigger as they do the devil." Rather than fighting for the Union, they expected the Irish to "fight to sustain our rights, if it finally comes to that."[1] With the memory of Know-Nothingism also fresh, another sympathizer wrote to the new president of the Confederacy, Jefferson Davis, urging him to make conciliatory remarks toward the Irish in the North who were "a weak point in the enemy's line," having been "objects of bitter and most intense persecution by an ignorant band of bigots."[2] While many

Irish living in the South did fight for the Confederacy against the Union, the vast majority of those who lived in the northern states remained loyal. "Whatever may be their opinion of slavery, or the wrongs of the South," warned the *Irish American*, "they will not countenance a destruction of the government which has naturalized, enfranchised, and protected them."[3]

Some felt that they had an obligation to defend the country which had given them refuge, and to fight for what one described as "the honest, noblest, purest and best cause that ever summoned men to arms."[4] James McKay Rorty, writing to explain why he had reenlisted in the 69th after a lucky escape following capture at Bull Run, wrote of his attachment to and "veneration for the Constitution, which urged me to defend it at all risks."[5] Even in Massachusetts, where, under the influence of Know-Nothingism, the Irish militia had been disbanded in 1855, and where in 1859 legislation had been passed which delayed naturalized citizens from voting for a two-year period, the Irish-run *Boston Pilot* could declare that the Irish "will stand up for the Union, and surround it like a wall of fire," urging its readers to "Stand by the Union; fight for the Union; die by the Union."[6]

The desire to stand by the Union was also closely allied to the desire to be seen to be standing by the Union. Writing shortly after the war, one historian asserted that if an Irishman had "fought as an American citizen, he also fought as an Irish exile," and there was a strong belief that participation in the conflict would help lessen the hostility between native-born Americans and the immigrants.[7] This was a common factor among all the immigrant groups. "The fight to end slavery," wrote the historian of the German-Americans, in a conclusion that was equally applicable to the Irish Americans, "was simultaneously a fight by the immigrants for social acceptability on the part of the native population,"[8] something which was particularly important to the Irish after a rancorous and violent decade of anti–Irish, anti-immigrant and anti–Catholic agitation. A Private Casey put it baldly in a letter to one of his officers when he wrote, "Let the Irish then do the fighting and we want all the credit."[9]

This desire for acceptability and respectability operated at different levels, depending on whether the individual belonged to the "shanty" Irish or the "lace curtain" Irish. Being seen to be fighting for and dying in sufficient numbers in defense of the Union, would, in effect, help provide upwardly mobile "lace curtain" Irish with an entree into respectable American society. This was certainly the perspective among many of the principal Irish American leaders. It was also implicitly and explicitly the line followed by Irish newspapers such as the *Irish American* and the *Pilot*, the latter of which it is said "not only reported on the war itself, but the war within the war, the battle to improve the status and position of the Irish in American society."[10] The *Herald*, in jubilant terms and with more than a touch of hyperbole, in late 1861 declared that the war had "united in an eternal bond of

4. Standing by the Union

generous brotherhood the native American and those sons of foreign climes who share with us the enjoyment of rational liberty." The *Irish American* urged its readers "to be true to the land of your adoption in the crisis of her fate," while the *Boston Transcript* proclaimed that "You have fought nobly for the Harp and Shamrock, fight now for the Stars and Stripes.... Your adopted country wants you."[11] Archbishop Hughes ordered the United States flag to be suspended from St. Patrick's Cathedral, and in a letter which he sent to be read at the first mass meeting of the war, held in Union Square on April 20, 1861, he recounted that, "It is now forty years since, a foreigner by birth, I took the oath of allegiance to this country," since when he had "known but one country.... This has been my flag, and shall be to the end."[12] The message was passed on somewhat less eloquently via the foot solders of the hierarchy in sermons throughout the North. A Father Creedon of Auburn, New York, recounted how, "This is the first country the Irishman ever had that he could call his own country," before describing the two classes of men he most despised, "cowards and traitors; those who can enlist and do not, and are either one or the other."[13]

Mixed up with these sentiments, and perhaps unique to the Irish in terms of foreign-born soldiers in the Union army, was the spur of Irish nationalism and a corresponding hatred of Britain. This combination of American patriotism and Irish nationalism was something which native-born Americans never comprehended or trusted, and also greatly contributed to the Know-Nothing suspicions during the 1850s, especially as regards the loyalty of Irish militia units. One historian has remarked that the United States, "as the first rebel nation against the Empire and refuge to the Fenians had long been held in special esteem among Irish separatists whose tendency was always to support Washington in its disputes against Westminster."[14] British sympathies were with the South, and, as the *Irish American* declared, "If any Irish-born man wants a better reason for adhering to the Union, we don't know it.... If England's interest be served by the destruction of this Confederation, it is ours to thwart her: which we mean to do to the utmost of our ability."[15] Northern Irish tended to feel their battles were Ireland's battles, as the fight against the south was a fight against the monarchistic and aristocratic class of southern leaders, similar to the Irish landlords. A northern war correspondent wrote that "one might have supposed that the year '98 had been revived and that these brawny Celts were again afield against their Saxon countrymen."[16]

There is no doubt that many Irish joined up in the belief they could acquire military skills and experience that could one day be put to use against Britain. Corcoran, like other Fenians, was initially opposed to his countrymen joining the army for fear that their movement would be decimated, a fear that was well founded. He eventually relented and urged that if an Irishman had to enlist, he should enlist in an Irish regiment. "When this unhappy civil war is at a close and the Union

37

restored," declared Corcoran, "there will be tens of thousands of Ireland's noblest sons left to redeem their native land from the oppression of old England." There was even a belief that prosouthern British opinion would lead to a confrontation and, perhaps, war with the United States, providing further opportunity for Irish freedom.[17]

Undoubtedly, the strongest factor in Irish enlistment was poverty. Faced with the choice of hunger or signing up, many Irish responded to the initial call more eagerly than others. A French visitor to New York in 1861 wrote how he "saw poor, famished Irishmen devour these seductive posters with their eye, fascinated as they were by the devilish hands pointing to the complacent listing of soldiers rations: bread, wine, meat, vegetables and beer."[18] A great many had lost whatever employment they had due to the depression which accompanied the secession crisis. Even before the election of Lincoln, some industries had anticipated the worst. The wholesale clothing industry, catering largely for a southern market, convinced that the South would not take its wares if Lincoln won the election, had stopped giving out work. After the election the situation deteriorated as southern customers repudiated their debts to merchants and manufacturers, and business failures mounted.[19]

Within a space of six weeks, at least 80,000 persons were said to have been thrown out of work, and those contemplating emigration from Ireland were warned by one writer that it would be "sheer madness" to come over at this time. Another wrote home in August 1861 that "the times is miserable in this contery ... [since] this rebellion has stoped all publick works ad men is going about in thousands that cant get any thing to Do." With "the business of the Country ... wholly prostrate," wrote another, "all the people who have lived by their labor and only from hand to mouth ... are going to war."[20] The Irish were not alone among immigrant groups in their predicament, as the *New York Herald* dryly remarked upon the high proportion of foreigners among recruits in New York during the first days of the war: "It may be a question whether the applicants are actuated by the desire of preserving the Union of the states or the union of their bodies and souls."[21]

Leading from the Front

Individual cases would have their own particular reason for enlisting, with the emphasis on the individual's circumstances and emotions. Thomas Francis Meagher was one of those who had several good reasons for joining the Union army, few of which would probably have been apparent even a few short months before he was offering the services of himself and his company of Zouaves to fight the Confederates at Bull Run.

Like the vast majority of his countrymen in the North, Meagher was a Democrat whose political beliefs were balanced by an intense dislike of Lincoln's Republicans

4. Standing by the Union

One of the least "posed" photographs available which captures something of the "loucheness" and the "mad, bad and dangerous to know" aspects of Meagher and members of Co.K, 69th NYSM, the "Irish Zouaves," 1861 (collection of Michael J McAfee).

on the one hand and a certain sympathy for the South on the other. "I could see none of the horrors that I had been taught to believe existed among them [southerners]," he wrote after touring the South in 1856, "I found a people sober, intelligent, high-minded, patriotic, and kind-hearted ... I saw no poverty."[22] In April 1861, he had argued with his father-in-law, an ardent Republican, for calling the Confederates rebels. "You cannot call eight millions of white freemen 'rebels' sir," Meagher had exploded, "You may call them 'revolutionists' if you will." Later that same evening in a New York restaurant he declared "candidly and plainly that, in this controversy, my sympathies are entirely with the South." Soon after, he left on a trip to New England during which Fort Sumter was fired upon. On his return to New York, Meagher was clearly aghast to find the temper of the city so changed. Never had he witnessed "such a change in public opinion as has taken place during the past week. I feel like one carried away by a torrent. The whole cry is—'The Flag! The Flag.'" The following day, as the 69th Militia took its boisterous leave of New York upon the *James Adgar*, Meagher's advertisement appeared in the *New York Daily Tribune* calling for the 100 "healthy, intelligent and active" young Irishmen. These volunteers were needed to go and fight those stout "revolutionists," with whom he had "entirely" been in sympathy three weeks previously, for a cause which Meagher now described as never "more sacred, more just, nor more urgent." Even his friends and allies were amazed. Cavanagh, later one of Meagher's biographers, wrote how he could not "comprehend the cause of so sudden and radical a change."[23] Such a *volte-face* can be easily enough explained as sheer undiluted opportunism. One did not need to have extraordinarily sensitive political antennae in those autumn months to realize that war was going to mean opportunity and advancement for many, and in 1861 Meagher was in dire personal need of both.

"The relative calm of the Irish community in New York," wrote the historian of the 69th Militia, "was shattered on May 27, 1852, when a good looking stocky stranger walked into the law office of Dillon and O'Gorman in William Street, and announced that he was Thomas Francis Meagher, lately escaped from Australia."[24] As with many who fought on the Union side in the war, Meagher has been treated kindly by historians. "Dashing," "gallant" and "colorful" are words that frequently crop up when the Irish Brigade and Meagher's contribution are discussed. In normally brief descriptions of his career prior to 1861, it is easy to see why his life should be described as "colorful." Highlights include his time as a Young Irelander and the 1848 rising; the escape to the United States from Tasmania; his subsequent careers at the bar, as a newspaper owner and a much-in-demand lecturer are all mentioned, as is his marriage to Elizabeth Townsend, daughter of a wealthy Fifth Avenue merchant. What such a superficial and picturesque resume conceals is that in 1861 Meagher was almost a has been, a fleeting hero now in search of a role. After his celebrity status waned soon after arriving from Tasmania, he had dabbled

4. Standing by the Union

in several areas, such as law and publishing, without much experience or success in any area. He was fortunate in his marriage, but was unable to afford a home of his own and was living with his in-laws. His main employment was that of an itinerant or vagabond public speaker on past glories on the ethnic circuit in the States. This was an uncomfortable and debilitating existence in the midcentury America, the equivalent of what modern politicians call the "cold chicken" circuit, upon which Meagher was stuck, waiting for something to turn up.

Such was his disillusionment with the United States that during the late 1850s he attempted to start a new career elsewhere after renewing his acquaintance with Ramon Paez, a Venezuelan, with whom he had attended Stoneyhurst College, the English public school. Paez's father would become president of Venezuela, and in 1858 Meagher had traveled with Paez to Central America, becoming involved in another unsuccessful scheme, the promotion of an alternative to the Panama Canal as the main route of interoceanic travel. On his return to New York, with the Paez family now in power in Venezuela, he began lobbying the new Republican administration of Lincoln to obtain the position of United States minister to that country. Given his well-known Democratic sympathies, and the fact that there were no doubt a great many deserving Republicans whose needs had also to be attended to, he was again unsuccessful. Then, like Corcoran discovered, as the long-talked-about secession of the southern states occurred and jaw jaw turned into war war, something quite big had actually turned up.[25]

It is hard not to disagree with much of the description of Meagher, certainly in relation to his activities during the Civil War, as being that of a "professional ethnic." This term has been used to describe someone who "exploited ethnicity to advance their personal status, to promote vaulting political ambitions, to improve their financial fortunes," and who "set a higher priority on their personal careers than on promoting the ethnic cause," Meagher being "the archetypal professional ethnic."[26] The more cynical historians have tended to see the participation of ethnic soldiers in general in the war as largely the product of their dire economic circumstances or as a more direct exercise in raising the status of ethnic minorities. Yet such a sweeping condemnation of Meagher's and indeed his comrades' motives is, to an extent, unfair. It certainly omits a degree of Irish nationalism and anti–British sentiment previously mentioned, which were also factors in Irish participation in general on the Union side, and of which Meagher must also have had his fair share. It is also quite credible that Meagher genuinely felt, as again many of his fellow comrades undoubtedly felt, that he was honor bound to support the country which had given him and so many of his compatriots asylum and the chance of a new start.

This is certainly the emphasis which most later accounts, admittedly written through a rose-tinted haze, would wish to place. Yet in the earliest full account of the Irish Brigade, that of Conyngham's written in 1866, only a year after the end of the war, Conyngham writes, "The Irish felt that not only was the safety of the great Republic, the home of their exiled race, at stake, but also, that the great principles of democracy were at issue with the aristocratic doctrines of monarchism."[27] A more general history published two years later claimed that "they [the Irish] were animated by a high sense of duty, and an earnest feeling of patriotism"[28]; while it was possible to find a soldier in the brigade writing in 1863 that, "In this country ... we have a free government, just laws, and a constitution which guarantees equal rights and privileges to all.... We have the same national, political and social interest at stake not only for ourselves but for the coming generations and the oppressed of every nation for America was a common asylum for all."[29]

What made Meagher unique was that he was like a composite of all the various motivations rolled into one, an individual melting pot of various desires, aspirations and needs. As recruiting for an all–Irish brigade began in earnest in September 1861, from a rented room over the Metropolitan Hotel at 596 Broadway, with "a solitary chair, a few benches, a single desk and a few placards on the walls," whomever looked at Meagher could no doubt see a bit of themselves and their individual motives in him, whether this was the Irish patriot, or the American patriot, or the "cute hoor" on the make, or someone who just needed a job. This is perhaps why he was, and would remain, popular with the vast majority of those who served in the brigade.[30]

Chapter 5

Commissioning a Brigade

Meagher's Maneuvers

Not everyone was entirely enthusiastic about Irishmen enlisting en masse to fight in the war. Irish opinion at home was extremely apprehensive at the start of the war. One local paper expressed the sentiment that it mattered not "whether puritanical North or slave holding South, carried off the laurels of victory.... Our concern was with another flag — the sunburst of Erin." *The Nation* expressed the hope that it would not witness "the horrors of civil war in the States" as "it is but too likely that Irish blood would flow on both sides ... we shall look out anxiously for news, not of victories and defeats, but of peace and reconciliation."[1] One unsurprising objection came from an Irishman writing from prison in Richmond after being captured at Bull Run. Aggrieved over the enlistment debacle, "Old Abe would not let the regiment go home," he wrote, "Well it served us right when we were fools enough to fight in such a cause; but I hope the time will come when Irishmen will mind their own business."[2]

Their own unfinished business in Ireland was the spur for an Irish revolutionary paper in New York, *The Phoenix*, which argued that the Irish should stay out of the war as "The first enemies the 69th will encounter will, in all probability be Irishmen, some of them their relatives, all of them friends ... in the death grip of one another, thousands of miles from the land which it would be their common pride to defend, and their common honor to die for."[3] Meagher, for his own reasons, would be much more enthusiastic for participation in the war, while also privately believing that it was "a moral certainty that many of our countrymen who enlist in this struggle ... will fall in the contest." But echoing Corcoran's judgment on the military value of the war to the Irish, Meagher declared that, "If only one in ten of us come back when this war is over, the military experience gained by that one will be of more service in a fight for Ireland's freedom than would that of the entire ten as they are now," especially as he regarded the militiamen as simply "Broadway militaires," unsuited to any serious military action.[4] In any case, whatever doubts people did have were merely brushed aside in the heady rush to enlist "for the duration" after Bull Run. Patriotism, patronage and personal ambition together proved a potent combination, with the latter two in particular, dangling the temptation of "a colonel's commission to be awarded to some distinguished, well-heeled citizen who had exerted himself to round up recruits."[5]

It was eventually August 3 before the 69th in its Bull Run conception as state militia was mustered out of service, and on August 21, a large majority of the members of the regiment decided to reenlist. This "new" regiment was given the same numerical designation, the 69th, but was termed New York State Volunteers. On August 23, the first mention of a projected brigade consisting of a number of Irish regiments appeared in the press. The exact genesis for the idea of a distinct Irish brigade is hazy, although it is quite possible that it was in the minds of any number of Irish given the tradition of Irish brigades fighting in the service of European powers. Certainly, one enthusiastic proponent was Meagher, who was the focus for the public recruiting campaign. Also involved was a committee of prominent New York Irish, including Richard O' Gorman, Judge Daly, Michael Phelan and Robert Emmet, which had been set up originally to organize a fund for the families of the 69th Militia.[6] The command of the brigade was initially to be tendered to another Irishman, Brigadier General James Shields, a veteran of the Mexican-American War of 1846–48. In the event, Shields would decline the offer. Apparently he felt, or was made to feel, that the brigadier generalship of a brigade of volunteers was beneath him, and was holding out for a Major General's command. According to Judge Daly's wife, it was Meagher who was instrumental in turning Shields' head from command of the Irish Brigade, allowing the "crafty Meagher" himself a clear run. "General Shields ... has destroyed himself," wrote Maria Daly, "Meagher, like the fox in the fable, has induced him to drop his pieces of meal in the Irish Brigade by telling him how much better he would be as a Major general, and flattering his vanity."[7] Although the official outcome of who would command the new brigade would not be known until February 1862, in the meantime, Meagher had firmly established himself as the prime contender for the position to such an extent that on October 21 he was able to dispatch his first general and special order under the title of acting brigadier. The maneuvering for this position probably began in Meagher's own mind back in April when he felt like he was being "carried away by a torrent" of support for the war and decided to raise his own company of Zouaves, and no doubt continued unabated during and immediately after the Bull Run debacle.[8]

Given the enforced absence of Corcoran in Libby Prison, Richmond, there was a question as to who would or should assume his leadership mantle, both specifically as regards the 69th, and also of the New York Irish in general.[9] The larger question was settled, if only temporarily, in remarkably quick time in favor of Meagher, who, militarily, was perhaps the least qualified or entitled to fill that position, but who, politically, was in a different league from his opponents. According to one historian, "Meagher's advantages included an unexcelled talent for self-aggrandizement, fierce ambition, and unmatched skill as an orator accompanied by the

5. Commissioning a Brigade

energy and willingness to travel the ethnic political circuit in pursuit of the twin goals of an Irish Brigade and a general's commission."[10] Meagher's maneuvering to achieve these ends would leave a trail of bitterness. One of those on the receiving end of Meagher's maneuvers to attain his goals was Alderman James Bagley, major of the 69th Militia. When the 69th, along with other New York Irish regiments, arrived back in New York in July, it was led in a parade up Broadway by the senior line officer, Captain James Kelly, who had made the regiment's official report following the battle. Lieutenant Colonel Nugent, who had returned from Fort Corcoran a few days before, marched behind the other officers. Bagley, who had not been at Bull Run, was criticized in the *New York Daily Tribune* for riding at the head of the regiment. In the same paper, a "warm friend of the 69th" published a letter saying that Major Bagley, upon whom command should now devolve, was not as competent as some others, and would it not be better to entrust the command to Captain Meagher instead?[11] As the drive to recruit new regiments began in earnest, there was growing resentment at the *parvenu*, Meagher, who, prior to Bull Run, had displayed little interest in the old 69th. At one meeting, the majority of officers in the 69th Militia had voted against tendering its services, with the motion for continuing in service apparently defeated "largely by the vote of a large number of officers who had been commissioned by the state but had remained at home" during the Bull Run campaign.[12] Meagher was obviously going to go ahead and recruit for the "new" regiment, the 69th New York State Volunteers. At one point during the dispute, Bagley's name was to head a list of signatures under a resolution publicly condemning Meagher for "certain remarks reflecting on the character of the officers and members" of the 69th Militia. These remarks were to the effect that "the best of the old 69th would be with him [Meagher]" while those who chose to stay behind were "impostors" and "there could be no regiment with the number '69' on their caps parading Broadway in their absence." Bagley's resolution, part of which read like a charge sheet against Meagher, stated that, "No speaker from whatever motive whether of malice, self-aggrandizement, or bid for popularity can injure the name or impair the standing of the 69th."[13] "I despise them and defy them," Meagher railed in response, and continued, perhaps protesting too much, that he despised and "utterly defy their gossip, their resolutions, their most venomous conspiracies and calumnies against me."[14]

Another possible "victim," despite eventually becoming colonel of the new 69th New York Volunteers, and eventually commander of the Irish Brigade in 1864, was Nugent, although his role is somewhat ambiguous. Nugent worked very closely with Meagher in the Irish Brigade. One account credits both of them, "on the very day that the 69th Militia returned to New York from the battlefield at Bull Run," with conceiving in the regiment's armory the idea of forming an Irish brigade.[15] Captain Lyons, a supporter of Meagher, writing in 1869, claimed that Meagher "authorized Col. Nugent to raise the first regiment [of the proposed brigade], to be known as the 69th" after having received permission from the secretary of war, Simon Cameron.[16] The sequence and substance of the events in Lyons account are somewhat misleading. Despite the fact that Nugent as lieutenant colonel was the ranking officer, and Meagher was, militarily speaking, one of the most junior captains, on August 22, Meagher had written to the War Department offering the services of the 69th. It was to "Colonel Thomas F. Meagher," on August 30, that the War Department replied accepting the services of the 69th. Shortly after this, on September 5, Meagher publicly denied that he had offered the services of the 69th, and also stated that he would not accept a colonelcy from the government. Two days later, it was then announced that the 69th had decided to open recruiting offices for the purpose of a reorganization of the regiment under the new colonel, Thomas Francis Meagher, with Nugent as the second field officer.

One verdict on this sequence of events was that they represented a "difficult and embarrassing maneuver to by-pass Nugent." This may have been the case, although Meagher was also reported to be the colonel of the Fourth Regiment organized for the Irish Brigade, the 88th New York State Volunteers. This regiment was formed around the nucleus of his former Zouave company and who were more popularly known as "Mrs. Meagher's Own." With Nugent becoming colonel of the 69th, it is also probable that he acquiesced in Meagher's schemes and indeed could have been the "warm friend of the 69th" who originally began the public lobbying for Meagher as the old 69th returned from Bull Run. Meagher by this time had already refused a number of other offers, including the colonelcy of the 63rd New York State Volunteers, who would eventually become the third New York regiment in the soon-to-be-formed Irish Brigade. He had also refused the offer of a captaincy in the regular army—which would have meant a permanent position as opposed to a commission in a volunteer unit which would cease once the war ended—as well as the post of colonel on the staff of General John Fremont in the West. A colonelcy or a captaincy was only small change however, and both of these appointments would clearly have removed him from his power base in the eastern cities, especially New York. Meagher had visions of much bigger prizes to be won. The public reason he gave for refusing the offer of the captaincy in the regular army was because of his "limited military practice and information" and he was "unwilling to leave the 69th ... as long as he can be of use to it." Presumably Meagher felt that "military practice and information" were not prerequisites for a brigadier general, as he then wrote to Simon Cameron on September 7 offering the services of an Irish brigade, which would consist of two regiments from New York, one from Philadelphia, and one from Boston. Meagher claimed that he could "organize an Irish Brigade of five thousand ... and have it ready in thirty days to march." Cameron replied to the effect that the application

5. Commissioning a Brigade

should have been made to the governor of New York, E. D. Morgan, who in turn accepted the offer on September 9.[17]

The formality of gaining acceptance had not prevented recruiting for the brigade to have already begun in earnest, with the appeals aimed at touching the range of motivations among the audiences. On August 29, Meagher was the main speaker at a "grand festival" for the widows and orphans of the old 69th held at Jones Wood in New York. According to one description, "Booths, stands, wagons and baskets occupied every available spot"; there were swings, merry-go-rounds, pipers and fiddlers, and "the sale and consumption of 'Fort Corcoran Lager Beer,' 'Bull Run Peaches,' and 'Manassas Gingerbread,' and edibles of all kinds of still more grotesque nomenclature." The attendance was estimated at between 30,000 and 70,000, and in the crush to gain admittance the entrance barriers were swept away in a torrent of people. In the confusion, a number of individuals made unauthorized entrance collections and were sternly warned to hand over the money in order to "save the trouble of a more pointed invitation." In his speech Meagher called on the "Irishmen of New York" to "stand to the last by the Stars and Stripes — the illustrious insignia of the nation that of all the world has been the friendliest sanctuary to the Irish race ... despite all the bereavements and abiding gloom it may bring on such homes, as this day miss the industry and love of the dead soldiers of the 69th."[18] In Boston the following month, where Know-Nothingism had been a strong force, and where Irish militia regiments had been disbanded in 1858, Meagher proclaimed that "in the centre of where this insult was offered to the Irish soldier — 'Know Nothingism' is dead ... the Irish soldier will henceforth take his stand proudly by the side of the native born ... and tell him that he has been equal to him in his allegiance to the Constitution." An all–Irish brigade was needed, he believed, as "Irishmen desire earnestly and passionately to be together in the fight for the Stars and Stripes," and because, "An Irishman never fights so well as when he has an Irishman for his comrade." Now was the time, roused Meagher, "Irishmen! Up! Take the sword in hand! Down to the banks of the Potomac!" and if any were able but unwilling they should "take the next Galway steamer home."[19]

Recruiting the ethnics

The proposed organizational plan of the brigade was relatively clear by early September. Philadelphia would provide one regiment, Boston another, and two from New York. The New York regiments, with Shields still the publicly preferred choice for brigade commander, would be commanded by Meagher and Nugent. There are discrepancies in some of the accounts with regard to designation of the brigades, as they were often termed the First Regiment, Second Regiment etc. The First Regiment was the first New York Regiment, the 69th. The Second Regiment was to be the one from Philadelphia, which was eventually the 116th Regiment, Pennsylvania Volunteers, commanded by Colonel Denis Heenan. The formation of this regiment was not authorized until June 1862, and the regiment did not subsequently join the Irish Brigade until that October. The Third Regiment was to have been from Boston, but due to local politicking, the regiment which did join the brigade did not do so until December 1862. In the meantime, the 63rd New York, a regiment not previously connected with the brigade, voted to join it, and became the Third Regiment, commanded by Lieutenant Colonel Patrick D. Kelly. The 88th New York, although the second of the New York regiments, was the Fourth Regiment of the brigade, initially with Meagher as colonel, succeeded by Henry Baker after Meagher became Brigade commander. At this stage a Fifth Regiment, apparently to have been the artillery component of the brigade, was also proposed with Meagher mentioned again as colonel, although this regiment never materialized in its intended form.[20]

Meagher's original concept for the brigade appears to have been almost that of an autonomous unit with its own artillery and cavalry units attached. Indeed, his schemes did not stop at a mere brigade, and for a time he entertained hopes of an entire division of Irish regiments, with himself a major general. The War Department's reply to such a request was almost magisterial, and should have given Meagher a forewarning of future difficulties. "Your proposals to have several regiments composed of Irish citizens now in service consolidated and placed under one command ... is not approved," wrote Adjutant General Lorenzo Thomas. "The sentiment of Union that has brought them into rank shoulder to shoulder with the natives of this and other countries is inconsistent with the idea of army organization on the basis of distinct nationalities, and to foster such organization among those who are fighting under the same flag is unwise and inexpedient."[21]

Although the War Department officially dampened that ambition, Meagher was to have ample trouble attempting to organize sufficient regiments to form the brigade, let alone a division. Despite the brouhaha and the verbal pyrotechnics that accompanied the initial recruitment for the brigade, many obstacles confronted its formation. There were particular problems with the regiments from Boston and Philadelphia, which meant that while both of these regiments probably had a majority of Irish when originally recruited, they were never as ethnically exclusive, as for example the 88th New York, which has been described as "practically an alien organization."[22] Ironically enough, one of the main problems in recruiting outside of New York was the very facet of recruitment which proved so attractive in prompting Meagher and others to become involved with volunteer regiments, namely, the power of patronage. Even before Meagher and others began to agitate for a regiment from Boston to be part of the Irish Brigade, Boston already had its own Irish regiment, the 9th Massachusetts, a fairly rough-and-tumble affair by all accounts.

5. Commissioning a Brigade

Three prominent Irish Bostonians were largely responsible for canvassing the formation of this regiment; Thomas Cass, a successful businessman, who became its first colonel; Patrick Donahoe, owner and editor of the *Boston Pilot*; and B. S. Treanor, editor of the *Irish Patriot*. It was again this latter pair who joined forces with Meagher in September 1861 to lobby Governor John Andrew to organize a second Irish regiment from Massachusetts. On September 23, Meagher made his "Down to the Potomac" speech in the Music Hall which has been credited with leading directly to the creation of the second regiment. However, Governor Andrew, no doubt driven to distraction by incessant and competing ethnic claims, had already made the decision, as on the same day a letter from Andrew was already on its way to Washington with a request for another Irish regiment.

His problems did not end there however. Maneuvering for leadership of the regiment began in earnest with Donahoe and Treanor having their own local and opposing candidates, while Meagher was promoting the claims of a group of officers from New York. A further dilemma was whether Andrew wanted his Massachusetts regiment to be subsumed into an Irish brigade largely dominated by the New York Irish, especially when one of his own local appointees, Major General Benjamin Butler, a powerful force in Massachusetts politics, was also eager for new regiments to join a New England force which he was assembling. As the pressures on Andrew mounted, his solution was worthy of Solomon; he would create two new Irish regiments. One of these, the 28th Massachusetts Infantry, would join Butler's force, while the second, the 29th Massachusetts Infantry, would be his contribution to the Irish Brigade. Alas for Andrew, this solution only presented him with two more headaches instead of one.

As it happens, the New York Irishmen made a clean sweep of the leadership of the two new regiments with William Monteith becoming colonel of the 28th Massachusetts, and Thomas Murphy, an officer from the old 69th, intended as colonel of the second new regiment, the 29th Massachusetts. The two regiments then went into camp, the 28th at a place called Camp Cameron, and the 29th at Framingham. Soon after, with reports reaching his ears of problems and discord in the camps of the new Irish units, Andrew sent his adjutant general, William Schouler, on an inspection trip. Schouler's report was damning, and included the rather startling discovery that the actual commander of the 29th was not in fact Thomas Murphy, but one Matthew Murphy, another Murphy from the 69th who had been mistakenly appointed instead of his namesake. Matthew Murphy, according to Schouler, was "seldom in camp," and, "The men are sorry when he comes and glad when he goes." When he learned that he was about to lose his post, Murphy threatened to return to New York. Andrew made it clear that he thought this sounded like good news, whereupon Murphy went to the camp of the 28th and made a speech urging his countrymen to protest, after which many of them promptly deserted.

This was too much for Andrew, combined with the fact that recruiting for both regiments was slow, the final upshot was that both fledgling regiments were merged to become a single regiment, the 28th Massachusetts, under Monteith. No doubt now thoroughly fed up with the antics of the Irish, the 28th was then assigned to Butler's New England force for an expedition to South Carolina before being eventually assigned to the Irish Brigade in December 1862, just in time to participate in the bloody slaughter at Fredericksburg on the Rappahannock River.[23]

While the history of the Philadelphia regiment was marginally less controversial, it was an equally slow process before it was able to join the Irish Brigade. The governor of Pennsylvania, Andrew G. Curtin, was to be equally as riled with the drive to recruit for an Irish brigade as was his counterpart in Massachusetts. Casting his net wide for recruits and regiments, Meagher was treading on the toes of these important local officeholders, both in terms of their desire to retain control over the process in their own states, but also in that they were obliged to supply the Federal army with a certain quota of recruits. To facilitate this, there were laws forbidding potential recruiters from taking men for out-of-state units. These were of little concern to Meagher. Governor Curtin was eventually obliged to write to Secretary Cameron complaining that "sundry persons," including a "Colonel Meagher," were recruiting men in his state to the great detriment of the service there, and could not something be done about it?[24] But Meagher was riding the moment, and the War Department was not about to take a chance at offending the largest ethnic group in the North with a war to be won. "In this grand struggle," the reply to Curtin read, "no effort must be relaxed to secure the full and earnest sympathy of all nationalities." Yet despite this elliptical approval from officialdom, Meagher's recruitment drive in Philadelphia in 1861 was not very successful. One southern sympathizer wrote that Meagher had raised no more than a "corporal's guard."[25]

A large part of the problem was that Philadelphia, like Massachusetts, already had its own Irish regiment, the 69th Pennsylvania Infantry, which had deliberately copied the number of their comrades and countrymen in the New York regiment of the same designation. Thus, when Governor Curtin eventually gave permission for another Irish regiment to be raised in the summer of 1862 under Colonel Denis Heenan, recruitment was painfully slow. The headquarters of the 116th — which took upon itself the lugubrious name of the "Brian Boru United Irish Legion" — had been opened in Philadelphia since early May. In August following the first series of battles in which the Irish Brigade had been involved outside Richmond, fresh appeals were made for volunteers to go and fight with the "gallant Meagher."[26] But it would still take the visit of a *bona fide* Irish war hero to the city before the regiment was able to enlist sufficient volunteers to allow it to join the Irish Brigade. The hero was Corcoran, who was finally released from his Confederate prison that August, and accepted an invitation to speak in Philadelphia on August 22, following which there

5. Commissioning a Brigade

was a spurt of enlistments.[27] Even so, the 116th was still understrength with only 630 men when, on September 1, it was ordered to Washington in the panic following the second and even worse Federal defeat at Bull Run. Subsequently, on October 6, it was ordered to Harpers Ferry on the Potomac to join the Irish Brigade, arriving on October 10, 1862. By that time the brigade it joined, which had been enlisted with such high hopes and expectations of glory, had already lost over 1,200 men since it had left New York the previous November.[28]

Au revoir to the "bould soljer boys"

Meagher's first general and special order issued as acting brigadier in the wake of Shields' refusal to accept the post of brigadier, ordered all officers and men to report to Fort Schuyler, on Long Island Sound, New York, which was to become the "alma mater of the Irish Brigade."[29] Life there was not too unpleasant for the new volunteers. Their days were punctuated by "a constant stream of visitors who made their way out to Fort Schuyler to see the 'bould sojer boys.'" In one reported vignette, a newly arrived lieutenant approached a group of soldiers lying on the grass, puffing on their pipes. After studiously ignoring any form of military etiquette at the approach of an officer, when asked if they liked their life in camp, the reply came, "Faith, I do; an' it's sorry I am that I didn't 'list years ago."

Sundays in particular were reported to be "especially brilliant," with excursion steamers leaving from the East Piers bringing "hundreds to visit and witness the dress-parades which usually took place on those days." On one occasion, the steamboat "was so crowded with passengers at Peck Slip that she could not make a second landing at Tenth Street for fear of the consequences of the great overcrowding." Little wonder that before a month was out, even Meagher, who "constantly visited it [Fort Schuyler], when his labors at the recruiting office would permit," was of the opinion that being surrounded by all of life's amenities was no preparation for warrior heroes.[30] Early in November, Meagher wrote to Secretary Cameron to request that the regiments be moved to another camp, as he was having "difficulty in reducing the recruits to order and docility in the vicinity of their homes — families and friends having constant access to them, and other distractions frequently occurring." A second similar request was made the following week, and on November 18, Cameron telegraphed, "Get your command ready for marching orders. We shall have quarters for you at Harrisburg in a few days."[31]

Preparations must have already been afoot, as on the same day, the 69th received immediate orders to move. The steamer *Atlas* brought the 69th from Fort Schuyler, and at noon the regiment as well as the officers from the other regiments lined up in front of Archbishop Hughes' residence to be presented with their battle flags. Hughes was a rather reluctant convert to the cause of Meagher and his

Brigade. Both had bitter rows during the 1850s. Hughes was convinced that the revolutionary Fenians, and by extension Meagher, although not then a member, were no better than the "red republicans" of Europe. This conviction was no doubt strengthened following Meagher's statements about the role of the Irish clergy during 1848. Hughes, apart from personal dislike of Meagher as a result of this, also feared that Irish militia units in particular, delayed assimilation and acceptance of the Irish in America, and encouraged Know-Nothingism. Now, at the start of the Civil War, in private he also opposed the formation of ethnic Irish regiments, and by extension an Irish brigade. He had written to the secretary of state, Seward, stating his belief that ethnic identifications for regiments and brigades would ferment trouble and division, and that the best policy was one of neutral numbers for regiments. Nevertheless, there was little he could do but publicly express support for Meagher and the brigade given the tide of emotion and hype which accompanied the initial recruitment drive. He also probably felt that participation in itself would be too significant a factor in gaining acceptance with the native-born Americans, than to risk a public row over the question of the desirability of ethnic regiments. On the other side, Meagher, a touch later than most, discovered that in politics you should never butt your head against a brick wall — particularly a church wall — and was willing to woo Hughes' public support for the idea of an Irish brigade, aware of how important this would be among the rank-and-file immigrants.[32]

Diplomatically enough, Hughes happened to be absent in Europe on the day the 69th was to move, and the ceremony had to be performed by the Very Reverend Dr. Starrs, his vicar general. The ladies committee for the Irish Brigade had prepared the embroidered colors, with six flags and six guidons, with the silver-plated mountings on the flagstaffs "executed in Tiffany's best style." The regimental flag was of "a deep rich green, having at the centre a richly embroidered Irish harp, with a sunburst above it and a wreath of shamrock beneath." Below the wreath, in a crimson scroll, was the motto, *Riam nar druid o spairn lann* (Who never retreated from the clash of spears). Three ladies presented the three sets of colors. Mrs. Chalfin did the honors for Colonel Nugent of the 69th; Mrs. Meagher, fittingly, presented Colonel Baker of the 88th — "Mrs. Meagher's Own"— with their colors; and, with the final composition of the brigade still undecided, Colonel Meagher, also acting brigadier, accepted the colors for the proposed Fifth Regiment from Miss Devlin.[33] Following the speeches, the 69th marched down Fifth Avenue and Broadway to the Battery, where they boarded the transports. Like the departure of the old 69th Militia for the Bull Run campaign, their exit was melodramatic. One newspaper reported how, "In many instances the scenes were quite affecting.... Wives clung to their husbands arms, and in a number of instances consolation was sought in a draught from a mysterious black bottle." Such scenes were repeated 10 days later as the 63rd Regiment also took its leave. The same newspaper recorded how, "Many men and

5. Commissioning a Brigade

women crowded into the ranks, and furnished the soldiers with liquor, and the consequence was that not a few of the 'bould sojer boys' became drunk. Rows and fights ensued, and much difficulty was experienced in getting the men on the pier, and then on board the transport. Several men determined to see their friends once more, and to get a parting 'nip,' jumped overboard, and endeavored to swim to the docks. Whether any were drowned is not known."

The 88th would be the last to leave on December 16, again amid similar scenes, with the acting brigade commander reportedly almost run down by a train in the melee. It is not difficult to concur with one of Meagher's biographers when he suggested that, "It must have been with a great sigh of relief that he removed the last drunken soldier from the embrace of his family and commenced driving his herd southward."[34]

Chapter 6

Frolics and Frustrations

"Men who will have frolics"

When the 63rd, 69th, and 88th regiments left New York, they numbered about 1,000, 745 and 800 respectively. According to Meagher, "a rough and tumble, drive ahead, rollicking, devil may care lot of fellows." Near enough one-fifth of these were already "blooded," having fought at Bull Run. Even if they could not quite be called veterans yet, they were a tough backbone to the brigade. The majority of the brigade was a fair cross-section of Irish immigrants, most of them being "brawny workers, canal diggers, track layers, highway workers, building laborers, hod carriers, cabmen, porters and streetcar drivers, with a seasoning of waiters and barkeepers." With a higher profile were those veterans "of the British army in India ... men who had served at Balaclava and Inkermann, and men who hastened to the colors from the Irish Brigade that fought for the Pope in '60 and '61 at Spoleto and Ancona."

Men such as John H. Gleason, who was presented a gold medal on October 5, 1860, for his services at the battle of Ancona. After arriving in New York, he joined the 63rd, entering Company H as a lieutenant before eventually rising to become a lieutenant colonel. John Gossen, who would serve on Meagher's staff, left Ireland to enter the military service of Austria, seeing action in Syria before transferring to the 7th Hungarian Hussars. Men such as these would have added color and romance to any outfit, adding their tales to those told around the campfires. The soldiers often sang about Ireland, which was generally referred to as either the "Old Dart" or just "Home," and songs about English oppression were favorites. When the stories turned to recent events, to the backing of "Johnny Flaherty's fiddle," Bull Run was "only second to Waterloo" in the accounts of the "veterans."[1]

The behavior and traits of the Irish in camp are easily recognizable. On several occasions, their coolness and response in battle was evidence that their time in camp was not entirely misspent. They had obviously worked hard and mastered the art of drill and maneuver. But when not working, they were hard men to control, irreverent and undisciplined. This was in large part due to their "pugnaciousness and the excessive fondness of many of them for strong drink."[2] The circumstances behind their departure from New York were symptomatic of this

6. Frolics and Frustrations

problem. "Pay day, and of course drinking," one chaplain from an Irish regiment remarked in a diary entry, "Such a picture of hell I had never seen."[3] The fondness of the Irish for drink was even written into the minutes of the Joint Committee on the Conduct of the War through the evidence of Brigadier General Fitz-John Porter. Porter was asked whether he suffered from drinking in his division. "Not much," Porter hesitatingly replied. "We have some men who will have frolics," he continued, before clarifying his answer by adding, "We have a great many Irishmen, to whom a frolic is as necessary about once a month."[4]

Anecdotes about the behavior of the Irish abound, and while many need to be taken with a large dose of salt, it is equally likely that not much embroidery was required. And neither are the anecdotes confined to the rank and file. Meagher himself was undoubtedly fond of a drink. So much so that one historian described him as "a notorious inebriate."[5] Even sympathetic observers such as William McCarter, who would serve as one of Meagher's aides, wrote of Meagher's "one besetting sin ... the besetting sin of so many Irish then and now — intemperance."[6] While commanding the Irish Brigade, personal excess appears to have been combined with entertaining on a grand and gaudy scale at every available opportunity. "Brilliant" was a word frequently applied to Meagher and his staff as they traipsed around. This was a trait that Meagher had carried with him from Ireland. "His [Meagher's] appearance is not vulgar," wrote *The Times* of the imprisoned rebel in 1848, "but 'pretentious,' and you see in it ... the usual characteristics of an *ad captandem* [publicity-seeking] orator."[7] With the Irish Brigade, Meagher had at last arrived, and he and his staff appeared determined to outdo all comers in terms of pomp and circumstance. The chaplain of the 88th New York described Meagher's "brilliant staff ... composed of gallant young officers, who were decked out not only with regimental gold straps, stripes and cords on their coats, trousers and hats, but they also had great Austrian knots of gold on their shoulders, besides numerous other ornamentations in gold which glittered in the Virginia sunshine enough to dazzle one."[8] On another occasion, a young officer recalled how, when his regiment arrived at the brigade's camp, they were visited by Meagher, who "came in state, splendidly mounted, and surrounded by a brilliant staff, the members of which seemed to wear a deal more gold lace than the regulations called for ... the canteen was passed around and the talk became animated." Other accounts testify to several more elaborately organized "banquets" and "feasts" presided over by Meagher. Most famous, or infamous, was the notorious "death feast" held while the dead and dying at Fredericksburg still carpeted the slopes outside the town. Even more damaging to Meagher personally were the stories which were printed after some of the most famous engagements in which the Irish Brigade fought, which accused him of poor leadership due to the effects of drunkenness, with the accusation of cowardice thrown in for good measure.[9]

Thomas Francis Meagher and the Irish Brigade

Not that excessive drinking on the part of the soldiers of the brigade could be blamed on a lack of spiritual guidance. One of the recruiting angles for the brigade was that volunteers were promised that each regiment would have a Catholic chaplain, and indeed, at no time during the war was the Irish Brigade without the services of at least one priest. While the quantifiable extent of religious observance throughout the brigade is hazy, there is no doubt that the combination of Catholicism and

Photographed at Harrison's Landing in July 1862, seated in the middle front row is Fr. James Dillon, chaplain, 63rd New York, with Father William Corby, chaplain, 88th New York, to his left. The presence of the chaplains with the Irish Brigade ensured that men from other units who were not so fortunate in having priests attached to their regiments "came to regard the camp of the Irish Brigade as their parish in the Army of the Potomac" (Library of Congress).

6. Frolics and Frustrations

Irishness was prominent, not only in the perception of, but also in the public face of the brigade. One soldier in the 28th Massachusetts described how, as his regiment marched past a Catholic church "the order was given to carry arms and we saluted with the colors, which was quickly obeyed by the men."[10] While Fathers McMahon and McKee served briefly with the 28th Massachusetts and 116th Pennsylvania respectively, the three best-known of the chaplains were those attached to the New York regiments. Of these, Father James Dillon of the 63rd was the only Irish-born chaplain. He was from the University of Notre Dame, and has been described as "impulsive and ardent." To these traits, no doubt, optimism could be added. Before the regiments of the brigade had left New York, Father Dillon had managed to organize the Irish Brigade Temperance Society.

Father Thomas Ouellet, a French-Canadian priest, was attached to the 69th. Described as a "perfect martinet in everything that pertained to his sacred duties," he was ever ready to scold officers and men alike from the pulpit. Father William Corby, attached to the 88th, would become the most noted of the three priests. Also from Notre Dame, he was said to be the antithesis of Ouellet in manner, being both "gentle and conciliating." As well as providing one of the best firsthand memoirs of life with the brigade, he would also be associated for posterity with his absolution of the remnants of the brigade just before they waded into shot and shell at the battle of Gettysburg.[11] The presence of Corby, Dillon and Ouellet ensured that men from other units who were not so fortunate in having priests attached to their regiments "came to regard the camp of the Irish Brigade as their parish in the Army of the Potomac."[12]

"The wisest man in the world"

February 1862 would see the culmination of Meagher's maneuvers to lead the Irish Brigade. The previous November he had told Judge Daly that "nothing would induce him to be a brigadier." Maria Daly recorded how the "two-faced Meagher" then proceeded to get others to lobby "some influential men in Washington" on his behalf.[13] Two days after Fathers Dillon and Ouellet celebrated midnight mass for the brigade, on Christmas Eve 1861, one of Judge Daly's friends' back in New York wrote to him saying that, "I believe it is certain Meagher is appointed to command the Brigade; his family have information on it."[14] Others, including a delegation of officers from the 88th New York—"Mrs. Meagher's Own"—had already been to lobby Lincoln on Meagher's behalf. The result of all these maneuvers was announced in February 1862, when Thomas Francis Meagher was named as a brigadier general by the Senate. On February 5, he formally took command with a full dress parade, which was reviewed by himself and Shields, who was there as Meagher's guest. "A numerous and brilliant staff and escort rode along the line," recorded one officer of the event, "This was followed by a grand banquet ... with the tables literally groaning under the weight of the tempting viands provided."[15] Three days later the new brigadier general and his command were ordered to join the division of General Sumner at Alexandria, at a place called Camp California, so called in honor of Sumner who had just returned from the West Coast.

Camp California it may have been, but that did not stop the Virginia winter from turning the roads and fields into mud flats. Father Corby wrote how he witnessed an officer crossing the street have "his boots sink so deep ... he was obliged to call a soldier to dig him out."[16] President Lincoln would no doubt have sympathized with the officer's plight. After the rout at Bull Run, the Union war effort was in danger of becoming equally as immobilized as the officer's boots. To replace the luckless McDowell, Lincoln had brought in a young and relatively untried general to try to bring order out of the chaos, and fashion an army that would beat the Confederates. George Brinton McClellan, the "young Napoleon," was to be the savior of the Union. But in early 1862, Lincoln felt that the war effort was even more bogged down than it had been when McClellan had taken command.

Although an outstanding organizer and administrator, McClellan was on less-sure ground militarily. Believing, or wanting to believe, wildly exaggerated reports of the number of Confederates he was facing, McClellan chose to remain inactive within the defenses around Washington, much to the disgust of Lincoln and his government. Also, McClellan's high-handedness and arrogance in dealing with members of the administration, including the president himself, had almost totally soured relations between the young commander and his political masters.[17] This arrogance also precluded sharing his plans with political superiors, much to their chagrin, causing one senator to remark: "If he was an old veteran who had fought a hundred battles ... or we knew him as well as Bonaparte or Wellington, then we could repose upon him with confidence," but otherwise, "we have no evidence that he is the wisest man in the world."[18]

Neither was McClellan pleased when he was eventually forced to reveal his strategy for defeating the rebels. Rather than attack the Confederate army two days march away to the southwest, McClellan proposed to march the entire Army of the Potomac off to the northeast to Annapolis. They would then be transported by boat down Chesapeake Bay to the town of Urbanna on the Rappahannock River, interposing themselves between the Confederate army and the Confederate capital, Richmond. The Confederates would then be forced to retreat in haste from Centreville to protect their capital, and could then be destroyed by the awaiting and prepared Federals. Richmond could then be taken and the war would be over. The president was unenthusiastic about the plan, seeing it almost as an attempt by McClellan to further delay having to confront the Confederate army. His secretary of state, William Seward, was also skeptical, but said he didn't care whether the army beat the Confederates at Centreville, or at the gates of Richmond, just as long as it beat them somewhere.[19]

6. Frolics and Frustrations

Back to Bull Run

In the end, the rug was pulled from underneath the Urbanna plan by the Confederate commander, Joe Johnston. Sensing that the Army of the Potomac would soon be on the move, and lacking McClellan's imaginary legions, he decided that his position was untenable. On March 7, the Confederates began to evacuate their lines at Centreville and retired toward Richmond. McClellan, with good military sense, decided to march his army out to the now-deserted fortifications as an exercise in logistics and marching. A successful military exercise it may have been, but it proved another disaster in terms of public and political relations. Here was McClellan, marching his grand army out to the rebel fortifications, but only after the rebels had abandoned them. Furthermore, the extent of the rebel camps was evidence that no more than 45,000 soldiers had been there. The apparent farce was further exacerbated when reports came back that many of the guns mounted in the fortifications were in fact "Quaker guns," namely wooden logs painted black for effect.[20] The Irish Brigade, as part of Sumner's division, had been part of the grand exercise. They left camp at three in the afternoon, carrying full packs, and marching into "a raw wind and a miserable drizzling rain."[21] The scene presented by the Army of the Potomac on the march was described by one of the brigade's officers. "On they march," he wrote, "dark puritans from the New England states; stalwart Yankees of bone and muscle; men from the west and Northwest; exiles of Erin, from Munster's sunny plains, from Connaught's heights and Leinster's vales; peasants from the Rhine."[22] When they arrived at Warrenton Junction, according to Meagher, "orders were given to encamp, and in five minutes the orders were carried out. All we had to do was to stack arms, and throw ourselves in the mud."[23] When they eventually arrived back at the old battlefield at Bull Run, the rains had washed out the shallow graves of the dead from that first encounter that seemed a lifetime ago. "Amid dead men's bones," Father Corby meditated on the costs of the war to the thousands of homes across the country, while General McDowell wept over the bones of "the light-hearted berry picking men he had led southward under the full moon of [the previous] July."[24]

McClellan, however, had prepared a fallback plan. Instead of landing at Urbanna, the scene of operations would now shift to the peninsula of land formed by the James and York rivers in eastern Virginia. Landing at Fort Monroe, his army would now strike north westward toward Richmond. He had little alternative but to do something quickly. The administration had just about run out of patience with the young Napoleon, and on March 8, Lincoln removed McClellan from his position as general in chief of all the Union armies, reducing him to the sole post of commander of the Army of the Potomac. It was against this background that the Army of the Potomac began to head for Alexandria to board the waiting transports, with the first boats setting sail on March 17. On that day the Irish Brigade was marching from Fairfax Courthouse and unable to enjoy the traditional St. Patrick's Day celebrations, making do with a blessing from Fathers Ouellet and Dillon that morning. Two weeks later their turn for transportation finally arrived and on March 31, the Irish Brigade marched to Alexandria's docks, escorted by the brigade band of Brigadier General Phil Kearny playing *Garryowen,* and boarded the *Columbia* and the *Ocean Queen,* bound for Fort Monroe.[25]

Chapter 7

Fort Monroe to Fair Oaks

"Fighting Dick" makes an appearance

One thing McClellan cannot be blamed for is the quality of his corps commanders at the start of the Peninsula campaign. These were appointed for him by Lincoln. The Irish Brigade was now part of the Second Corps of the Army of the Potomac, commanded by Brigadier General Edwin Vose Sumner. Even the generally sympathetic historian of the Second Corps, who served directly under Sumner, questioned whether "with his [Sumner's] mental habits and at his advanced age he should have been designated for the command of 20,000 new troops." Sumner's corps consisted of two divisions, the First and Second, commanded by Israel Richardson and John Sedgwick, respectively. Each division contained three infantry brigades. The Irish Brigade, commanded by Meagher, was designated the Second Brigade of the First Division. The other two brigades in the division were commanded by Brigadier Generals John Caldwell and Otis Howard. The division commander, Richardson, was known as "Fighting Dick," a sobriquet he had earned during the Mexican War. He was also known as "Greasy Dick," a sobriquet he continually earned because of his personal dress sense. Richardson would walk around camp "with a battered straw hat on his head and his hands in his pockets, looking like a seedy old farmer [with] no insignia of rank visible."[1]

One of most repeated stories regarding Richardson and the Irish Brigade concerns his first review of the brigade as they were making their way toward Alexandria to board the transports for Fort Monroe. To his delight and lasting affection for the brigade, on passing the lines he was greeted by resounding cheers and hats flung in the air. Little did he realize that Captain Gossen had arranged this welcome. Just before Richardson arrived, Gossen had addressed the men, telling them that "the brave old fellow ... has sent to our camp three barrels of whiskey, a barrel for each regiment; and we ought to give him a thundering cheer when he comes along." Unsurprisingly, given the nature of the gift, the expectant soldiers duly obliged. Of course no whiskey ever appeared. Gossen, whom Richardson later threatened to cashier were he not "such an incorrigible rascal," kept a low profile for a while. The soldiers no doubt put the "disappearance" of the whiskey down to their rapacious officers.[2]

They could certainly have done with some of that whiskey during those early April days on board the *Columbia* and *Ocean Queen*. When they reached Fort Monroe, the weather was too bad to allow them to disembark. They had to remain ship-bound for five days, eating only short rations of salt pork, hardtack and coffee. When they eventually were able to disembark, they had to wade ashore up to their armpits in freezing water. Once ashore, they found that no quarters had been prepared for them, and had to share with units from General Howard's brigade, who had arrived three days earlier. Even more disappointing for the soldiers was the fact that by the time they disembarked, the campaign itself had already stalled outside the historic town of Yorktown, less than 20 miles up the Peninsula.[3]

Stuck in the mud

McClellan had arrived at Fort Monroe on April 2 with a spring in his step. No doubt he was glad to be away from the intrigues in Washington. With perhaps an unconscious acknowledgement of his recent lack of initiative, he wrote to his wife claiming that, "The grass will not grow under my feet."[4] Although he had set over half his army in pursuit of the Confederates within 36 hours of his arrival on the Peninsula, faced with the first sign of resistance by the heavily outnumbered Confederates at Yorktown, McClellan halted and began to call up his siege guns. The Confederate general, Joe Johnston, a soldier not dissimilar to McClellan as regards being cautious, probably recognized a kindred spirit when he remarked, "No one but McClellan could have hesitated to attack."[5]

A month went by as McClellan gathered his siege equipment outside Yorktown. But just as he was ready to open what he believed would be an irresistible bombardment, as at Centreville, the Confederates stole the thunder from his guns. On the night of May 3, the Confederate army abandoned their works and headed back up the Peninsula. After initial disbelief, then claiming a "brilliant victory," McClellan set his troops in pursuit. At a place called Williamsburg, Johnston turned to fight a delaying action which turned into a fair-sized battle, which was badly mishandled by Sumner, who was leading the pursuit. At a cost of about 2,000 casualties on both sides, the Union pursuit was delayed long enough for the Confederate army to get back behind the defensive line at Richmond, for which the Army of the Potomac and its siege equipment now headed.

The Irish Brigade took no part in the battle at Williamsburg and indeed had seen little by the way of soldiering since their arrival on the Peninsula. Apart from manning picket lines, they had spent several days helping to unload supplies at Ship Point. They also frequently found themselves as working parties attached to the engineers, building roads, mortar emplacements, bomb shelters, and a system of approach lines as the siege developed.[6] At least outside Yorktown, they had managed to escape

7. Fort Monroe to Fair Oaks

Fort Monroe with its "no end to cold rain, sleet and mud." Their camp was bearable enough and life began to take on a settled rhythm. A chapel of sorts was even erected, made from a circus tent belonging to Father Dillon. On May Day, the "rustic chapel" was decorated with wild flowers, and massgoers "carried a prayer book in one hand, and in the other a bit of wood to kneel on in the mud."[7]

Life was reasonably secure behind the lines, but camp life claimed lives as easily, if not more so, than great battles. Diseases were the great killer, accounting for more than twice the number of Union army losses of those either wounded or killed in actual combat. Soldiers were invariably healthier when actively campaigning than in camp, as the constant exercise appears to have counterbalanced the appalling effects of the basic army diet of salt pork and hardtack. Half of the deaths from disease came from intestinal ailments, mainly typhoid, diarrhea, and dysentery. Half the remainder came from pneumonia and from tuberculosis.[8] Death often visited in more mundane forms. One member of the brigade was killed in camp at Yorktown by a falling tree. Like many soldiers of the day, in the absence of dog tags, he had a note in his pocket. The brief testament informed the finder that the soldier's name was Patrick Casey, Company B, 69th New York State Volunteers, and "Anyone finding this note on my person when killed will please write a note to my wife and direct it as follows; Mrs Mary Casey, Number 188 Rivington Street, New York."[9]

On May 5, the brigade set off for Yorktown, prepared for battle, unaware that Johnston had already flown the coop. The march was miserable. One Irishman wrote of "night and dreary rain and wind; hungry, thirsty and shivering with cold."[10] There was a driving rainstorm during which large chunks of the brigade got scattered on the march. Still expecting to go into action, Meagher was distressed at the thought of his outfit being found wanting, or simply not being found at all, at the first time of asking. "Great God," he exploded to one of his officers, "The Irish Brigade will be brought into action at daybreak, and the work of a brigade will be expected of them, while I have scarcely two hundred men. Are these the men I expect at some future time to free Ireland with?"[11] In the event, the brigade never fired a shot. The following morning they continued up to Williamsburg, where again, the fighting had finished. On Sunday, May 11, they returned to Yorktown. From there they were sent via three transports up the York River, disembarking at Cumberland Landing on the Pamunkey River, less than 20 miles from Richmond. Two days later the brigade eventually made their way to a place called Tyler's Farm, on the north side of the Chickahominy River, to make camp.[12]

A day nearly spent racing

On Saturday, May 31, several hundred members of McClellan's host camped in front of Richmond felt in need of some distraction from the rigors of soldiering.

"Feeling the ennui of camp life at Tyler's Farm rather oppressive for their restless and mercurial natures," the Irish Brigade had arranged to go to the races. The going would be on the heavy side. It had been raining consistently over the last few weeks, and on the previous night there had been a truly torrential downpour. No matter. The self-styled "Chickahominy Steeple-Chases" were to go ahead. The main race was to be open to "all horses the property of and ridden by officers of the Irish Brigade. Best of three heats over the course." Generals Richardson and French were to be the judges, and the prize was "A magnificent tiger skin, presented by General Meagher — the spoil of his own gun in South America."

Local houses were ransacked for bits of scarlet, blue and green as clothes of every description were rejigged into jockey's outfits. One officer had a pair of yellow pants with a red shirt and cap, "with a furiously bobbing tassel and top boots lent by General Meagher." Captain Gossen, riding Colonel Nugent's bay gelding, Mourne Boy, had red pants made from "flaming red curtains," and a jacket inside out with a huge smoking cap, "bedizened with beads and gold fringes." After "much cheering, laughing, betting, false starts, beautiful jumps, serious tumbles, amusing spills, dislocated shoulders, and all the adjuncts of a well-conducted race, Major Cavanagh, on Katy Darling, came to the winning post in fine style, and carried off the tiger skin." Further festivities were just getting under way, in particular a mule race for the drummer boys, when, from south of the river, "the evening breeze ... brought the roar of the distant battle." Richardson and French hurriedly left as the mud-splattered officers of the brigade, costumes discarded and "accoutrements hastily donned," set about getting their men under arms. The Confederates had finally decided the time was right to try to put an end to McClellan's "artillery and engineering" tactics, and had attacked his corps south of the Chickahominy.[13]

Joe Johnston, the Confederate commander, had caught the Federals on the hop. With the majority of McClellan's army north of the Chickahominy, Johnston had decided to attack the two corps south of the river. With the Chickahominy swollen and in flood from the recent rains, this would hopefully delay or prevent any reinforcements from arriving.[14] The downpour on Friday night had further augured well, as the bridges which McClellan had been trying to construct across the Chickahominy to keep his various corps in contact, already in a perilous condition, would surely not now be passable. Johnston's plan called for a converging attack on the Union corps, who were positioned about a half mile in advance of a place called Seven Pines. The attack was planned to start at 8 a.m., and as such, Major Cavanagh was indeed fortunate in being able to secure his tiger skin before the battle got underway.

The man to whom Cavanagh owed the most thanks for this opportunity was Confederate General James Longstreet, whose bungling and arrogance was the chief contributor to what has been described as "unquestionably the worst-conducted

7. Fort Monroe to Fair Oaks

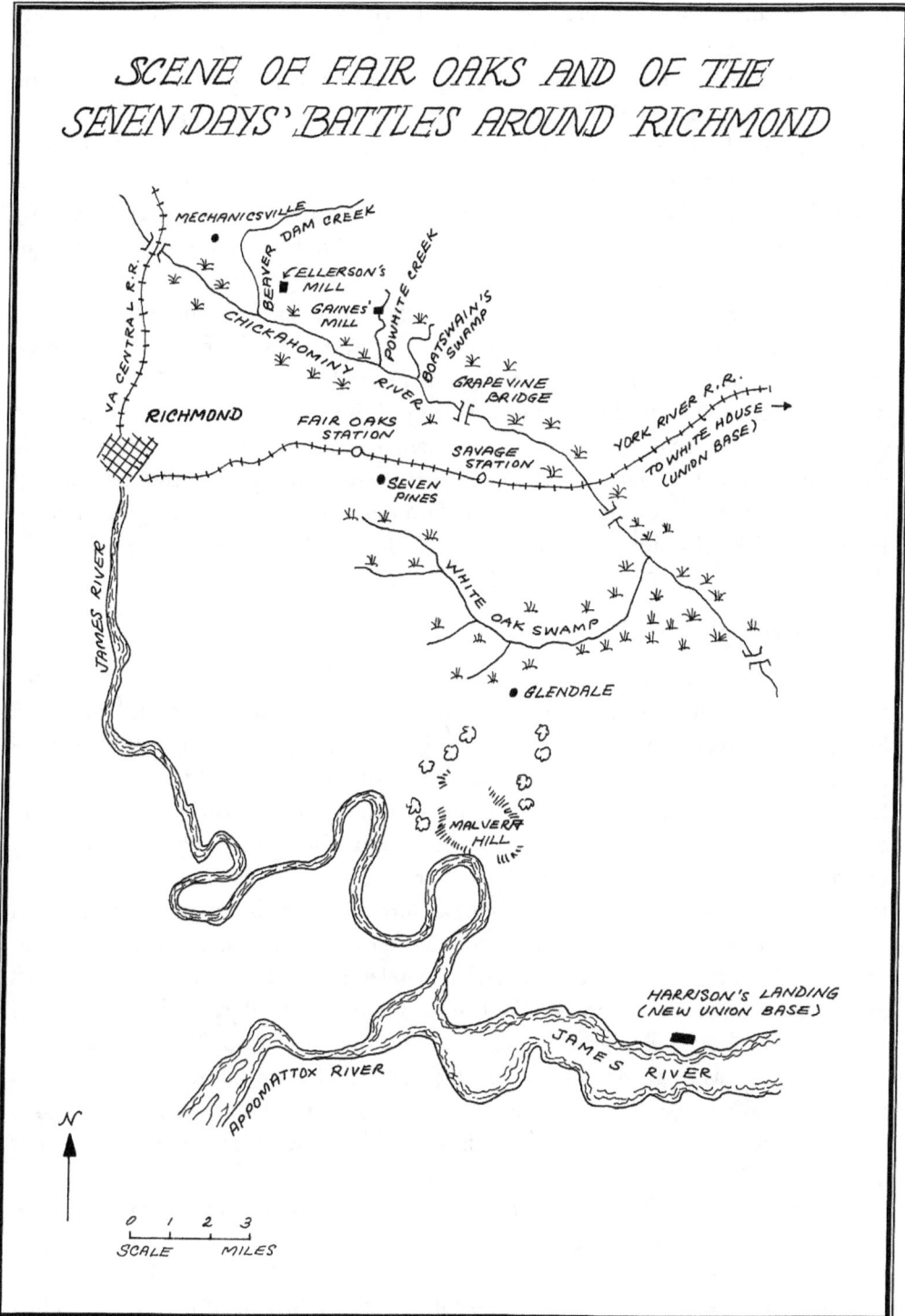

large-scale conflict in a war that afforded many rivals for that distinction."[15] Largely because of Longstreet, the majority of the Confederate forces never managed to get into position, or even make contact with the Federal army that day, leaving one division under General Daniel Harvey Hill to launch an unsupported attack at about 1 p.m. . Hill, who was one of the ferocious warriors which the Confederate army would throw up, crashed into the Federals and swept them back toward Seven Pines. By 3 p.m. the Federals had managed to regroup, and were reinforced by other troops coming up from their rear. Although holding well, they would be in trouble if any of the other Confederate divisions could get into the action.

Shortly before 5 p.m., this appeared likely to happen. Two more Confederate divisions had reached the railroad stop of Fair Oaks, less than half a mile from Seven Pines, when they came under fire from four Federal regiments which had become detached from the main fight. Unless reinforced, four regiments were not going to delay two divisions very long. Then, in a remarkable turn of events, further Federal reinforcements began to arrive, but they were arriving from the direction of the "impassable" Chickahominy. It was Sumner's corps, with Brigadier General John Sedgwick's division in the lead, with Richardson's following close behind.[16]

Their time had come

Sumner was the hero of the day. When McClellan, who was in bed with malaria north of the river, heard the firing soon after the battle started, he ordered Sumner to be ready to advance the Second Corps across the river should they be needed. If Sumner had obeyed this order literally, the day could have been lost. Like the old soldier he was, Sumner reacted to the sound of battle "the way a veteran fire horse reacted to the smell of smoke," and marched his two divisions right up to the river.[17] He was also conscious of the criticism of his handling of the battle at Williamsburg, and would try to make sure his leadership would not be found wanting a second time if the need arose. When, at 3 p.m., as the Federal troops were regrouping at Seven Pines, McClellan telegraphed Sumner to march to his assistance, Sedgwick's division was waiting at Grapevine Bridge, while Richardson's waited at the Lower Bridge, the men standing in ranks ready to cross. All they needed to do was to get across the Chickahominy. This would not be an easy task as the normally sluggish stream was sweeping past in full flood, with both bridges already underwater, and looking like they would be wrenched free from their ties and carried off at any minute.

As the crossing was about to start, an engineer warned Sumner that it was not possible to use the bridges. Sumner was not having any of it. "Can't cross this bridge!" he bellowed, "Sir, I tell you I can cross. I am ordered." Sedgwick's and Richardson's men started across with only the weight of the men and the guns stopping the bridges from being swept away. It was too much for the Lower Bridge, which soon collapsed, leaving Meagher and his men to follow Sedgwick's men across the submerged Grapevine Bridge, or "Devil's bridge" as Corby christened it that dismal night.[18] "Our men were obliged to wade (part of the bridge having been swept away) nearly up to their middles in water," wrote Richardson.[19] Only one of the batteries managed to make it across, and even that was bogged down as the logs which were laid to make a corduroyed road either side of the bridge were swept away. Richardson detailed the 63rd New York, under Colonel John Burke, to help bring the artillery through these swamps and to guard the bridge. For the other two regiments in the brigade, even once across the bridge, it was still three miles to Fair Oaks. Through "the dark dismal swamps of the Chickahominy" the men splashed and dragged their way, through what one soldier described as "the most damnable bog I ever went through, clear up to our knees in solid mud," with "horses plunging up to their bellies ... teamsters whipping, swearing and flogging the helpless animals."[20]

The first of Sedgwick's men began to arrive at Fair Oaks around 5:30 p.m. But it was nearer midnight, on "the blackest night ever known," before Meagher's men reached the field. Once there, they found themselves having to bivouac on the ground where part of Sedgwick's force had been fighting hours previously. "The scene of that day's terrible conflict," wrote Meagher, "was impressed upon us startlingly by the appearance of numbers of surgeons and chaplains with lanterns in hand searching over the ground to the right and left of our advance in column for the dead and wounded, who they said were scattered in every direction around." With the lanterns of the surgeons and chaplains moving about in darkness, the brigade spent an uncomfortable night listening to "the saddest moans on every side." As it became light they could see for themselves the debris from the previous evening: the killed, wounded and maimed, broken guns and caissons, dead horses and abandoned equipment. But there was little time for reflection as at first light the following morning, the Confederates attacked again.[21]

During the night, the remaining Confederate troops eventually reached the battlefield, and some of these were now attacking the section of the line held by Richardson's division. Richardson's three brigades were posted facing south along the line of the Richmond and York River Railroad, about a quarter mile east of Fair Oaks. French's brigade was in the first line, with Howard's and Meagher's forming the second and third lines. At 6:30 a.m. the Confederates burst out of the woods across the railroad cut from French's men. For an hour French's men fought off the Confederates while taking heavy casualties. Running out of ammunition, and with some of French's men beginning to fall back, Howard's brigade then moved forward in support, followed by Meagher's. While they had been waiting in the woods, Sumner and his staff had ridden by. "Riding in front of our ranks," as Meagher

Soldiers working on Grapevine Bridge—or "Devil's bridge" as described by Father Corby—which the Irish Brigade crossed on the night of May 31, 1862. The work party has been identified as soldiers of the 5th New Hampshire, the 64th New York and the Irish Brigade (Library of Congress).

described the scene, "[Sumner] addressed a few words of encouragement and confidence to our men, reminding them that they had been held back ever since they joined the service, but now their time had come."[22]

Led by Nugent, the 69th moved by their left flank through the woods and down to the railroad cut, before stopping to take up position on the extreme right of the Federal line. For a few minutes it was all quiet to their front as the firefights continued farther down the line. Then, suddenly, the Confederates attacked from out of the woods south of the railroad, to be met by the fire of the 69th. "Our fire was sustained with fearful consistency," wrote Nugent, "until the enemy was silenced.... Our firing only ceased with the retreat of the enemy, leaving us in undisputed possession of the railroad, which we still hold."[23] The 88th, meanwhile, had continued past the position of the 69th, working their way through the dense wooded terrain on the north side of the tracks, before coming under fire on reaching a clearing. "On emerging from the wood," wrote Colonel Kelly, "I found I had only two companies."[24] Unbeknown to Kelly, the other eight had been halted temporarily in the woods by a staff officer. Kelly got his two companies into battle lines and they charged down to the railroad track. They were soon joined by the missing eight companies and the 88th began to pour a "fire so telling, that the enemy were compelled to retire, leaving their dead and wounded in the woods." All along the Federal line the Confederates were either held or repulsed. At about 2 p.m. the battle finally spluttered out, leaving both sides in roughly the same positions they were in before the fight began, except for Sumner's corps, which was now south of the river.[25]

"The saddest shot of the war"

Fair Oaks was an inconclusive, disordered affair. Its main significance is often seen to lie in an event which occurred during the first evening. Riding down toward Fair Oaks, the Confederate commander, Joe Johnston, was seriously wounded. This shot has been described as "the saddest shot of the war," leading as it did to Johnston's replacement by Robert E Lee.[26] Lee's military genius would repeatedly confound the numerically and logistically superior Federal armies for another three years. And it was going to be an increasingly bloody business. Fair Oaks itself had proved to be a costly 24 hours. Union losses were over 5,000, while Confederate losses were over 6,000 — higher totals, for each side, than Bull Run and Williamsburg combined. The war was getting tougher and the numbers of casualties were being ratcheted upward.

For the Irish Brigade, overall losses had been relatively light, with seven killed, 31 wounded, and one missing. Although one soldier wrote his father, "We have won a glorious victory after three days fighting. The 88th crowned itself with glory,"[27] the casualty figures for the Irish Brigade contrasted with those for Howard's brigade, which had 95 killed, 398 wounded, and 64 missing; the figures for French's brigade were, 32, 188, and 22 respectively.[28] What the soldiers of the Irish Brigade had been asked to do, they had done competently and bravely. But it was Howard's and French's brigades who had already broken the back of the Confederate assaults on the second day. Also, while Howard and French were conspicuous in leading their brigades — Howard losing an arm — one of the few references to Meagher is of him and his staff, "riding from line to line, cheering on the men."[29] Although Meagher was barely glimpsed during the actual fighting, despite having only two regiments in action, one of the most celebrated of contemporary battle portraits, published in *Harper's Weekly*, was of Meagher apparently leading the charge of the Irish Brigade at Fair Oaks. In his official report, which, according to one critical historian, was "long on platitudes and short on details," Meagher himself did not

Harper's Weekly's fanciful depiction of Meagher "leading" the charge of the Irish Brigade at Fair Oaks. According to Colonel John Brooke of the 53rd Pennsylvania, it was only "after the battle Meagher moved forward across an open field on his front to the edge of the wood beyond, and in which wood the fighting had been done" (Library of Congress).

claim to have taken part in such a charge.[30] Neither did he claim to have much control over his regiments. "For further particulars," he wrote, "of which I cannot pretend to be personally cognizant, I refer you with pleasure to the reports of the officers commanding the two regiments of my brigade engaged."[31]

This did not stop him from heaping praise on his men. While he would not be the first nor last commander to talk up the performance of the troops under his command, given the relative losses between the brigades engaged, the tone of Meagher's report must also have rankled with his fellow brigade commanders. While the march across the Chickahominy by his regiments was "performed with unremitting celerity, ardor, and eager readiness for action ... on the line of march we met several soldiers and other parties returning from the field of action, who informed us that the Federal arms had met with a severe reverse, and that as some New York troops were implicated it was specially incumbent on us to redeem the honor of our State and the fortunes of the day." Not only that, but in almost wild overexaggeration of the contribution of the 69th and 88th on June 1, Meagher wrote that had not his men performed so gallantly, "I believe the issue of the day adversely to the Army of the Potomac would have been materially influenced."[32] The reports of

7. Fort Monroe to Fair Oaks

Colonels Nugent and Kelly, who had been at the sharp end, were much more businesslike. "Where men only seemed desirous of emulating each other in bravery," wrote Nugent, "I find it impossible to name any one as more courageous or prompt than another." Kelly was similarly low key, except "to mention a drummer-boy named George Funk, who acted most heroically during the engagement, and who followed closely on the track of the retreating rebels, bringing in a prisoner, whom he delivered to General Sumner."[33]

Despite these matter-of-fact accounts, it was the seemingly orchestrated public praise for Meagher and the Irish Brigade that was most prominent in the reporting of the action at Fair Oaks, causing much indignation among Meagher's fellow commanders. In a letter to the *New York Herald*, on its reporting of Fair Oaks, Colonel Edward Cross of the 5th New Hampshire decried the praise which the Irish Brigade has received in comparison to Howard's. "It is a fact," wrote Cross, "that the brigade of the lamented and gallant Howard bore the brunt of Sunday's battle.... All we ask is simple justice, no fulsome flattery, no distorted praise. The facts will suffice for Howard's brigade."[34] In his private journal, Cross was more forthcoming about what he felt was "distorted praise." "Gen Thos F. Meagher was *drunk* on the march to the battlefield (on the night of May 31)," he recorded, "and while the army was being posted behaved in a very disgraceful style, shouting and riding about in a manner highly unbecoming an officer and a gentleman, especially on such an occasion."[35] While such a description may tell us as much about Cross as it does about Meagher, Cross also recorded more than once that Meagher was nowhere to be seen during the fighting on June 1.

Fair Oaks would prove very much a pyrrhic victory for Meagher with regard to his standing among his fellow officers. Another of the most damning criticisms of Meagher in later years would be made by Colonel John Brooke, who commanded the 53rd Pennsylvania Volunteers in French's Brigade at Fair Oaks. Brooke would also see Meagher in action while in command of the brigade at Sharpsburg which followed Meagher's command into action, and was back in command of a regiment at Fredericksburg for the charge on Marye's Heights. In his report on the action of June 1, French wrote that while "the most desperate efforts were made to break our line," the 53rd Pennsylvania, "led on by the gallant Colonel Brooke, repulsed them again and again."[36] When the historian of the Second Corps contacted Brooke in 1884 regarding Fair Oaks, he was scathing about Meagher's role. "After the battle," wrote Brooke, "Meagher moved forward across an open field on his front to the edge of the wood beyond, and in which wood the fighting had been done." This was the "charge" pictured in *Harper's Weekly*, Brooke wrote. With possibly his observations of Meagher on this and later fields of battle in his mind, Brooke continued unsparingly. "I had a high regard for the bravery of the Irishmen," he wrote, "but despised Meagher, who never, to my personal knowledge, did any service in battle while commanding that brigade ... as a soldier he was the sorriest charlatan I ever knew."[37]

Despite these early misgivings being voiced elsewhere, after Fair Oaks, spirits in the brigade were obviously high. Meagher filed his official report from "Camp Victory." The majority of the men, however lightly engaged, had been in their first proper battle, or in the parlance of the time, had "seen the elephant." They received praise for their conduct from McClellan himself, as well as from a distinguished foreign observer, the Spanish general Prim, who visited their camp. "Spain had reason to appreciate Irish valor," Meagher reportedly told Prim, "Spain and Ireland were old friends from ancient times, and their soldiers had often fought side by side together on many a hard fought battle." The generals and their "brilliant staffs" then galloped off to "thundering cheers" from the assembled soldiers, causing Prim to remark, "I don't wonder the Irish fight so well: their cheers are as good as the bullets of other men."[38]

Chapter 8

"Column of Generous Friends"

Lee plays for high stakes

Following Fair Oaks, the Irish Brigade remained on the front line for another 15 days, during which time there was a new addition to the brigade, the 29th Massachusetts. The new regiment was needed to bolster the numbers in Meagher's small brigade, but was neither Irish nor Catholic. Burial details and picket duty were the main occupations of the men, amid "the vitiated atmosphere and the water of the vile swamp in which we lay entrenched." The lowlands of the Peninsula, never pleasant at the best of times during warm weather, were made much worse by the stench of the dead from the battle. For weeks after, the surrounding area stank of rotting corpses. As the rains washed away the earth over makeshift graves, one soldier described how "here and there a leg or hand or head could be seen protruding in all its ghastliness." The toll kept rising, "with pickets engaged unremittingly," and snipers active on both sides, "the crackling of firearms was incessant." It was with some relief that, on June 16, the brigade was ordered to a new camp behind the lines, with their belongings finally brought south of the Chickahominy from the old camp at Tyler's Farm.

The effect of Fair Oaks on McClellan was predictable enough. It made him even more cautious and deliberate in his approach to Richmond. Grapevine Bridge was repaired, and eight additional bridges were constructed to ensure there could be no repetition of the panic during the battle of Fair Oaks. Miles of fortifications sprang up in front of the Federal lines, built of "huge logs ... a deep ditch outside them," with an abatis in front which covered the ground "with a wreck of splintered trunks and broken limbs, and a torturing web and trap of stumps and branches, as impervious and inextricable as an Indian jungle."[1] It was hard to tell the besieged from the besiegers. But the approach, however slow and deliberate, was unremitting. Certainly from the point of view of the Confederates. The new army commander, General Robert E. Lee, like his predecessor, knew that if his army remained entrenched, sooner or later, McClellan would be ready to attack, and it would be difficult to resist.

Lee soon began to build up the defenses outside Richmond, behind which a small number of defenders could hold off much larger numbers of attackers. By doing this, Lee hoped to free up the majority of his army for maneuver and attack. In a reversal of Johnston's plan for Fair Oaks, Lee planned to strike the Federals north of the Chickahominy, sending his largest corps, that of Major General Ambrose Powell Hill (no relation to D.H. Hill), across the river. Powell Hill would attack the Federal corps from the front, while Stonewall Jackson's men, recalled from the Shenandoah Valley, would assail them on their northern flank. Once the Federals were routed, Lee would then send over Longstreet's and D.H. Hill's troops, and the Confederate army would then sweep down the north bank of the Chickahominy, isolating the bulk of McClellan's army south of the river from their supply base at White House Landing. It was a gambler's throw. Altogether, Lee would have less than 85,000 troops at his disposal. His plan allowed for only 25,000 of these to remain south of the Chickahominy in the early stages of the assault, while the bulk of his force attacked Porter. Facing these 25,000 were the three Federal corps, with not much less than 80,000 between them. Should McClellan divine what Lee's plan was, and send these corps head on against the thin Confederate line, Richmond was lost and the game was up.

The battle of Mechanicsville, the first major battle in what would become known as the Seven Days' battles, began on June 26.[2] It was uncannily similar to Fair Oaks in many respects. This time however it was Stonewall Jackson who played the villain's role instead of Longstreet, failing to get his troops in position on time. A. P. Hill, fed up with waiting, crossed the Chickahominy at 3 p.m. and proceeded to attack the Federals, whose main line of defense was just east of Mechanicsville, behind Beaver Dam Creek. Attacking such a strong position head on, and without any flanking support, Hill's men were practically slaughtered. Looking back on Hill's assault in later years, a watching Confederate officer wrote how, "We were lavish of blood in those days."[3] At 10 p.m. the battle died out. Although Hill had not even dented the Federal defenses, the mind of its commanding general did not prove as steadfast. Within hours after the fighting died down, McClellan was making plans for retreat.

Stopping a rout

As such, Mechanicsville was almost as good as a Confederate victory. Lee had certainly won the initiative. The following morning, Porter's corps pulled back to another defensive position, equally as formidable as Beaver Dam Creek, and equally behind a sluggish stream, this time known as Boatswain's Swamp. A mile to the west was the gristmill of Dr. William Gaines, and it was as Gaines Mill that the next and bloodiest battle of the Seven Days' would be known. On the afternoon of the June 27, A.P. Hill's troops again attacked another strongly entrenched Federal position, unsupported, without much success, but with plenty of casualties.

8. "Column of Generous Friends"

Porter's troops had been magnificent. For the best part of two days they had held off repeated assaults, with the "Irish Ninth," the 9th Massachusetts, one of the volunteer regiments, holding the center of the Union line. After running out of the 60 rounds of ammunition they had been issued that morning, "We took the ammunition from the boxes of the dead and wounded and fired that also," wrote one member of the regiment.[4] As tiredness and persistent Confederate pressure began to take its toll, Porter asked for reinforcements. "I am pressed hard, very hard," he wired McClellan, and unless further reinforced, "I am afraid I shall be driven from my position."[5]

At 7 p.m., in a charge led by General John Bell Hood's legendary Texas Brigade, the Confederates finally broke Porter's resistance. The only question once this happened was whether there would be a complete rout, or whether Porter would manage any sort of ordered retreat. With the rebels advancing up the plateau from the front and both flanks, some Federal units were retreating stubbornly. Others were either surrendering or were making their way pell-mell for the bridges across the Chickahominy. It could have been worse than Bull Run, when to the surprise of the advancing Confederates, from the retreating Federal columns up ahead could be heard the sound of cheering rising above the noise of the battle. There were over 70,000 troops just south of the river as the battle to the north approached its climax and Porter sent his plea for help. McClellan sent him 5,000. The brigades of French and Meagher.

"In the late afternoon," wrote Richardson, Sumner ordered him to "detach two of my brigades to the assistance of General Porter on the opposite side of the Chickahominy." French and Meagher's brigades "were accordingly detached, under the command of the former officer."[6] With Captain George Armstrong Custer of McClellan's staff acting as guide, the two brigades had crossed the Chickahominy at Grapevine Bridge. Soon after, Meagher described how they were met by "an immense cloud of dust, through which teams and horsemen hastily broke, [which] indicated something more than a repulse for our arms. These teams and horsemen were followed by crowds of fugitive travelers on foot, whose cry was 'They had been cut to pieces.'"[7] French then directed Meagher to deploy some of the 69th New York to drive back the runaways. Captain Felix Duffy's company was thrown forward, with fixed bayonets. According to French, this "had great effect, being vigorously executed." After almost having to fight their way through their own troops at the point of bayonet, to reach the front line, Meagher's men were soon making their presence felt, and heard.[8] A French military observer noted how they "came in shirt sleeves, yelling at the top of their voices."[9] Such was the volume of cheering with which they signaled their arrival, other Union troops in the vicinity at first thought it was a rebel force which had succeeded in surrounding them. "We were much concerned as to the cause of the cheering which took place to our rear," wrote Colonel G. K. Warren of the 5th New York Volunteers, "fearing they were a rebel force that had succeeded in getting in our rear."[10] This "column of generous friends," as one relieved officer in Porter's command later described them, forced their way "through the flying masses," and made their way to the top of the hill. Forming into line, "with one wild shout [they] swept down upon the enemy."[11] Other of Porter's troops soon rallied behind the reinforcements and as the fighting died away, "Meagher's brigade stood panting and elated between the army they had saved, and the army they had vanquished."[12]

"The finest fun"

As at Fair Oaks, the Irish Brigade had proved that they could be relied upon in a crisis, even if by the time they arrived the Confederate assault had already begun to splutter out in confusion and darkness. "Although they [Meagher and French] came too late to give us the aid required to drive back the already retiring foe," wrote Fitz-John Porter, "they gave renewed courage and confidence to our men, whose regiments formed under their protection and were all withdrawn that night."[13] Porter may or may not have had his own reasons for depicting his ability to handle the situation with "an already retreating foe." A Confederate cavalryman was later to recount how, "after a severe struggle our men gave way and retired in great disorder," largely due to Meagher's brigade which offered "heroic resistance," holding their ground "with determination which excited the admiration of our own officers."[14]

Whatever the extent of the deed, the men of the Irish Brigade had once again performed it handsomely. In his official report, McClellan commented on how "by their example, as well as by the steadiness of their bearing, (they) reanimated our own troops."[15] No doubt, many other brigades in the Army of the Potomac who were equally as reliable, but there was something in the foolhardy and reckless manner they went about their business which set the Irish somewhat apart. In fact, one wonders what the newest arrivals to the brigade, the 29th Massachusetts, made of their comrades. This 29th was in no way related to Governor Andrew's aborted attempt to form two Irish regiments in Boston during the previous autumn. These had been consolidated into a single regiment, the 28th Massachusetts, then stationed on the coast of South Carolina, although soon destined to join the Irish Brigade as well. The 29th, whose colonel was Ebenezer Pierce, was "uncompromisingly old Yankee, a mustering of names that would have sounded familiar in the forecastle or on the quarter-deck of the *Mayflower*." They would provide "an unlikely matching with their ancient political foes the Irish," and indeed, not so ancient, considering the prominence of Know-Nothingism during the 1850s.

Although Meagher would later claim them as "Irishmen in disguise," the 29th

8. "Column of Generous Friends"

would remain unmoved by his antics, listening "coldly, in a pinched and critical silence" to his "flights of Celtic eloquence."[16] Neither would they have been impressed by the ostentatiousness, some would say gaudiness, of Meagher's entourage. One reporter thought Meagher's gold-bedecked staff to be "fox hunters ... a class of Irish exquisites ... good for a fight, a card party or a hurdle jumping — but entirely too quixotic for the sober requirement of Yankee warfare."[17] A regular army officer, describing "Yankee warfare," remarked that in battle, how "very Bostonian and unemotional" New England soldiers could be, unbothered about striking heroic attitudes. They had "no poetry in a fight," he thought.[18] The Irish regiments, however, had poetry to spare. In a passage written by an army surgeon after the battle of Fair Oaks, he described the Irish Brigade "in all the glory of a fair free fight." "Other men go into fights finely, sternly, or indifferently," Doctor Ellis wrote, "but the only man that really loves it after all, is the green immortal Irishman. So there the brave lads from the old sod, with the chosen Meagher at their head, laughed, and fought, and joked as if it were the finest fun in the world."[19] Even allowing for the clichés running into each other, the description does seem to catch the essence, the exuberance, and the naiveté of the brigade in their fights during the early years of the war. It was this spirit, this almost uniquely Irish élan, which biographers and historians of the war would hand down.

Not everyone was entirely taken in by the exuberance of the Irish camp. The day following the battle of Fair Oaks, the correspondent of the *New York Herald* had visited the brigade. "Every adjunct of the place was strictly Hibernian," he wrote, "The emerald green standard entwined with the red, white and blue; the gilt eagles on the flag-poles held the Shamrock sprig in their beaks; the soldiers lounging on guard, had '69' or '88' the numbers of their regiments, stamped on a green hat-band; the brogue of every county from Down to Wexford fell upon the ear.... When anything absurd, forlorn, or desperate was to be attempted, the Irish Brigade was called upon. But, ordinarily, they were regarded, as a party of mad fellows, more ornamental than useful, and entirely too clannish and factious to be entrusted with power."[20] Nor was everyone especially enamored by the very public "exuberance" with which the fighting prowess of the Irish was reported. Similar to Colonel Cross's letter to the *New York Herald* following Fair Oaks, the tension between the "style" of the Irish and that of their more restrained comrades is neatly captured in French's official report on the battle of Gaines Mill. Almost resentful of "the enthusiasm of the Irish Brigade, which has gained universal applause," French wrote that it was unfair to make any comparison with "the unobtrusive courage of the American soldier, who does his duty cheerfully, although unnoticed."[21] Such tensions were not helped by other descriptions that appear to catch "exuberance" of another sort on the part of the brigade commander, the "reckless, rollicking, irrepressible, irresponsible Meagher."[22] One historian of the Peninsula campaign wrote that at Gaines Mill, Meagher had "led his Irish Brigade with the courage found in a bottle, galloped about drunkenly trying to rally everyone he saw." One of French's men reportedly watched Meagher ride into a group of walking wounded and single one man out, before striking him "over the head with his sword, knocking him down, then gallop[ing] on...."[23] Whether or not related to this incident, two days later Meagher was temporarily placed under arrest.[24] After rejoining the brigade on June 30, he was to find himself again embroiled in controversy after another incident at the battle of Malvern Hill in July 1. While the valor and unique contribution of the soldiers in the Brigade was being recognized and would remain largely unblemished, Meagher himself never quite seemed able to make it fully around the track without some questioning of his performance and temperament. With each passing battle, he was cumulatively building up a reputation that would eventually be a significant contributor to his reluctant departure.

Chapter 9

To Malvern Hill

The big "skedaddle" begins

With the coming of darkness, the fighting at Gaines Mill died down. The enthusiasm of their rush against the Confederates had carried Meagher's men "far to the front," where they "lay in close proximity to the enemy."[1] Sometime before midnight, a party from the brigade was sent out of their lines to get water from the well of a nearby farmhouse. On their way back they passed two other soldiers who walked by in silence. It was only after the war that the Irishmen found out that they had let two Confederate generals, D.H. Hill and Alexander R. Lawton, pass them by unaccosted. "We met the party [from Meagher's brigade] going back, and saw them go into their own lines," Hill later recalled, "Not a word was spoken by them or us."[2] Three months later at a town called Sharpsburg, in Maryland, the Irish Brigade would suffer dearly for allowing Hill his free passage through the lines that night.

As Porter's troops made their way to Alexander's and Grapevine bridges, the Irish Brigade remained north of the river as part of the rear guard. With Porter's men safely withdrawn, French then ordered his and Meagher's men to pull back across the Chickahominy. The 88th New York would be last to cross and had orders to destroy the bridge. Meagher, never one to miss a melodrama, handed Captain Clooney of the 88th New York a box of matches with orders that they be used to burn the Irish flags rather than allow them to be captured.[3] South of the Chickahominy, some of the Federal generals did not prove as cool-headed under pressure as Hill and Lawton. Soon after Hill had his silent encounter with members of the Irish Brigade, McClellan had a rather noisier one with some of his generals. For McClellan, his worst fears had been realized. Lee had cut off the Army of the Potomac from its supply base at White House Landing, and it must now retreat to a new base on the James River, Harrison's Landing. Two of his division commanders, and not a few of the rank and file, were aghast at the decision. The division commanders — Joe Hooker and Phil Kearny — and a number of brigade commanders went to see McClellan that night to protest the decision. Hooker and Kearny wanted to attack. They were sure that the Confederate lines were thin south of the river and all they wanted was the chance to prove it.

McClellan pooh-poohed the idea. Lee, he believed, still had half his army, 100,000 men or more, ready to strike south of the river. He had to save his own army to fight another day. Kearny was unrestrained in his fury. One officer at the meeting later wrote that Kearny had denounced McClellan "in language so strong that all who heard it expected he would be placed under arrest until a general court martial could be held."[4] But McClellan did not want to fight that battle either, and nothing was done. The "big skedaddle," as the men called it, or the "change of base," as McClellan preferred to call it, began early the following day, June 28, with the bridge builders at work in White Oak Creek, the main barrier between the Federal army and the James.

Burning bridges

After crossing the Chickahominy, the Irish Brigade rejoined the rest of Sumner's corps back at Fair Oaks. At dawn on the following morning, Saturday, June 29, the corps began to head back east along the line of the railroad, bound for the Meadow Station crossing of the Chickahominy. The move, like the whole of McClellan's "change of base," was a hurried affair. Tents were to be abandoned, along with "all articles not indispensable to the safety or the maintenance of the troops." Regrettably, for the chaplain of the 88th, into that category fell all his belongings, including the chapel tent, and a book containing all the sermons he had ever written.[5]

The same time as Sumner's corps was starting its withdrawal from Fair Oaks, Lee had received information which confirmed in his mind what McClellan was up to following the withdrawal of Porter's troops across the river. He immediately set his army off in pursuit to destroy the Federal army. Sumner's troops rejoined the rest of the Federal rear guard, now around Savage Station, arriving around 2 p.m. Just after 5 p.m., the pursuing Confederates ran into the Federals. Shortly before, General Heintzelman had explicably withdrawn his corps, leaving the left flank of the Federal position exposed. At 5 p.m., Generals John Sedgwick and William Franklin were making their way to where they supposed Heintzelman's corps to be, only to discover that they were riding straight into a line of advancing Confederates. "In as dignified a manner as the circumstances would permit," the generals managed to hastily turn back for their own lines. Franklin then went to look for Sumner, the senior commander on the field, to inform him of the impending attack. Sumner was asleep when Franklin found him, but quickly ordered the brigade of Brigadier General William Burns from Sedgwick's division forward to meet the attack. Burns soon needed support himself and sent word back for reinforcements. Sumner, still assuming Heintzelman's troops were at hand, initially did not think reinforcements necessary, and it was only when Burns sent his "last

9. To Malvern Hill

mounted man, urging and demanding reinforcements" did Sumner start sending units forward to Burns' support.

As the attack started, the Irish Brigade, along with the rest of Richardson's division, was behind the main line near Sumner's headquarters. Following his realization that Heintzelman was gone, Sumner himself galloped up, white hair streaming behind him. Waving his hat in the air, he directed the two nearest regiments from the division—the 88th New York, and the 5th New Hampshire from Caldwell's brigade—up ahead to reinforce Burns. "A mass of men came up in my rear in full yell," Burns later recalled. "I halted the crowd and asked for their commander. I am Major Quinlan of the 88th New York, Sir," came the reply. Burns quickly got them in line along the Williamsburg Road facing the Confederate batteries that were raking the immediate area with grapeshot and canister. On the command "Double quick, charge.... They went in with a hurrah, and the enemy's battery fell back." Shortly after this charge, for which Quinlan would be awarded a Congressional Medal of Honor, the rest of the Irish Brigade came up and were also involved in silencing other Confederate batteries, this time managing to spike the guns when they discovered they could not haul them away. Eventually, with roughly equal numbers engaged and neither side being able to gain the advantage, "the fighting in front of Savage Station settled down to a bloody stalemate as the daylight faded." That night, a thunderstorm broke and the rain came down in torrents.

As darkness fell, the Federals continued their withdrawal. The sick and wounded were abandoned in the houses and outbuildings around Savage Station which were serving as a field hospital. At about 3 a.m. on the morning of June 30, the first units began crossing over White Oak Bridge. Richardson's division, with the Irish Brigade again bringing up the rear, was the last to cross at 10 that morning, again destroying the bridge behind them.[6]

"Hell seemed to have opened on us"

Two hours later the pursuing Confederates, under Stonewall Jackson, arrived at the destroyed White Oak Bridge. They could see there were Federal batteries and troops on the far side, ready to dispute any attempt to cross. These troops were commanded by Franklin, and largely consisted of one of the divisions from his own Sixth Corps, and Richardson's division from the Second Corps, including the Irish Brigade. Just before 2 p.m. Jackson ordered his artillery, 31 guns in all, to open on the Federal positions.

Having carried out their preparations under cover of a ridge, the Confederate bombardment, "the severity of which," according to Franklin, "I had never heard," caught his troops by surprise.[7] Some of the officers from the Irish Brigade were making themselves at home in a nearby farmhouse where the owner proved

81

to be "affable and hospitable," while most of the other troops were also relaxing and taking shelter from the heat. They were soon awoken "by the thunders of artillery, the shriek of shells, and the horrid humming of their fragments. Hell seemed to have opened on us." The "fearful violence" of the battery fire caused "a regular stampede amongst teamsters, waggoners, and some artillery men, in which some of the troops also joined ... moving at a rate of speed not recognized by any of the books of tactics."[8] General Franklin thought that the stampede of the mules, which went through Meagher's troops, disabled "more men than were hurt in the Brigade during the remainder of the day." Some of Jackson's cavalry, and Jackson himself along with D.H. Hill, then made a brief foray across the creek only to be repulsed and forced to re-cross. The battle for the crossing appeared to be about to begin in earnest, but in fact had effectively ended. Jackson, believed by later historians to have been suffering from a form of nervous exhaustion following his adventures in the Shenandoah Valley, promptly sat under a tree and went to sleep. As the opposing artillerists settled down to throwing shells at each other for the rest of the afternoon, one Confederate wrote, "It looked to me as if on our side we were waiting for Jackson to wake up."[9]

As a result of Stonewall's sleep, the main attack on the Federals that day was left to the corps of Longstreet and A.P. Hill, who attacked the Federal center just east of Glendale. The fighting was as bloody and as intense as any during the Seven Days,' and the Confederates pressed the Federals hard, breaking their line. But as was often the case, the Federals were reinforced late in the day, this time by four brigades from Franklin's command at White Oak Bridge. First to arrive at about 5 p.m. were two brigades from Sedgwick's division, who were followed later by Meagher's and Caldwell's brigades from Richardson's division.

After dodging shells for most of the day at White Oak Bridge, the order to move probably came as somewhat of a relief to Meagher's men. During the day Meagher himself had been intensely restless, and was described riding his horse up and down the firing line "apparently oblivious of any personal danger." When requested to dismount and take cover, he replied, perhaps still smarting from his arrest the previous day, "No, I'll not dismount. If I am killed, I would rather be killed riding this horse than lying down."[10] Another report had him on foot helping to manhandle some Federal cannon in position. When they were then running out of ammunition, according to the artillery officer, General Meagher rather bizarrely "volunteered to ride to General Richardson and have ammunition sent to me as soon as possible." The ammunition never arrived.[11] Toward sundown, the request came from Sumner for more reinforcements, and the brigade headed off down the Long Bridge Road.

As they neared the sounds of battle around Glendale, they encountered "a stream of men, cannon, and horses coming to the rear, wounded, disabled, and stragglers."[12]

9. To Malvern Hill

After similar calls at Fair Oaks, Gaines Mill, and Savage Station, an officer in the Irish Brigade wrote, "It was our fate to march into the battlefield under the most — to other men — depressing circumstances ... it is only when the black need comes that we press forward to the work.... [B]ut our cheers reanimate — our élan gives them hope."[13] As the brigade charged past him to their work that late June evening, Sumner is reported to have said, "Boys, you go in and save another day."[14] With the Confederates pressing forward in the twilight, a soldier in a Pennsylvania regiment described the arrival of the Irishmen. "Just then a great noise was heard on the left and rear; all eyes were instantly turned in that direction.... A brigade of troops was pouring from the woods, marching under a banner of strange device, which in the dusk of the evening could not be distinguished. 'My God!' exclaimed Colonel Roberts, 'What is that?' The next moment the Stars and Stripes emerged from the wood, and the answering shout went up: 'It is the Irish brigade!'" Quickly getting into line of battle, "The 'fighting Irishmen' threw aside their hats and coats, rolled up their sleeves, gave a tremendous cheer, and then following their gallant commander, charged across the field against the murderous fire of artillery ... on went the Irish brigade, over the field and into the woods beyond; so completely routed the enemy, that he did not again renew the conflict on that portion of the field."[15]

The Federal brigades, fresh to the battle, effectively shored up the position at the center of the Union line which the Confederates had managed to break. Both sides had fought themselves to a standstill. At a cost of nearly 4,000 Federal and Confederate casualties, the columns of the Army of the Potomac were stretched but did not break on June 30. McClellan's wagons continued on the way to their new base, and Lee was once again denied his Cannae. At 1 a.m. July 1, the troops from Richardson's division withdrew from the lines at Glendale. "We pulled up stakes again in the night and skedaddled," was the verdict of one soldier.[16] Marching behind Meagher's brigade, one of Caldwell's men recalled the drudgery of the march following the battle as being characterized by "darkness and toil," until at about 5 a.m., they "began climbing a hill and were greeted with the advancing dawn." They had arrived at the next Union line of defense, Malvern Hill, and went into bivouac on the right flank, protecting the road to the new base, Harrison's Landing.[17]

"Some of us will never come back"

The stretched concertina that had been the Army of the Potomac during the retreat of the last week now once again collapsed together as a single mass with its back to the James River. Lee's army, spread out like a fan during the chase from Mechanicsville, also now converged to the area directly north of the Federal position. After Gaines Mill, Malvern Hill was probably the strongest defensive position the Army of the Potomac would hold during the entire war. It was just a mile long from north to south, and about three-quarters of a mile wide. On either side were two streams; on the right flank were seven divisions, while the left flank was faced by high bluffs known as Malvern Cliffs. This left a narrow front, facing north, with a long slope up which the Confederates would advance with little or no cover. Directly facing them would be hub to hub Federal artillery, and 18,000 soldiers from two Federal divisions.

Ironically, the main danger for the Federal army was the actual narrowness of the front they had to defend. Lee's soldiers had already displayed their tenacity in attack, and no matter how many Federal divisions were on hand, only so many could be squeezed into the narrow front. If, as at Gaines Mill, they were attacked by equal numbers of determined Confederates, these might just be able to break though. Some of Lee's officers thought it was not worth the risk. Even as aggressive and fearless a warrior as Daniel Harvey Hill warned Lee that, "If McClellan is there [on Malvern Hill], we had better let him alone."[18] Lee would have none of it. In his judgment, McClellan's army was near the breaking point, and it might take just one more push to sunder it. After personally scouting the area with Longstreet, Lee decided he would not let McClellan go without one more attempt to destroy him. After a botched artillery bombardment and a confused set of orders, the Confederates attacked. "Up the long slope they went," wrote one historian, "brigade after brigade, and the Federal guns knocked their lines all apart and covered the hillside with broken bodies."[19] Harvey Hill thought that the courage displayed by the charging Confederates was "sublime," but against such odds, "It was not war — it was murder."[20]

Despite the Confederate casualties and the subsequent judgment that Malvern Hill was a decisive, almost casual or inevitable victory, throughout the battle, the outcome did not always appear so assured. "The battle was desperately contested and frequently trembled in the balance," wrote Henry Hunt, the man directing the Federal artillery.[21] As they had done before and would do again, the men from the South proved, as the saying went, "they took a lot of killing." It could also possibly have turned out like Gaines Mill, not just because of Confederate gallantry, but also because Fitz-John Porter nearly committed similar tactical errors. When he had been hard pressed north of the Chickahominy during June 27, he had delayed calling for reinforcements, and when they did arrive, they had to be fed into the line piecemeal to shore up weak points. On Malvern Hill, as his brigades became hard pressed, Porter sent "an urgent request" to Sumner, but asked for only two brigades.

He was lucky even to get these. Although there were seven divisions to hand in the immediate rear of Porter's lines, Sumner felt that his own position was threatened, and his response to Porter's request was to send only one brigade, that of Caldwell's. When Heintzelman, who was with Sumner at the time, and who had been

Porter's corps commander during the early stages of the Peninsula campaign, saw Sumner's response, he sprang to his feet and exclaimed, "By Jove! if Porter asks for help, I know he needs it and I will send it."[22] The immediate upshot of this was that Heintzelman sent one of his own brigades, that of Brigadier General Dan Sickles, and Sumner sent another of his. Once again, it was the Irish Brigade. So it was that for the fifth time during the Peninsula campaign, Meagher's men found themselves ordered to advance during the falling darkness to shore up a hard-pressed line. Many of the men had already began to settle down for the night, and on hearing of the order to advance, one officer remarked that "some of us who have prepared our supper will never come back to eat it." The officer, Captain Joseph O' Donoghue, was one of the first to fall.[23]

"Like a stonewall"

As the Irishmen made their way across the plateau, Sickles' brigade went into position in support of Caldwell's men, who, even though only a short time on the scene themselves, had already "suffered severely." The Irish Brigade, or at least the 69th and the 88th New York — the 63rd and 29th Massachusetts having being detached en route to support some batteries — carried on until they were met by Porter, who started to lead them to the front himself. The 69th was commanded by Nugent, the 88th by Major Quinlan. As they moved forward, they passed the mortally wounded Colonel Cass of the 9th Massachusetts, his jaw shattered by a ball, being brought to the rear. "As they recognized a fellow-countryman," wrote one observer, "they gave a yell that drowned the noise of the guns."[24] Porter led the men "beyond our lines into the woods held by the enemy."[25] The historian of the Second Corps, who, "had no love for Meagher and little for the Irish Brigade" described the arrival of the 69th and 88th.[26] "Anyone who has ever been in action," wrote Francis Walker, "knows how easy it is to recognize the firing of fresh troops; and the writer has never forgotten the outburst which announced that the Irish men had opened up on the Confederate column, now halfway up the slope."[27] By now the ground in front of the Union line was carpeted with dead Confederates, and "in some places the bodies were in continuous lines and heaps." As the Irishmen went forward, a line of Confederates "suddenly rose and opened with fearful volleys upon our advancing line."[28] "It was one sheet of molten lead," recalled an officer of the 69th. But the soldiers of the 69th and 88th stood firm, "sustaining each other like genuine brothers."[29] It was reportedly on Malvern Hill that a Confederate officer was heard to remark, "Here comes that damned green flag again." After their repeated experiences on the Peninsula, it would appear to have been as appropriate a time as any to make it.[30] "I turned to the [Irish] brigade," described Porter, "which had thus far kept pace with my horse, and found it standing 'like a stonewall'

... returning a fire more destructive than it received." The 69th was supported by the 88th and "as soon as the 69th had exhausted its ammunition, the 88th took its place, and again the 69th took the line when the 88th was out of ammunition." Volley after volley they fired, "strewing the hill with dead and wounded" all the while picking up the guns of their dead and wounded comrades when their own became too hot to handle.[31]

Even more dramatic scenes were to follow. As part of a last desperate charge, the Confederate 10th Louisiana regiment, largely Irish themselves, came to blows with Meagher's men. The Louisiana Tigers as they were known, had been recruited from "New Orleans toughs and Mississippi rivermen, mainly Irish, and all skilled at alley fighting with hatchet and bowie knife." It must have been an extraordinary scene. Around and above them were "jets of flame darting from thousands of rifles; hissing fuses marked the flight of innumerable shells crossing the plain from every direction," while on the slopes of Malvern Hill, the struggle between the fellow countrymen was almost primeval, the worst nightmare of the *Boston Pilot* come true. As the Tigers rushed their countrymen in Union blue, "Nugent charged with both regiments and met the enemy in a hand to hand encounter" during which "bayonets were brought into play, muskets were reversed, and men were brained and clubbed to death." In his report, the brigade commander of the 10th Louisiana wrote how "the terrible fire poured by the enemy in our front, caused the line to waver and finally to break."[32] When Sumner subsequently saw the pile of damaged and broken guns of the Irishmen he was initially outraged, thinking they had been abandoned by stragglers, until it was explained to him by one soldier that the guns had been used in an unorthodox fashion. "When the rebs went for our biys with bowie knives," went the explanation, the "biys went for the rebs in the way they wor used to."[33] One of Lee's generals described the scene where the opposing brigades clashed as "a slaughter pen." But the Federal line held, and the Confederates withdrew, leaving over 5,000 of their dead, wounded, or missing on the field. Malvern Hill had been a costly misjudgment for the Army of Northern Virginia.[34]

"A singular crawling effect"

The lifting of the morning fog brought the full panorama of horror. A line of bodies marked the furthest limit of the Confederate attack, but scattered behind them down the slope, "Five thousand men lay ... covering the ground like a ragged carpet that lived and made incoherent sounds." A Federal soldier wrote how, "A third of them were dead or dying, but enough of them were alive and moving to give the field a singular crawling effect."[35] A temporary truce was declared later that morning. "The parties from both armies gradually approached each other and continued their mournful work without molestation from either side," wrote one Confederate

9. To Malvern Hill

officer, "being apparently appalled for a moment into a cessation from all hostile purposes by the terrible spectacle presented to their view."[36] One of the Federal dead was Sergeant Haggerty of the 69th New York, brother of Lieutenant Colonel Haggerty, who was killed by the bullets of the 4th Alabama at Bull Run, and "whose noble example of patriotism and soldiership it was the passion of Sergeant Haggerty to emulate."[37] One of the wounded was Lieutenant John Donovan, also of the 69th, who had been shot through the eye. When he met with Judge Daly's wife the following September, Donovan recounted how, while lying wounded and unable to move "he felt someone touch him with his sword." Looking up, he saw a Confederate officer standing over him. "Why don't you get up?" asked the officer. "Because I cannot," replied Donovan. "Where do you belong?" asked the officer. After Donovan replied that he was from the 69th New York, the Confederate proceeded to berate the wounded Irishman; "Then, sir, you vagabonds are speaking to General [D.H.] Hill of the Confederate Army. You have a bad wound. You seem to have lost your eye. You are an Irishman, I suppose. That what you've got for interfering to prevent the Southern people from maintaining their rights." "I lost that eye in the cause of the old Union and the old flag," replied Donovan, "and I am prepared to lose the other in the same cause if I get a chance. And if I lose that I can go blind."[38]

The rest of his uninjured comrades in the brigade were not called on to make any such similar sacrifices that day. Their guns hadn't cooled from their day's work, when Porter had received orders from McClellan to withdraw to Harrison's Landing. Even the normally cautious Porter was reluctant to abandon the site of his hard-won victory, and spent the night "urging McClellan to move forward on Richmond at daylight." General Kearny was less circumspect. "I say to you all," he told his fellow generals, "such an order can only be prompted by cowardice or treason." McClellan was not deflected, and by daybreak the troops and trains were well on their way, with only a regiment of cavalry and one of infantry acting as rearguard. The eight-mile march was a sad affair. Maybe Lee's judgment had not been that far out. The march began "as a regular stampede, each man going off on his own hook," but in the midst of a torrential downpour, "what began as a stampede ended as a rout." "The soldiers who had fought so magnificently for the last week," wrote General Couch, "marching by night and fighting by day, were now a mob."[39] They carried with them the memory of the previous night, as in the darkness, "the Federal guns continued firing, bathing the smoky crest of the hill in a pulsating dull red light, so that it looked like a depiction of the maw of hell."[40] For many, the Seven Days' had been such a descent.

Chapter 10

Rebels Resurgent

"Coffee-coolers and skedaddlers"

On the morning of Sunday, July 6, Fathers Corby and Ouellet summoned the brigade to mass in a newly erected chapel at Harrison's Landing. Corby was to be the celebrant, Ouellet was to provide the sermon for the day. Many of their flock were still tired. The weather was warm, and coffee and breakfast appeared to be a more favored option among many. Ouellet, the pastoral equivalent to a Phil Kearny, decided to shake his troops out for action. He stormed down the streets between the tents, and with some well-aimed kicks sent pots and pans flying, much to the chagrin of the men. He then went back to deliver his sermon, and once again launched into the backsliders. "The good came here this morning to thank God for their deliverance from death," he thundered, "and the rest who remained to satisfy their appetites were fellows that were *coffee-coolers* and *skedaddlers* during our retreat."[1] Subsequently, when Father Ouellet was in camp, coffee would have to wait until after mass.

Ouellet was only doing his duty, just as the men in the brigade had done theirs during the battles of the Seven Days.' They had been in action as much as if not more than any other brigade, and they had the gaps in their ranks to prove it. While the reputation of the Irish Brigade as an organization was in the ascendant, Meagher's main achievement during the Seven Days' appears to have been to reinforce his reputation as having a "suspect" temperament. Compounding earlier reports of drunkenness, and his arrest in the middle of the Seven Days,' Meagher had capped off the campaign with another erratic episode on Malvern Hill. While on their way to reinforce Porter, the 63rd New York under Lieutenant Colonel Fowler had been ordered to wait in support of an upcoming battery. Shortly after, Meagher and his staff came by. "What are you doing here, while your comrades are being slaughtered?" demanded Meagher, "Follow me!" Fowler told him he was under orders from General Porter to remain in position. Meagher was not best pleased on discovering that his orders "were consequently without weight." "The fiery Meagher," wrote Corby, "was wild with rage, while he dashed down the front of the regiment and back again to the right where Fowler stood." "You are a disgrace to the Irish Brigade," he fulminated at the hapless Fowler, ordering Captain Gossen to take the lieutenant colonel's sword, and place him under arrest.

10. Rebels Resurgent

Then, with the evening sky over Malvern Hill lit by the thousand flashes of the desperate struggle, this peculiar Irish drama turned into farce as Meagher called upon the men of the 63rd New York to follow him. Only two companies elected to do so. "Having reached the top of the hill," wrote Corby, "the companies were halted, when it was decided to return to the regiment, that all might act together." On returning in confusion, the men were then ordered by their chaplain, Father Dillon, to "Lie down, boys, and wait for orders." This they promptly did until the said battery eventually arrived, and off they went. Lieutenant Colonel Fowler soon rejoined his regiment and was wounded at Sharpsburg in September.[2]

If the Seven Days' fighting had proved that some of the commanders were unfit to command, it had also proved that they were unworthy of the troops they did command. Almost without exception, the men had behaved well, losing dignity and discipline only during the final retreat to Harrison's Landing. If one was looking for heroes on the Federal side, many of the artillerists, Fitz-John Porter, Sykes' regulars, or indeed the Irish Brigade, could have fitted the bill quite handsomely. The brigade had been called into action under severe circumstances on four of the seven days, and had not been found wanting. "I wish I had twenty thousand men like yours," and, "I envy you the command of that Brigade," were remarks Meagher was said to have received from McClellan and Porter respectively during the Seven Days' battles.[3] After Malvern Hill, where the valor of Peter Rafferty of the 69th would earn the brigade a second Congressional Medal of Honor, it was reported that Sumner said he thought he could whip Lee's army with "the Irish Brigade and Petit's battery."[4]

Posthumous encomiums about any and every brigade in the Army of the Potomac were not uncommon, especially in the ethnic papers, but the exploits of the Irish Brigade do lend a well-earned, if not a literal, credence to the remarks. One historian of the brigade has written that the brigade had become "one of the small number of combat units that correspond to high trumps in a card game," whose "wild determination" in a fight would provide a division or corps commander with the "absolute assurance that nobody was going to be let down." And they had the scars to prove it. Through a combination of disease and battle casualties, the brigade had lost about 20 percent of its original strength since the three New York regiments had left Annapolis back in March. The 69th had lost heavily, being reduced from 750 to 295 men; the 88th lost 200, leaving 400 men; the 63rd, which had not seen as much action, was down from 750 to 550.[5] While the frequency with which the brigade was called upon during the Seven Days' was partly due to the exigencies of the retreat rather than deliberate choice, the use, or overuse of the brigade as some would see it, would fast become a point of controversy among the Irish population of the North. This was something that Meagher would have to face later in July when he returned to New York to try to enlist more recruits.

Fire in the rear

On July 16, Meagher received approval from McClellan following a request to be allowed to go to New York to try to recruit replacements for his depleted regiments. "The General Commanding relies upon General Meagher to use his utmost exertions to hasten the filling up of his regiments," wrote McClellan's assistant adjutant general, "and to rejoin his command at the earliest possible moment."[6] Despite hunting on his "home patch," and using all his old oratorical skills, Meagher's mission was a failure. Less than 200 new recruits would eventually enlist in the brigade that summer. Part of the problem was common to all Federal recruiting efforts at that time. So confident had the government been early in 1862 of defeating the rebellion, that Secretary of War Stanton had actually closed recruiting stations in April. By May, this was beginning to be seen as a mistake, and the War Department discreetly began to urge state governors to start raising some new regiments. In June, to little fanfare, recruiting stations were reopened. But enlistments were painfully slow. The original spurt of volunteers in the wake of Fort Sumter and Bull Run had provided the Union armies — east and west — with over 600,000 men. The first and most readily available layer of men had thus been already scooped up. Future enlistments would prove more troublesome. One governor reported that, with a booming war economy and a busy summer on farms, many possible recruits "have engaged in other pursuits for the season." Even as resourceful a man as Governor Andrew of Massachusetts could only declare that the call for more men "finds me without materials for an intelligent reply."[7]

Following the setback of the Seven Days,' the tempo was stepped up, with Lincoln and Seward using the state governors to front a more public appeal for recruits. But the casualty lists from the battles outside Richmond had only further contributed to deflating the attempts at repeating the enthusiastic parades and rallies of 1861. The Irish press at home had never been strongly in favor of participation in the war. "Though entertaining the highest regard for Mr. Meagher," the *Galway Vindicator* had written following the battle of Fair Oaks, "we were amongst the first of the Irish national journals to warn our countrymen in America against being led away by his eloquence.... It is an unfortunate civil war in which the Irish should have taken no active part but as mediators."[8] Now, hard on the heels of the Seven Days' battles, erstwhile supporters of the war, such as the *Irish American*, were beginning to strike a more than somber note. "From the melancholy record of killed and missing and wounded which we publish," said the *Irish American*, "it will be seen how heavily our gallant regiments suffered in the continuous series of battles."[9]

It was going to take a varied carrot-and-stick approach by the government to achieve the target of 300,000 new recruits. This would include payment or part payment of bounties, drafting some men for nine months instead of three years, and allowing the new recruits to join new regiments, with the incentive of 30-odd officers' commissions, rather than insisting that existing regiments be replenished. It was against this background that Meagher left Harrison's Landing and headed to New York. Meagher was in fact hoist by a number of petards in his attempt at recruiting. One angle, which he might have been able to exploit, was the use of a basic romantic appeal to the fighting instincts of the Irish, to join their fellow countrymen in their time of need, with maybe a dash of Fenian rhetoric thrown in for good measure. It was this tactic, plus an appeal to come to the aid of their adopted country, which had paved the way for the recruitment of the original regiments. But the original rush of adrenaline had passed. Twelve months later, he was he facing many men who were once again hearing the jingle of money in their pockets after the unemployment of the previous years. If they did want to enlist, there was the prospect of substantial amounts of bounty money elsewhere. Meagher was also trying to mine a bedrock of hardened Democratic supporters, whose antipathy toward the Republican cause had merely been suspended during the early euphoria of the war. Meagher, a well-known Democrat himself, was in an awkward spot. When he addressed a call for volunteers to a meeting on July 25, he was heckled from the audience with cries of, "Why don't the Black republicans go?" Meagher's somewhat undiplomatic reply, "Anyone who makes a remark like that, I denounce as a poltroon and a coward," could not disguise the patent hostility of many of his countrymen to the war.[10]

As well as his Democratic credentials being suspect, Meagher's personal motivations were further questioned with regard to the casualties the brigade had suffered. This was partly fuelled by suspicion that they were deliberately overused because the Irish were well known as Democrats. There were also mutterings about Meagher's personal leadership. Not only was it said that he was an ineffective camp commander whose men suffered poor sanitary conditions and poor food, but he was also an ineffective field commander. Back in the previous August, when he had refused the colonel's commission, his own admission of inadequacy for command had been printed in a letter in the *Boston Pilot*. "With my limited experience and very imperfect knowledge of military affairs," he wrote, "it would be grievously culpable in me at this crisis of the national interests, when a great disaster [Bull Run] has to be reversed, to assume a post which I feel, and everybody knows, I am incompetent to fill."[11] Although the thickets and swamps of the Chickahominy would have confounded more experienced commanders, Meagher's failings and flailings would have done nothing to dissipate his own stated "limited experience and very imperfect knowledge of military affairs." While his leadership at the next great battle, Sharpsburg, would perhaps give greater cause for accusations of incompetence, Meagher's often wildly erratic performance during the Seven Days' battles only served to highlight his own admitted inadequacies. Allied to this, and in some respects more damaging, was the charge that his desire for personal acclaim had led him to expose his men recklessly. One soldier writing home told of how he was "speaking to a sergeant here that served under Meagher who told men that he was a gentlemen and a soldier, but that he wanted to gain so much praise he would not spare his men."[12] Not so, Meagher would answer, with not a little desperation appearing in his convoluted attempt to answer these charges. Long ago Irishmen had "established for themselves a reputation for fighting, with a consummate address and a superlative ability," he told a rally in New York. It was also accepted, he went on, that "Galway beats Bannagher, and Bannagher beats the devil; and if the boys of the Irish Brigade had not, with an untoward innocence, shown themselves, the first chance they had, as trustworthy as their blessed old sires, and just as eager and ravenous for a fight ... the Irish Brigade would not have had any more fighting to do than anyone else...."[13] Not surprisingly, arguing that the brigade's casualties had been due to his compatriots' inherent love of fighting and dying brought few recruits that summer.

Indeed, why should Meagher be believed when even his own men camped on the James did not believe it, as their letters home and to the papers showed. The failure to capture Richmond was "all owing to the damned abolitionists that are in Congress," wrote one officer in the 69th regiment, "If we only had 20,000 more men ... we would be in Richmond today instead of where we are." Not only did the soldiers suffer because of political interference from the "Black Republicans" in Washington, but "it is my humble belief that they wanted General McClellan and his army killed or captured," wrote the same officer.[14] Such extraordinary sentiments had been fuelled by McClellan's paranoia over his relations with Lincoln and the Republican administration, which had pervaded a large section of the Army of the Potomac. It was believed that the radical Republicans had not wanted McClellan to win in the Peninsula, as this might have led to a *rapprochement* between the North and South, and the continuance of slavery. Rather, they wanted a long, drawn-out, bitter, and destructive war which would guarantee the end of slavery. "Does the President (controlled by an incompetent Secretary) design to cause defeat here for the purpose of prolonging the war," Fitz-John Porter wrote from Harrison's Landing to a newspaper editor in New York. "Was there ever such a government, such fools, such idiots," wrote another officer. "I hate or despise them more intensively than I do the rebels."[15]

As these sentiments became a matter of public debate in the newspapers, Irish recruits stayed away in droves. It was a trying episode for Meagher. He remained ostensibly a Democrat, and a strong "McClellan man"; but his own position and status was dependent on his being able to maintain a viable command in terms of regimental numbers. He railed against the efforts of "an army of implacable conspirators in the rear," meaning his erstwhile Democratic colleagues who were intent on frustrating the administration's war efforts by discouraging recruitment. "There is treason here among us," he said, "He was fully aware that there were some traitors in our midst who went about opposing recruiting and preventing many good men from entering the army."[16] In August, Meagher returned to Harrison's Landing, somewhat disoriented and increasingly disillusioned, and with less than 200 new recruits to follow along.

Back at Harrison's Landing, Lincoln finally decided to pull the rug of the Army of the Potomac from underneath McClellan. On July 13, Lee, now confident he had the measure of McClellan, dispatched some of his forces northward to attack the Federal Army of Virginia which had been formed under Major General John Pope. Lincoln decided that the main thrust of Federal action should move back north also, and on August 3, McClellan, to his disgust, received orders "to withdraw your army from the Peninsula to Aquia Creek." The grand campaign was over and if Lincoln could have had his wish, so would have been McClellan's career. He offered the command of the Army of the Potomac to Major General Ambrose Burnside. Burnside refused. But once, in taking the step of offering the post, this Rubicon had been crossed, McClellan's days were numbered.

If any further evidence of McClellan's unfitness for high command was required, plenty more was available with regard to his actions during the Second Bull Run campaign. This next major encounter between the Confederates and Federals led to perhaps the most unsavory episode in the history of the Army of the Potomac. In the lead up to, and during the battle itself, which was fought over the last two days of August, Pope was completely outgeneralled, and his army almost entirely routed and demoralized. What might have made the difference was more support from the Army of the Potomac, and while this is arguable, the point was that it was not forthcoming.[17] After the battle, the victorious commander, Robert E. Lee, took yet another bold decision. He couldn't maintain his army where it was, nor could he attack the Washington fortifications; to withdraw south seemed fruitless, both in terms of maintaining morale, and also finding provisions for his army in war-ravaged Virginia. The only alternative was to throw the dice again. He would invade the North and take the fight to the enemy, living off the fat of their land. On September 4, the advance units of Lee's Army of Northern Virginia, "a most ragged, lean, and hungry set of wolves," splashed across the shallows of the Potomac at White's Ford, and on into Maryland.[18]

For the Irish Brigade, Second Bull Run was only a noise offstage and the source of confused marching. After making their way back down the by-now devastated landscape of the Peninsula, through Yorktown and on to Newport News, they boarded transports bound for Aquia Creek. From there the brigade was put on railcars and shipped to General Burnside at Falmouth.[19] Two days later, as the crisis atmosphere around Washington deepened, they were shipped back again to Alexandria, and then further down the Potomac to Fort Corcoran on Arlington Heights, "our old camping ground which we left in 1862."[20] On August 30, they were ordered to march west, in the direction of Manassas to support Pope, but were stopped just outside the fortifications of Washington. It was at this point McClellan was proposing to his superiors that Pope be left to get "out of his scrape" with Robert E. Lee, and he wanted to keep as many "reliable troops in and near Washington" as possible.[21] He was overruled, and the troops continued their march, but arriving in time only to cover the withdrawal of Pope's defeated army. Four days later they were in position northwest of Washington, ready to begin the pursuit of the Army of Northern Virginia.

Soft beds and hard battles

The Irish Brigade, like the rest of the Army of the Potomac, actually enjoyed their tramp through the Maryland countryside in search of Lee's legions. On September 6, they left camp at Tennallytown, northeast of Washington, and headed off up the National Road. With McClellan wanting to cover Washington and Baltimore, as well as looking for Lee, the advance was cautious and slow, with the soldiers having to cover less than 10 miles a day. Easy marches, a friendly country, good weather and good roads all marked a sharp contrast to the deprivations on the banks of the Chickahominy. On the march through Maryland, the historian of the 29th Massachusetts described the Irish Brigade "moving along the road with its tattered flags, the clothing of its men being almost as ragged as its banners."[22] As the division marched through one town after another, with smiling girls, cold water and provisions of all sorts left out for the passing lines of marching men, one soldier was moved to call out, "We're in God's country again."[23]

On September 13, the brigade was due to march through the town of Frederick. With the weather having been so warm the previous night, many men chose to sleep rough in the fields, among and on top of the haystacks. At reveille, Captain Gossen slid down from one of these, only to land on someone sleeping below. "My ribs are broken, you scoundrel! Who the devil are you?" spluttered Gosson's unfortunate victim. General Meagher's *aide de camp* was not going to be spoken to like that by any enlisted man, regardless of the circumstances. "And who the hell are you?" replied Gossen, "Get up out of that," only to be confronted by the disheveled figure of none other than the division commander, General Richardson. "Bless my soul, General Richardson," exclaimed Gossen, and proceeded to offer his embarrassed apologies, finally becalming the general with an offer of a drink of whiskey from his pocket flask, which of course, no self-respecting aide of General Meagher would be without.[24]

10. Rebels Resurgent

Later on, the corps passed through Frederick, going into bivouac about a mile outside the town. The atmosphere was relaxed as the men lolled about in the fields. An officer from a new regiment that joined the Second Corps at Frederick looked on in wonder at the hardened veterans and commented on the "celebrated Irish Brigade," describing them as a "'free and easy' going crowd."[25] Fathers Corby and Ouellet absented themselves briefly to visit the Jesuit's residence in the town to avail themselves of "a square meal."[26] Well into the night of September 13, there was a stir in the camps with officers coming and going. Rumor had it that Lee's army had been found and tomorrow would see fighting. What had happened was that two Federal soldiers, who were relaxing in a field just outside Frederick, discovered a package. The package turned out to be three cigars wrapped in a piece of paper. The paper was headed "Headquarters of the Army of Northern Virginia Special Orders No. 191," and was nothing less than a copy of Lee's most recent instructions to his commanders, which also outlined their exact whereabouts. The following morning, McClellan's army headed off in pursuit of Lee.

On September 14, some of Lee's troops fought a holding action at the gaps through South Mountain, through which McClellan's army would have to pass. After severe losses on both sides, the Confederates withdrew. Next morning the pursuit began again, with Richardson's division in the lead. As they made their way past the town of Boonsboro there was evidence of the Confederates' hasty retreat to be seen everywhere. "On every side, men and horses, dead and dying," wrote Corby, who would dismount occasionally to hear the confessions of the wounded and dying men. Up ahead, some Confederate artillery delayed the pursuit, but quickly withdrew as the infantry started to outflank them. Just outside the village of Keedysville, the pursuers came under more sustained fire, this time from Lee's army. As described by Meagher, the Army of Northern Virginia was "in full force, drawn up in a line of battle on the heights near Sharpsburg and overlooking the Antietam."[27] There they waited until McClellan arrived before going into camp on either side of the road, to wait for the inevitable clash of the armies.

Lee's men were strung out along a ridge about four miles long, which paralleled the north-south course of the river. McClellan spent September 16 riding back and forth along his lines on the opposite side of the river, trying to gauge the lie of Lee's defenses, while formulating his plan of attack for September 17. While McClellan was preparing his battle plan, the Army of the Potomac had remained basically idle during September 16. The men probably spent some time writing letters to their loved ones. They knew what was coming, sooner or later. During the morning, the most exciting event was provided by Gosson and a surgeon from the brigade, Francis Reynolds. They decided to have a steeplechase, which took place in full view of the Confederate pickets the far side of the river, but rather than shooting, the southerners "shouted their approval and tossed their hats in the air."[28] Elsewhere, wrote one of McClellan's staff officers, "Nobody seemed to be in a hurry.... Corps and divisions moved as languidly to the places assigned to them as if they were getting ready for a grand review instead of a decisive battle."[29] In the center of the Federal lines, the Irish Brigade had moved up almost to the banks of the Antietam and lay on their arms just north of the Middle Bridge across the river. There they spent a cold and disturbed night as a succession of mules, horses, and soldiers clanked through their position to get water from the river. On the way into position they had been marched to the ammunition wagons, and in an ominous portent, had been issued 80 rounds per man, twice the usual allocation.[30]

Chapter 11

"The Longest Saddest Day"

"We must get out of this"

September 17 would prove to be the bloodiest day in American history. On the Confederate side, the battle would be known as Sharpsburg. The Federals would call it Antietam. More Americans, 23,000, would be killed or wounded during what one Confederate officer described as "the longest saddest day" than in any conflict before or since.[1] The carnage started at first light as the sound of firing rose from beyond the woods off to the northwest on the far side of Antietam Creek. The initial assault was made by Joe Hooker's division. As Hooker advanced southward, a battle line of Confederates was seen emerging from the woods near a whitewashed church, known as the Dunker Church. It was the division of John Bell Hood, on their way to repulse Hooker's advance with such abandoned fury and frenzy that Hood's division itself would be decimated. At 7:20 a.m. McClellan ordered Sumner to take his men across the creek in support of Hooker. He was not to take Richardson's division at this time, however, until his position in reserve could be taken by another division brought forward from the Fifth Corps. After waiting to be replaced, it would be another hour and a half before Richardson's men would cross the creek to join their comrades.[2]

Sumner quickly got his other two divisions, those of Sedgwick and French, to wade across the creek to their front. Once across, in what the historian of the Second Corps described as "ill regulated ardor," Sumner marched off toward the Dunker Church at the head of Sedgwick's men. Waiting up ahead was a trap, with Confederate units positioned on three sides. When the full horror of the position he had led these men into dawned on him, Sumner cried out, "My God, we must get out of this," and galloped off to the rear to try and warn the following brigades. "Back, boys, for God's sake, move back!" he called out, "You are in a bad fix." But it was too late. "In less time than it takes to tell it," wrote one participant, "the ground was strewn with the bodies of the dead and wounded." Sedgwick's division of veterans was practically slaughtered. Nearly half—2,500—were killed or wounded in the space of the first 15 minutes of the Confederate assault, before the remainder scattered northward and eastward out of the woods.[3]

The gleam of bayonets

The consequences of Sumner's advance were not confined to Sedgwick's division. Sumner was a corps commander. He had two other divisions under his command on the field that day — French and Richardson's, the former of which was meant to be following directly behind Sedgwick. Yet Sumner had gone marching off at the head of Sedgwick's troops, "so full of fight, so occupied with the thought of engaging the enemy, that he did not see to it that French, who followed Sedgwick was brought up within supporting distance."[4] Not only was French not within supporting distance when the Confederate onslaught began, but, "for want of precise direction," he had marched his division off to an entirely different part of the battlefield.

After fording the Antietam in the wake of Sedgwick's men, French lost sight of the leading division, driven so far and so fast ahead by Sumner. Approaching a local farmstead known as the Roulette Farm, French saw some troops off to his left. Without specific orders from either Sumner or McClellan, French ended up swinging to the southwest, taking up position on the left of the troops he had seen. In doing so he came under fire from some Confederates to his front. As French's men advanced, the scattered Confederates fell back, a few of them taking shelter in the farm buildings. As the Confederates fell back, William Roulette, who had been sheltering in his cellar, emerged shouting, "Give it to 'em. Drive 'em! Take anything on my place, only drive 'em."[5]

Driving them would not prove easy. South of the Roulette buildings the ground rose steadily before French's men for about 400 yards before dipping down again toward a country lane 100 yards away. The lane divided Mr. Roulette's farm from that of his neighbor, Mr. Piper. Like many such lanes, years of usage had sunk the level of the lane below the level of the surrounding sides. According to one Irish soldier, this lane, this sunken road, would prove to be "the most hotly contested point of the day."[6] The first part of the road ran east from the Hagerstown Pike for about 500 yards, then bent slightly toward the southeast for another 500 yards before turning sharply to the south, eventually winding its way down to the Boonsboro Pike. Posted in the road were two tough brigades belonging to the command of Daniel Harvey Hill, one of the Confederate generals who had cannily slipped by the men of the 88th New York the night following the battle of Gaines Mill. Because the level of the road had been eroded well below the level of the surrounding fields, except for where it shallowed out at the kink in the road after 500 yards before dipping again, the road formed a natural trench for the defenders. It was further strengthened by Hill's men who had used nearby fence rails to build a protective breastwork. On the Miller farm south of the sunken road were more Confederates who would be able to fire over the heads of their

11. "The Longest Saddest Day"

comrades at any advancing Federals. If you were going to attack the sunken road from the north, as French was intending to do, then, as the historian of the Army of the Potomac wrote, "It was as nasty a strong point as the army ever ran up against."[7]

In the sunken road, one of the Confederate brigade commanders observed the advance of the first Federal troops. "It was a thrilling spectacle.... The banners above them had apparently never been discolored by the smoke and dust of battle. Their gleaming bayonets flashed like burnished silver in the sunlight. With the precision of step and perfect alignment of a holiday parade, this magnificent array moved to the charge.... I thought, if I did not say, What a pity to spoil with bullets such a scene of martial beauty." But spoil it he did. As the first brigade crested the hill and began their march down toward the sunken road, the Confederates waited until they literally could not miss, "so close that we might have seen the eagles on their buttons."[8] The order to fire was given and an unbroken sheet of flame erupted from end to end of the sunken road. In less than five minutes French's lead brigade suffered more than 450 casualties. Nor did it get any better after that. While hugging the ground for protection, it almost appeared to some of French's men that the very blades of grass were moving so much they seemed to have a life of their own. One remarked that it looked like they were being swarmed by crickets before realizing it was spent bullets and not crickets that were skipping through the grass.[9] A reporter for the *Irish American* wrote that "those who were eye witness to the struggle did not suppose it possible for a single man to escape."[10] Looking down on the sunken road, the Federals on the crest of the hill could see lines of Confederate reinforcements disappear from view into the dip behind the sunken road on their way to join their comrades. The road itself was becoming so overrun with men that the rear lines were loading weapons and passing them to the front rank to fire, allowing the defenders to produce a tremendous amount of concentrated firepower.

Given the Federal disarray to their front, Hill was planning to launch a counterattack on French's exposed left flank. Some of the Confederate brigades moved out around the extreme right of Hill's line and were advancing forward to the crest of the hill. It was doubtful whether French's troops could have resisted. As they moved out of the sunken road, off to their right, where no Federals should have been, some soldiers had appeared. They were attempting to tear down the rail fence which formed the northern border of one of Mr. Roulette's plowed fields. They took some severe punishment before disappearing back down the other side of the fence. Minutes later a full Federal battle line appeared to take their place, bearing a green flag with a harp and sunburst emblazoned upon it. As if on cue, Sumner's third division — Richardson's — was beginning to come up in support, with Meagher and the Irish Brigade leading the way.

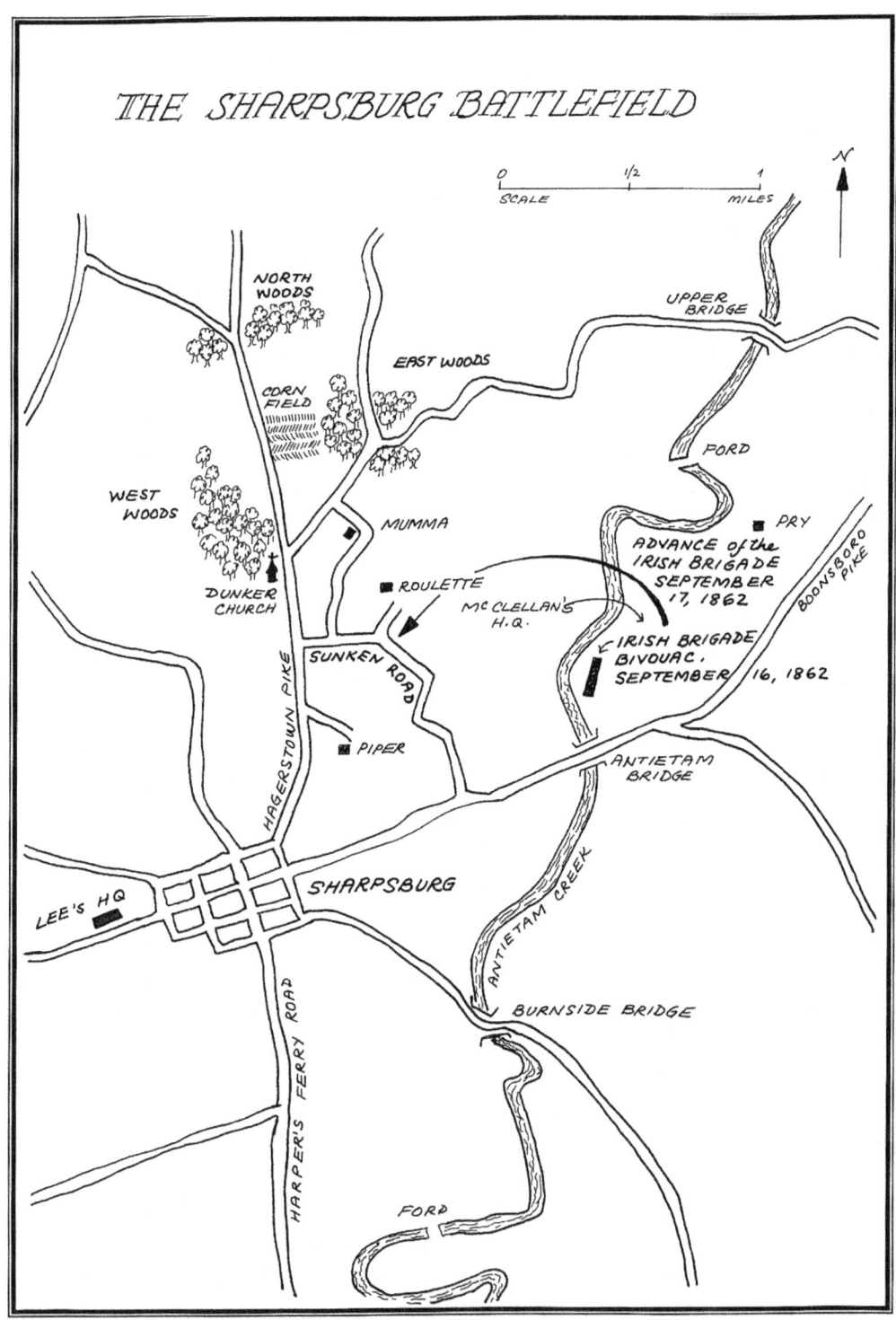

11. "The Longest Saddest Day"

"A well earned reputation"

After their uncomfortable night near the creek bank, the dawn brought fresh trials to Meagher's men. Breakfasting in the dark, they waited for orders to move. Once the battle had begun, the Federal artillery drawn up on the hills above them started to shell the Confederate positions across the creek, which attempted to reply in kind. Shells screamed overhead from both sides. Some landed short in the creek, others spent themselves in adjoining fields. One landed amongst the men of the 63rd New York. Nearby, Sergeant Matthew Hart watched in horror as the fuse burned its way back to the casing. Miraculously, the shell failed to go off, and Hart would no doubt dine out for a long time recounting his own personal miracle.[11]

The sounds of the battle across the creek rose and fell. Sedgwick's, and then French's men, had already forded the creek farther up, but still no orders came for the brigade to cross. Then, after 9 a.m., as some units from the Fifth Corps began to move in around their positions, the order came to ford the creek. Despite the wait, there was certainly no sense of urgency lacking in the movement. After making their way a mile or so along the bank to the ford, the men waded the creek in waist-deep water. After crossing, they were ordered to wring out their socks and fill their canteens. One soldier in the 88th New York did not bother with the socks. He hadn't taken his boots off for a week during the march through Maryland and he feared that he would not be able to get his swollen feet back into them once removed.[12] Another overheard Meagher, who apparently spent the night "sleeping on the ground without even a fly tent to cover him," tell his orderly to brush off his uniform, to which the soldier thought, "We'd all have a brush soon." From the southwest, they could hear the sounds of the heavy firing as French's assaults began.[13]

As Richardson formed his division for the advance, the Irish Brigade was placed on the right, Caldwell's on the left, and Brooke's taking the rear center. They climbed the high ground on the west side of the creek and began making their way southwest, "coming nearer and nearer," wrote one soldier, "to the dreadful and deafening discharges of musketry ahead."[14] As the fighting over by the Dunker Church abated through pure exhaustion and the sheer scale of the slaughter, the consequence of French's original decision to redirect his advance at the sunken road now shifted the entire focus of the battle to the struggle for this country lane. As they neared the center of this maelstrom, the circumstances of which they knew little, Richardson ordered his men to stop and remove all unnecessary equipment. The Irishmen, already well known to the quartermasters for shedding any excess baggage at the drop of a hat, responded eagerly. "The men of the Irish Brigade instantly obeyed this order with a heartiness and enthusiasm," wrote Meagher, "which was rare to expect from men who had been wearied and worn by the unremitting labors of nine months campaign."[15] As the advance continued, off to their right they could see some farm buildings — Roulette's — while, as on other battlefields, they began passing the remnants of previous assaults. Up ahead to their right, on a slope rising south from the farmhouse, they could see the men of French's division. Some were hugging the ground trying to get some protection from the artillery bombardment, others firing to their front from where could be heard the almost continuous roar of musketry fire.

In the hollow before they advanced up the final slope to their front, the brigade fell out of columns and into battle lines, with the 69th New York on the right, the 63rd New York in the center, and the 88th New York on the left. The 29th Massachusetts lined up behind in reserve. At the top of the hill, extending about halfway across their line of advance was a rail fence that ran along the edge of a plowed field. Meagher called for volunteers to take it down before the brigade advanced. In itself, it was a daunting task. It seemed likely that before long the fence would disintegrate on its own as splinters flew in every direction from repeated hits by bullets and cannonballs. But several dozen men from the 69th New York and the 29th Massachusetts dashed forward up the slope, coming under fire from Confederate snipers as they did so. Some members of the 88th moved forward to try to provide covering fire as the volunteers set about their work. Once at the fence, the snipers were the least of their worries as they came under direct fire from the men in, and those now advancing from, the sunken road. Bullets snatched the rails from their hands and tore into their clothes.[16] One soldier in the 29th Massachusetts remembered that "as one would grasp a rail it would be sent flying out of his hands by rifle shots." Most were left dead on the crest of the slope or hanging from the fence rails. The survivors raced back down the slope to rejoin the waiting lines.[17]

Fence or no fence, the brigade prepared to advance. As he heard the command "Attention! Forward! Guide! Center! March!" Father Corby, who was following behind the brigade on his horse, knew he too had his duty to perform. "I gave rein to my horse," he wrote, "and let him go at full gallop till I reached the front of the brigade, and, passing along the line, told the men to make an Act of Contrition.... I had time only to wheel my horse for an instant toward them and gave my poor men a hasty absolution."[18] As they reached the crest of the slope, the Irishmen halted and delivered a volley into the sunken road. They in their turn were greeted with a sheet of fire that was, according to one Irishman, "the most severest and most deadly ever witnessed." Still, "the hottest fire from artillery and musketry could not stop them from advancing repeatedly towards the enemy's lines at double quick, and with a cheer."[19] Their advance was sufficient to send the Confederates who had ventured out from the sunken road scuttling back, securing the left of the Federal center. But the men of the brigade could do nothing but recoil from the calamitous fire coming from the Confederates, who they could barely see below them behind their breastwork.

11. "The Longest Saddest Day"

On the left of the line, "the most destructive storm of leaden hail had in an instant killed or wounded every officer but one and more than one-half the rank and file," wrote the reinstated Lieutenant Colonel Fowler of the 63rd in his report.[20] Losses in the 69th on the right were no less severe. After the original color bearer of the 69th was wounded, Captain McGee picked up the emerald flag. As he waved it over his head, a bullet clipped it in two. Another went through his cap before he retrieved the broken staff, and "displaying coolness and bravery ... bore its folds aloft throughout the battle."[21] But individual acts of gallantry, either by brigades or soldiers, were not going to break the Confederate line. The charge of the Irish Brigade collapsed within 50 yards of the sunken road, while the survivors could do nothing but hug the ground and return fire as best they could. There they remained, trying to do as much damage to the men in the sunken road as was being done to them. Still clinging to his hope that an "impetuous" charge might dislodge the Confederates, Meagher sent Captain Gosson with an order for Patrick Kelly of the 88th. As described by Kelly in his report, "an aide rode up and ordered the Sixty-third and Eighty-eighth to charge and take the enemy's colors if possible. I at once gave the order, and my regiment advanced about 20 or 30 paces; but seeing that I had no support, I halted, and inquired for Colonel Burke (of the 63rd), and asked why he did not advance. Captain O'Neill, of the Sixty-third, said he would advance with me if he had any one to command the regiment, but not knowing who was in command he did not wish to do so." Kelly could not have known that Colonel Burke had dismounted earlier and hid behind a fold in the ground, unable to face the Confederate fire, a deed for which he was later dismissed.[22] With their double issue of ammunition almost gone, the Irishmen were finally relieved by Caldwell's brigade.

It was not before time. Caldwell's men had followed the Irish Brigade onto the field, but remained stubbornly and cautiously to the left rear of Meagher's men as they exchanged fire with the Confederates in the sunken road. For what seemed like a long time they had watched helplessly as the Irishmen's colors fell and rose. Caldwell himself was clearly shook by the casualties being taken by the Irishmen up the slope to his front and was only slowly and reluctantly moving his brigade into position on the left flank of the Irish Brigade. As the situation became even more desperate with their ammunition running out, Meagher rode down the slope. "Colonel, for God's sake come and help me," he pleaded with Colonel Barlow of the 61st New York, Caldwell's lead regiment. Barlow told him he could not until ordered to do so by Caldwell. As Meagher galloped back up to the crest of the slope, his horse was hit by a Confederate bullet, throwing its rider, after which Meagher disappears from the accounts of the assault, as he did from the battlefield. About this time Richardson himself arrived on the scene and demanded to know why Caldwell's men were not moving to support the Irish Brigade. "Where's General

Thomas Francis Meagher and the Irish Brigade

Caldwell?" he demanded. "Hiding behind a haystack," was the response from some of the men. "God damn the field officers," exploded Richardson as he personally took charge of the advance.[23] "By order of the staff officer of General Richardson," wrote Barlow in his report, "we then moved to the right in front, and formed behind the crest of a hill on the left of the Sixty-third Regiment, Irish Brigade," before advancing to the crest of the hill "and bravely engaging the enemy."[24]

As Caldwell's men finally moved to their relief, the remaining members of the Irish Brigade made their way to the rear, carrying out this maneuver in parade ground fashion, with "regiments breaking to the rear in companies, those of Caldwell to the front, as steady as when on drill." It was as dauntless a gesture as anything witnessed during the war. As the 88th New York passed Richardson, he stood up in his saddle and shouted, "Bravo, 88th; I shall never forget you."[25] But there were over 500 members of the brigade who remained dead or wounded in the area of the sunken road, with the 63rd and the 69th each losing around 60 percent of their numbers. One officer simply wrote that "the brigade had been cut away."[26] Well could McClellan write in his official report that at Sharpsburg, "the Irish Brigade sustained its well earned reputation."[27]

Dead of the Irish Brigade photographed by Alexander Gardner on the battlefield at Sharpsburg on September 19, 1862. In 1988, the bones of four Union soldiers were unearthed by relic hunters on the Sharpsburg battlefield. It was later established that the men had been members of the 63rd New York. As one of the men had been a private in his late 40s, his identity could be narrowed down to a choice of three — James Gallagher, a stonecutter from Kilkenny; Martin McMahon, a laborer from Clare; or James McGarigan, an Irish American. He had died with a rosary around his neck after three bullets smashed his breastbone while the brigade approached the crest above Bloody Lane. The remains of the soldiers were reburied, after a Catholic mass, in the National Cemetery at Sharpsburg (Library of Congress).

11. "The Longest Saddest Day"

"The end of the Confederacy was in sight"

The Irish Brigade was the fourth wave of brave soldiers to break before the sunken road within the space of three hours. It would take the eventual advance of Caldwell's brigade, the left of which overlapped the Confederate position in the sunken road, and some confused orders in the Confederate ranks, before the prize was won. The final tally of dead and wounded in the battle for the Sunken Road was 5,600. Around the sunken road lay most of the 3,000 Federal casualties, while the majority of the 2,600 Confederates lay along the road itself. One of Caldwell's men believed that the carnage along the length of the road was so great he could have walked it from end to end without touching the ground. Later, as the fight continued, with the Federals now occupying the road and Hill's men rallying in

The story was told that following the battle, when local citizens volunteered to help clear the field of the wounded and dead, an old woman was so shocked by the carnage she saw on the road between her neighbors' farms, she got on her knees to pray for the men who lay in this "bloody lane" (Library of Congress).

the fields to the south, this same carpet of dead and wounded became the "ghastly flooring that we kneeled [on] for the last struggle."[28] The story was told that following the battle, when local citizens volunteered to help clear the field of the wounded and dead, an old lady was so shocked by the carnage she saw on the road between her neighbors' farms, she got on her knees to pray for the men who lay in this "bloody lane."[29]

Soon after midday, the situation around the sunken road stabilized. As around the Dunker Church and the corn field, the soldiers in the immediate area had fought themselves to a standstill. Fresh Federal reinforcements could have yet carried the day. The Confederate line was so thin as to be transparent. "Lee's army was ruined," wrote one Confederate officer, "and the end of the Confederacy was in sight."[30] Yet despite having fresh divisions on hand, McClellan held them back, still fearing Lee's imaginary legions. As the fighting around the sunken road died away, the last drama of the bloodiest day occurred as Ambrose Burnside's division forced a crossing of the lower bridge across the Antietam, ever after known as Burnside's Bridge. This was something Burnside had been attempting since 10 that morning. But hopes for a decisive breakthrough faded fast. At that moment Confederate reinforcements arrived on the field at the right time, and in exactly the right place to drive the Federals back down to the banks of the creek. The battle for Sharpsburg was effectively over. As night fell, "the armies settled into the exhausted and dazed sleep of men who have raced through hell."[31]

Chapter 12

To Fredericksburg

The continued fall of a "convivial spirit"

Lee finally withdrew his battered army back across the Potomac on the night of September 18. Lincoln was furious. Although Sharpsburg had been a very bloody draw, it was Lee's army that was in the greatest danger, outnumbered and lacking supplies north of the Potomac. On October 1, Lincoln visited McClellan who was still at Sharpsburg. As he stood looking out over the vast expanse of the Army of the Potomac in camp, Lincoln asked a companion if he knew what the sight before them was. "Why, Mr. Lincoln," came the surprised reply, "this is the Army of the Potomac." "So it is called, but that is a mistake," said Lincoln, "it is only McClellan's bodyguard."[1] On November 5, McClellan was replaced by Ambrose Burnside as commander of the Army of the Potomac. On November 10, with a final review and with little fanfare, McClellan took his leave.[2]

If McClellan refrained from any dramatic scenes during his departure, the commander of the Irish Brigade was not one to miss such an opportunity. Within the brigade, the removal of McClellan "created among the troops universal feelings of the most profound sorrow, sadness and gloom."[3] During the review, Meagher had the color bearers of the brigade throw down their banners before McClellan in protest at his dismissal. McClellan halted and ordered the colors to be picked up before he would proceed. It was a grand gesture, but gesture it remained. The following week a number of officers put in their resignations, resignations that Meagher's depleted brigade could ill afford. On November 19, he issued General Order No. 10, writing that it was his duty to refuse all requests of resignations. Loyalty to the flag ought to precede loyalty to an individual. He reminded his men that "the great error of the Irish people, in their struggle for an independent national existence, has been their passionate and blind adherence to an individual instead of a principle or cause."[4] Fine words, which might have done him much good in Washington if he had left his pronouncements on McClellan's dismissal at that.

Unfortunately, as with his recruiting attempts two months previously, Meagher had to try to face two ways, professing support for the Republican war effort, but being critical of the Republicans for their political agenda. In a letter to a prominent Democratic friend in New York, Samuel Barlow, which was printed in the *New*

York World, he described McClellan's departure as "a most painful yet noble scene." "The Army of the Union," he continued, would never forgive "the gentlemen of the White House ... for the mistake or crime [which] had been committed by them."[5] This was certainly not what the "gentlemen of the White House" would wish to hear from one of their generals in the field, and certainly not one whose reputation was beginning to become as tarnished as Meagher's.

Officially, Meagher was reported as having his horse shot from underneath him at Sharpsburg, and had to be carried unconscious from the field. In some accounts he had been killed.[6] But no sooner had the battle ended than other reports began to circulate. "Meagher was not killed as reported," wrote one of McClellan's staff in his diary the day following the battle, "but drunk, and fell from his horse."[7] "General Meagher rode a beautiful white horse," the adjutant of the 132nd Pennsylvania, who had observed the Irish Brigade's approach across the fields toward the sunken road, later wrote, "but made a show of himself by tumbling off just as he reached our line. The boys said he was drunk, and he certainly looked and acted like a drunken man. He regained his feet and floundered about, swearing like a crazy man."[8]

The official reports of his superiors were less accusatory, but still carry an air of uneasiness. While unrestrained regarding the valor of the brigade itself, McClellan confined mention of its commanding general to a brief reference, stating that Meagher was "disabled by a fall from his horse, shot under him."[9] Hancock, who succeeded to division command after Richardson was mortally wounded, wrote simply that Meagher "had his horse shot under him in the action of his brigade, and, in falling, received bruises which prevented him from returning to the field until the next morning."[10] Other, sharper knives, were out. "The General in question ... was not in charge at all!" wrote the correspondent of the *Cincinnati Gazette*, Whitelaw Reid — whom the *Irish American* described as a "miserable scribbler" — "did not lead or follow it [his brigade]! He was too drunk to keep the saddle, fell from his horse ... several times, was once assisted to remount by General Kimball ... almost immediately fell off again ... too stupidly drunk to answer the simplest question ... about the disposition of his brigade."[11]

Although the case is unproven, the circumstantial evidence against Meagher to the charges of inebriation, or incompetence, or a combination of both, was becoming almost unarguable. Even sympathetic observers, who never went as far as overtly accusing Meagher of drunkenness at Sharpsburg or elsewhere, were circumspect when nearing the scene of some of the controversies surrounding him. Corby, unrestrained in his romanticism of life with the brigade and its men, could write about Meagher in defensive tones, with little enthusiasm for the man. "It is to be regretted," wrote Corby, "that at times ... his convivial spirit would lead him too far."[12] In his memoirs, Private William McCarter, who briefly served as an aide

12. To Fredericksburg

to Meagher before Fredericksburg, recalled an incident two months after Sharpsburg. While on guard duty on the night of November 13, McCarter came across Meagher who "was very drunk, looked strangely wild and only prevented himself from falling down by his grasp of the center pole [of his tent]." Seconds later, Meagher suddenly let go of the pole and "plunged" towards a large campfire a few yards ahead of him, only to be rescued by McCarter. During the incident, McCarter damaged his musket. The following morning, when he arrived in Meagher's tent to copy some papers, "a beautiful new musket with new bayonet was there given me," although "General Meagher never made any direct allusion to this incident."[13] It was a story both touching and bathetic.

Immediately following Sharpsburg, there was also further evidence of disquiet from within the brigade itself. On September 19, only two days after the battle, the quartermaster of the 88th New York, Patrick Haverty, wrote to Judge Daly in New York to lobby for a promotion for Colonel Nugent of the 69th. "Many officers who have not performed half the effective service he has have been appointed," wrote Haverty, and the judge "would only be carrying out your own axiom, that Irish Brigades should not only have popular officers but ones thoroughly acquainted with their duty. If necessary, a document can be forwarded from all the officers of his own [the 69th], the 63rd and 88th regiments, recommending him for promotion. General Meagher is not wounded but the fine horse he brought on here from New York was shot from under him."[14] It is possible that the implicit criticism of Meagher's leadership in Haverty's letter had been brewing at least since the Seven Days' battles, but were made all the more pertinent by Meagher's failings in leading his brigade at Sharpsburg.

Meagher's name does have to join a queue when discussing the command failures that led to the slaughter at Bloody Lane. Arguably at the top of the list was McClellan himself, for a number of things. These included his continued timidity in striking at Lee even after finding the "Lost Orders," and remaining inactive during September 15 and 16 while Lee was able to regroup his scattered army. Next would have to be Sumner for his "ill regulated ardor" in leaving two of his divisions adrift on the battlefield while he headed off to disaster with Sedgwick's men. By the time Meagher's name appears in the frame, those of the division commanders, Richardson and French, as well as the brigade commanders, would also have to be examined for allowing their men to be sucked into making a frontal assault on the sunken road. Unlike the Seven Days,' Meagher was conspicuous in leading his men at Sharpsburg up to the time he parted company with his horse. Whether or not he was drunk, it was the tactics he employed that added greatly to the losses of his men. Meagher had envisioned a charge from another era of warfare. His orders had been for the brigade to stop at the top of the hill and deliver two volleys with their "buck and balls," before charging down the slope to rout the Confederates with the bayonet. Meagher hoped that the volleys from his men would sufficiently weaken the defenders of the sunken road to allow them to succumb to "the impetuosity and recklessness of the Irish soldiers in the charge." "I felt confident that before such a charge the rebel column would give way and be dispersed," he would write in his report.[15] Such a strategy would have been hard on the attackers when attempting to assault any modestly defended position. At the sunken road, these tactics were as suicidal as they were amateurish. Meagher was not the only officer during the war, both experienced and inexperienced, that would order such charges. His leadership, however, was also subject to so many other doubts and misgivings that such mistakes could be less easily forgotten or forgiven.

A modest man

Following Sharpsburg, the movement of the Army of the Potomac to Fredericksburg was to have been the first advance in the new strategy of McClellan's replacement, Major General Ambrose Burnside. Burnside was a modest man, with much to be modest about. His experience in the war to date had been to lead a brigade at First Bull Run; a successful if small-scale operation off the North Carolina coast; and a less-than-successful command of the Union left at Sharpsburg. "Few men," wrote one contemporary, "have risen so high upon a foundation so slight."[16] He had already twice refused command of the army, believing himself unfit for such a command. It might have saved quite a few soldiers' lives had his superiors taken him at his word.

Burnside began well enough. His plan was to outflank Lee's army by crossing the Rappahannock River at Fredericksburg. This would place him between Lee and the Confederate capital of Richmond, forcing Lee to give him battle at a place of Burnside's choosing. Early on the morning of November 15, Sumner's Right grand division, one of the three wings into which Burnside had reorganized the army, left their camps at Warrenton "like a sprinter at the bark of a starter's gun." They were followed on November 16 by the Grand Divisions of William Franklin and Joe Hooker. There was little of the dead hand of McClellan's caution in this advance. The previous month on their way to Sharpsburg, it had taken Sumner's command a full week to cover the 40 miles from Tennallytown to Frederick. This time they covered the same distance in 60 hours, arriving in Falmouth on the Rappahannock River opposite Fredericksburg on November 17. The following day the other grand divisions took up positions to the northeast and northwest of Falmouth. Unfortunately, they could go no farther. Somewhere along the line there had been a cock-up. The pontoon bridges which Burnside had requested be at Falmouth to effect his crossing were nowhere to be seen, and indeed, would not appear until eight days later.[17]

12. To Fredericksburg

After the bad experiences that the Army of the Potomac had had with rivers, the Chickahominy and the Antietam, and the danger of getting trapped on the far side by Lee, Burnside was too wary to attempt a crossing. He would wait for the pontoons to arrive. While he waited, Lee's army began to arrive, taking up position on the heights just outside the town, preparing to meet the Federals should they be foolish enough to attack.

Exit the "honorary Irishmen"

The losses suffered by the Irish Brigade at Sharpsburg left it in a precarious position in terms of having sufficient numbers to carry on effectively as a unit. "The poor little brigade was woefully cut up," wrote Meagher to his wife in late September, "I have not more than 350 in camp today — the best of my officers have been killed."[18] Of the meager number of replacements that had come down from New York with Meagher prior to Sharpsburg, 75 had fallen in the battle. Recruitment to the brigade, already slow, now practically ground to a halt. Enlistments dropped so dramatically that at least one state official informed Governor Morgan that he believed a secret organization was at work to stop Irish enlistments.[19] But there was no need for any secret organization. The Irish American community, particularly in New York, from where the highest regimental losses had come, was in a state of shock and anger. "It would be well if Republicans had done their duty in this war as well as Irishmen," wrote one correspondent from Brooklyn to the *Irish American*, "Meagher's Irish Brigade [has fought] as bravely and lost as heavily as any of the armies in the Union."[20] There was a growing sense or suspicion that the Irish Brigade was overused, or even expendable. In her diary the week after Sharpsburg, Maria Daly recounted a story she had heard regarding an Irish man seeking to enlist in an American rather than an Irish regiment. When asked why he would not join the Irish Brigade, he replied that he had "a wife and family and when the Irish are all by themselves they do a deal of fighting and get killed. Now your Yankee chaps don't fight much, so I'd rather go with them, you see, as I don't want to get killed either."[21] In Boston, the *Pilot* was now calling for an armistice. "The slaughter of our officers is fearful," it declared, "Enough of blood has been shed and enough of treasure has been wasted to justify such a thing."[22] Those Irish who were enticed to enlist did so in Corcoran's new Irish Legion which also began recruiting that autumn.

During October it was reported that Meagher was proposing that his "now little crowd" be united with other Irish units such as Corcoran's and Mulligan's in the west in order to form a division under Shields.[23] Nothing ever came of this. The "little crowd," or what the *Irish American* was now beginning to call "our noble little brigade," was to be reprieved however, not by consolidation or by the addition of fresh recruits to the existing ranks, but by the addition of new regiments.[24] The first of these was the 116th Pennsylvania, commanded by Denis Heenan. Recruiting for this regiment had begun in Philadelphia in May 1862. As in New York, it was a slow process, and it would take a visit to the city by Corcoran in August before any substantial numbers began to enlist. Although generally referred to as an Irish regiment, the 116th had a bare majority of Irish troops. For this reason, the regiment did not carry the green Irish flag alongside the Stars and Stripes but the more common state flag.

By the end of the month, the regiment was still understrength with less than 700 men when it was ordered to Washington in the wake of the panic following the defeat at Second Bull Run. If the men of the 116th needed evidence that the mood in the North toward the war had changed from the previous year, they certainly found it when they arrived in the capital on September 3. With the stragglers from Pope's defeated army still prominent on the street corners and in the bars, the dust-covered rookies of the 116th received a somewhat frosty welcome. "No-one minded new soldiers," wrote one officer, "the good people of Washington had become accustomed to the music and the marching." The following month, the regiment was ordered to proceed to Harper's Ferry to join the Irish Brigade, which had been camped there since the week following Sharpsburg. They arrived there on October 10. That evening the regiment was visited by Meagher. True to form, "the canteen was passed around and the talk became animated" before the commanding general and "his brilliant staff" made their exit.[25]

The interlude at Harper's Ferry was brief, but it provided a well-deserved rest for the members of the brigade, with "racing, evening parties and amusements ... the order of the day."[26] Then, on November 2, they were again in motion, this time headed for Warrenton as part of McClellan's last advance. At Warrenton, they were joined by yet another new regiment, the 28th Massachusetts, commanded by Colonel Richard Byrnes. "As we approached the Irish Brigade," wrote Private John Ryan, "General Meagher had the other four regiments all drawn up in line with open ranks. As we marched through, the other regiments ... all presented arms and we brought our guns to a carry. General Meagher and his staff rang out, 'Three cheers for the 5th Irish Regiment of the Brigade.' The cheers were given with a will and were returned by the 28th."[27] By this time, the 28th already had a colorful history concerning its commanders. Following the shenanigans in Boston the previous year, Governor Andrew had amalgamated the original 29th Massachusetts with the 28th. The consolidated regiment had ended up in Burnside's Ninth Corps, where in some respects the boisterous Irishmen were as out of place as the 29th Massachusetts were with the Irish Brigade. "You must keep your men away from that 28th Regiment," their brigade commander told another officer, "you know they are all Irishmen and would just as soon fight as eat."[28] The original commander of the

12. To Fredericksburg

28th, William Monteith, through a combination of drink and incompetence, had been court-martialed and dismissed from the service. Following a string of further officers who were unable to cope with command of the regiment, Governor Andrew finally reached outside the pool of volunteer officers and appointed Richard Byrnes. Byrnes was a professional soldier in the U.S. Fifth Cavalry and proved to be a capable commander, briefly commanding the remnants of the original Irish Brigade in 1864 before being killed at the battle of Cold Harbor.

The cost of the 28th Massachusetts joining the Irish Brigade however, was that it lost the 29th Massachusetts. The latter outfit, comprising as it did true-blue Yankees, had always sat uncomfortably amongst the somewhat less puritanical character of Meagher's men, even if they had managed to fight well together during the Seven Days' and at Sharpsburg. So well in fact that Meagher had deemed them "honorary Irishmen," presenting them a green flag to match that carried by their fellow regiments in the brigade. The compliments were graciously received until it was apparent that the New Englanders were then expected to carry the flag into battle with them. This was too much for the Massachusetts men. The matter was only settled peaceably by affecting an exchange between the Second and the Ninth Corps, with the 28th Regiment, which had originally been intended to join the Irish Brigade, at last joining Meagher's men, while the 29th took their place in the Ninth Corps.[29]

While the New Englanders were no doubt somewhat relieved to be leaving the Irish Brigade, they took with them a respect, and a certain sense of awe regarding the qualities of their Irish comrades. After their first battles with the brigade during the Peninsula, Meagher had addressed the 29th, complimenting them on their bravery. Afterward, Colonel Pierce, who had lost an arm in the action at White Oak Swamp, wrote from his hospital to Governor Andrew of Massachusetts. "During this period [since joining the Irish Brigade]," wrote Pierce, "the regiment had added to its reputation by the mere fact of its being connected with the Irish Brigade; and it has been our endeavor that the brigade should not by our acts lose any of their already acquired reputation." Of Meagher's speech and compliments to the 29th, Pierce concluded that it was "the proudest moment the regiment had seen."[30]

Hancock the Superb

On November 10, the brigade paraded along with the rest of the Corps for McClellan after his dismissal, before setting off for Falmouth on November 15, as part of Burnside's flanking strategy. As well as having a new army commander, the brigade had a new division commander in the shape of General Winfield Scott Hancock, "Fighting Dick" Richardson having been another victim before the sunken road. Hancock was a handsome, charismatic figure, one of the very few commanders in either army about which it is rare to find even a mildly critical remark. "He is magnificent in appearance, lordly, but cordial, and is remarkably generous, giving everyone ample credit for what he does," wrote one officer. Following a gushing report by McClellan after one of the battles during the Seven Days in which Hancock was highly praised, he acquired the sobriquet, "Hancock the Superb."

Another notable attribute was that "in an army where the officers were notably profane," Hancock "was outstanding for the vigor, range, and effectiveness of his cursing," with the air "blue all around him" when he was in full flow.[31] One story concerns the sheep-stealing mania that seized the troops while they were in Virginia that autumn. Hancock, who was "particularly sensitive to the slightest imputation of indiscipline," came across several members of the Irish Brigade who were about to kill a sheep in violation of explicit orders. While "the less guilty members of the party, being less closely engaged, caught a glimpse of the coming doom in time to climb a high fence and escape," one unfortunate trooper was caught with his bayonet in hand and the prostrate body of a sheep on the ground before him. Hancock drew his sword and made for the soldier. "Arrah dear General, don't be the death of me now," pleaded the Irishman, "I didn't do it, indade I didn't." "You infernal liar," roared Hancock, "I saw you you scoundrel." Whereupon the woolly victim in question jumped up off the ground, gave a loud "baa" and galloped off, closely followed by his would-be nemesis, amid great shouts of mirth from Hancock and his staff.[32]

As they continued on their way down to Falmouth, Hancock reportedly had another occasion to witness members of the brigade in action, this time against less harmless opposition. As they approached a ford across the Rappahannock, the Confederates had a battery in position guarding the crossing. At a word from Sumner, members of the brigade plunged into the water, crossed to the opposite bank and captured two of the artillery pieces, prompting Hancock to remark that he "never saw anything so splendid." Such *élan* would soon be on display again just outside the town of Fredericksburg, but at a much greater cost.[33]

Burnside's Bridges

Following their rapid march, Sumner's corps had been camped across the river at Falmouth since November 17. Although the missing pontoons had arrived on November 25, it had been too late. Longstreet's command was entrenched in the heights outside the town, and Jackson would soon join him. Their position appeared impregnable, and it was assumed that the Army of the Potomac had no choice but to go into winter quarters before resuming campaigning again in the spring. "There is no immediate prospect of any fighting here," one soldier in the Irish Brigade wrote to his wife, "and it is doubtful if we will have any this winter as the roads

12. To Fredericksburg

will be unfit to move troops on as soon as winter sets in."[34] The camps and the ground at Falmouth were miserable, but the troops "settled down in earnest; built log huts, roofed them with tents, and built chimneys of sticks and mud — for there was plenty of mud." There was something to look forward to however. The flags of the regiments had taken a fair battering since they were received in 1861, and it was proposed by a civilian committee in New York that the brigade be presented new flags. A party of officers returned to New York for the presentation ceremony, while a Captain Martin was sent to Washington to procure suitable supplies for the subsequent banquet to be held in Falmouth. The date was set for December 13.[35]

Then, on December 9, word got around the camps that Sumner had convened a meeting of all the corps, division and brigade commanders. When one Irish soldier heard another camp rumor that the army was going to cross the river and assault Lee's army, he was sufficiently distressed to seek out Father Corby. "Father, they are going to lead us over in front of those guns which we have seen them placing, unhindered, for the past three weeks," reported the soldier incredulously. "Do not trouble yourself," Corby replied sanguinely, "your generals know better than that."[36] The following night, December 10, the Federals began the attempt to lay the pontoon bridges across the Rappahannock. Back in New York, Maria Daly recorded that the new regimental flags had been presented to the representatives of the brigade. "The old, tattered, and bullet ridden ones [were] consigned to the care of Mr. John A. Devlin.... McClellan was expected to present the flags, but did not arrive. Capt. Magee, on the part of General Meagher, consigned in a very soldierly, unaffected speech, the old flags to Mr Devlin's care.... It was very touching to see the old, faded, tattered standards which I had seen in all their first freshness, and the officers of the brigade, with their honorable scars, who received the second ones."[37]

As the new flags were making their way to Falmouth, the rumors around the camps were proving to be all too true. The meeting on December 9 had been called because Burnside had reached an extraordinary decision, which Sumner wished to discuss with his commanders. The commanding general was reluctant to go into winter quarters as he knew that he had been appointed to give battle to Lee's army. He was then left with various options about how to get across the Rappahannock. Through a logic all of his own, he reached the conclusion that as no sane man would expect him to try to cross at Fredericksburg and attack the entrenched Confederate army, this is exactly what Burnside proposed to do, thus catching the rebels unprepared. It was the sort of logic whereby someone puts his head in a bucket of ice and his feet in a basin of boiling water, and believes he should feel just fine. Burnside's plan called for a two-pronged assault on Lee's defenses. It appears that the main assault was to be delivered by Franklin's Grand Division against Lee's right flank south of Fredericksburg. Once a breakthrough was achieved there, Sumner would then be able to smash through the Confederate positions facing his troops outside the town, and complete the destruction of Lee's army. Hooker's Grand Division was to remain in reserve.

Well covered by artillery with an open ground across the river to their front, the bridge builders opposite Franklin had little trouble completing their work. It was a different story opposite Fredericksburg. As the darkness and the fog lifted on the morning of December 11, the Federal bridge builders were only halfway across the Rappahannock. From the buildings on the opposite bank came the crackle of musketry fire from a brigade of Mississippians under William Barksdale. It would take an artillery barrage and three regiments sent across the river, using some of the pontoons as boats, before the Confederates were dislodged. The following day, Sumner's men finally marched down to the riverbank and began crossing into the town. There was little firing from Lee's artillery positioned on the heights outside the town. This surprised many. But one veteran had his own forebodings. "They want us to get in," he said, "Getting out won't be so smart."[38]

Chapter 13

Visions of Hell

Another river to cross

During Wednesday, December 10, the men of the Irish Brigade were given three days' cooked rations, and 80 rounds of ammunition — 40 rounds to fill their cartridge boxes and 40 rounds for their pockets. The amount of ammunition alone was sufficient to indicate to one private in the 116th Pennsylvania that "hot, bloody work was anticipated," as 40 rounds was the "normal allotment for what might be termed an ordinary battle of engagement."[1] That night, the brigade had marched in silence toward the riverbank at Fredericksburg, then waited while the pontoons were laid. As dawn arrived on December 11, they heard two signal guns fired by the Confederate artillery which marked the attempted Federal crossing of the river. Soon after came the sound of musketry fire as Barksdale's men drove the bridge builders from their work. As the artillery bombardment began, in the cold morning air, "Clouds of sulphurous smoke rolled back from the masked artillery, the air became loaded, suffocating, with the odor of gunpowder." Apart from the church spires and the tallest chimneys, the town itself remained hidden from view, still under a heavy fog. "One could not see," wrote one member of the Irish Brigade, "but could hear the walls crumbling and the timbers crashing; then a pillar of smoke rose up above the fog.... Flames leaped high out of the mist."[2] Some of the waiting Irishmen drifted over to some Confederate prisoners. One of them rather unwisely suggested that the rebel canoneers across the river, who did not appear to be firing back, might have "skedaddled" in the face of such a bombardment. The face of one prisoner turned "crimson with rage as he indignantly and contemptuously replied, 'Ah, you'll hear from them at the right time.... You thick-headed Yankees won't know what hell and damnation is till you meet them over that river.'"[3] When the bombardment eventually finished, the sound of musketry rose again, not dying away until almost darkness, as the Confederates withdrew from the town, back to their comrades on the heights beyond.

The following morning, December 12, as the brigade prepared to cross the river with the rest of the division, they were cheered by the watching 14th Brooklyn while the band of the 9th New York struck up the brigade's marching tune, *Garryowen*. But it was a subdued crossing. They could not have been under much illusion about what awaited them if they had to try to assault Lee's men outside the town. If they were, the undertakers passing out their cards as the soldiers crossed over the pontoons, advertising their "patriotic services" should have soon dispelled them.[4] For some, their luck ran out early. A drummer boy with his drum slung on his back, toppled over and fell down into the water and was presumed drowned.[5] If they cared to think about it, the men of the Irish Brigade might have felt they had not had much luck with rivers and rebels. First the Chickahominy, then the Antietam, and now the Rappahannock. Yet the sight of so many men massing at the crossing seemed to one soldier that nothing less than victory could await them on the far side. Following the battle, he rued his misplaced optimism. "I was not aware," he wrote, "that hell personified was so close at hand and ready for our destruction."[6]

For many Federal soldiers, the town of Fredericksburg, already partially destroyed under the Federal bombardment, became "a city given up to pillage." For whatever reason, a growing hatred of southerners and the South, a sense of foreboding, or of anger and frustration that they were going to be misused and mangled once again, Federal soldiers literally sacked the historic town. As described by one soldier, "Books and battered pictures, bureaus, lounges, feather beds, clocks, and every conceivable article of goods, chattels, and apparel had been savagely torn from the houses and lay about in wanton confusion in all directions." Some danced around in women's dresses and underwear. One member of the Irish Brigade was seen walking off with a feather mattress about him; another was seen "wearing a white satin bonnet of some fait 'secesh bride,'" while yet another treasured a ten gallon coffee-pot.[7] Little effort was made on the part of the officers to stop the looting. Darius Couch, commanding the Second Corps, ordered a provost guard placed at the bridges to at least prevent his men from returning across the river with their plunder. That evening, "an enormous pile of booty was collected there."[8] One citizen of the town later complained bitterly about the pillaging of both Federal and Confederate armies during their alternate stays in Fredericksburg. "The rebel army took everything I had," he said, "and the Yankees got the rest."[9]

As the surreal scenes in the town died away with nightfall, the men of the brigade bedded down for a night that was described as one of "the most dismal and miserable ever experienced." "The cold was bitter and penetrating," wrote another, and like the night before Sharpsburg, the soldiers were ordered not to build any fires being so close to the enemy.[10] We hunted up pieces of boards," wrote one soldier in the 28th Massachusetts, "and lay them down on the mud and then lay down and covered ourselves in our blankets."[11] Small groups in the 116th Pennsylvania "bunked together on a bed composed of small branches of trees laid on cold, muddy and wet ground." Others were massed so close they were unable to lie down, and "it was a fortunate man who could secure a cracker box to sit upon during the weary hours."[12] On the exposed heights outside the town, Confederate soldiers died of exposure while blanketed in freezing fog. Many looked forward to the dawn and the prospect of a battle "whose horrors could not be worse than those of the night."[13] In the town, "Everything was quiet during the night," wrote a captain in the 69th New York, "a fearful calm ensued ... that is said generally to precede a storm."[14]

The Killing Ground

Throughout the war there were countless individual and collective acts of gallantry and heroism, but perhaps only during Pickett's Charge on the third day of the Battle of Gettysburg did soldiers behave with more valor than they did in the doomed assaults on the heights outside Fredericksburg. What lifted this assault above the mere heroism of others was that the soldiers, the majority of whom, like the Irish Brigade, were ordinary volunteers, knew before they began their charge how hopeless was their task. Many were able to see the fate of the wave of men who had gone in before them, yet they marched out of the town, got into battle lines, and made their way unflinchingly through and around the bodies of their dead and wounded comrades.

"I think there was a cruelty in the plan of the Federal attack," a Confederate officer later wrote, "which cannot be excused."[15] Much of this "cruelty" lay in the ground across which Burnside expected his men to attack. In 1862 the town of Fredericksburg extended from the riverbank about a quarter of a mile in the direction of the heights outside the town. These were commonly known as Marye's Heights, after Colonel Marye, a local resident. Two main roads ran westward from the town. One of these, the Plank Road, carried on over the heights and on toward the hamlet of Chancellorsville. Hanover Street in the town itself became known as the Telegraph Road when it reached the outskirts of the town, and ran almost parallel to the Plank Road, until it reached the foot of Marye's Heights. Here, a branch of the road continued up the hill, remaining parallel to the Plank Road, while the main road itself turned sharply southward before following the line of the hill until it reached an old railroad cut, before again turning westward. In an ominous echo of Sharpsburg, that portion of the road which ran southward along the base of the hill, in effect squarely across the line of the Union advance from the town, was for much of that distance sunken below the level of the ground. On the town side of the road stood a stone wall about four feet high.

Between the wall and the town was a plain about 800 yards wide and across which the Union troops would advance. The town itself was on a little plateau. Marching out in columns of fours, all the time within artillery range from front and both flanks, the troops would find the ground sloping slightly down for a distance of about 200 yards. There they would reach a wide ditch or canal carrying

The Irish Brigade advanced up these slopes, under constant artillery fire as soon as they left the shelter of the streets of Fredericksburg. "We cover that ground now so well that we will comb it as with a fine tooth comb," said General Porter Alexander, in charge of the Confederate artillery, "A chicken could not live on that field when we open on it" (National Archives).

the spillway from a paper mill farther to the north. When Burnside had originally presented his idea of an attack to his corps commanders, Couch had warned the commanding general that this canal might prove a serious obstacle to advancing columns, as it could be crossed in only two places, namely, at the road crossings. Burnside dismissed Couch's objections. The canal simply did not exist. He himself had been stationed at Fredericksburg earlier in the year and was well acquainted with the ground. But the canal was there, and even more difficult to cross as one of the bridges had been partially torn up, with troops having to cross single file on the stringers.[16]

Once across, the ground rose again to form a bank, behind which, at least protected from musketry fire, the columns would turn left and right to spread out into battle lines, two ranks deep. Once the lines moved over the top of the bank, they had another 400 yards to go across an open plain to reach the foot of the heights marked by the stone wall. It was said that during the Great Hunger of the 1840s the crop of corn raised on these fields at the foot of the heights was sent to Ireland to help relieve the suffering.[17] Here and there were houses and fences, particularly at a minor fork in the Telegraph Road about 150 yards from the stone wall, near which stood a large square brick house. Toward the town side of this house was another slight rise in the ground. The rise was slight enough to be almost unnoticed under ordinary circumstances, but it would provide a man lying face down on the ground protection from the fire coming from directly ahead. For many men on December 13, it would prove to be as big as a battlement.

The attackers would need all the help they could get, for soon after the assaults began, they would find themselves advancing into the sustained fire from four ranks deep of Confederate infantry, almost hidden from view behind the stone wall. A position of already great natural strength had been further strengthened by the Confederate defenders who had thrown earth in front of the wall from the roadside, to the extent that the wall itself was almost invisible from the front. When the attack began, waiting behind the wall for the Union advance would be three regiments from Thomas Cobb's Georgia Brigade—many of whom were Irish—and the 27th North Carolina from General William Kershaw's brigade. "We have a magnificent position, perhaps the best on the line," Cobb is reported to have said.[18] As well he might. The hills behind his men rose in terraces from where more Confederates could pour their fire on any attackers, while curved along the crest of the hill was the Confederate artillery. A nervy General Longstreet was inspecting the positions of his men before the battle started when he came across an "idle cannon." Turning to his chief of artillery, General Porter Alexander, Longstreet suggested that the gun should be put in line with the others to better cover the plain in front of the heights. Alexander demurred. "General, we cover that ground now so well that we will comb it as with a fine tooth comb," he replied, "A chicken could not live on that field when we open on it."[19] Just after 11 a.m., scattered musket fire was heard from the direction of the town and then a heavy line of Federal troops could be seen driving the advanced Confederate pickets back toward Marye's Heights. Burnside's Right Grand Division was preparing to go into action.

"We might as well have tried to take hell"

Driving back the Confederate pickets were three regiments from Kimball's brigade of French's division, the 4th Ohio, the 8th Ohio and the 1st Delaware. It was an eerie Fredericksburg that morning in which the Federals had prepared to advance. A heavy fog hung over the wrecked town. Assorted stragglers were still on the prowl, some still wearing the women's clothes they had looted, while the streets were littered with the debris from the looting the night before. Just after 8 a.m., Couch received his orders from Burnside to prepare his men "for the purpose of seizing the heights in the rear of the town." For the initial assault Couch had chosen

French's division, with Hancock's division to follow. It was almost the assault on Bloody Lane all over again, with Kimball's men again leading the charge.[20]

Commanding the 1st Delaware was Major Thomas Smyth, who would later command the Irish Brigade during the opening campaigns in 1864. In the 8th Ohio was 17-year-old Irish-American Thomas Galwey, later associate editor of the *Catholic World* and professor at Manhattan College. The 8th Ohio had done some plundering of their own the night before and almost every man had half a box of tobacco on his back, wrapped up in his blanket. Couch, who was in the street watching their deployment was furious when he saw the extra baggage the men were carrying into battle, and "very indignantly ordered the tobacco to be cast aside." It was quickly done and the men "went forward at a run," cheering loud enough to be heard by the waiting Confederates in the Sunken Road.[21] They were the first troops to encounter the destroyed bridge over the canal on Hanover Street and were forced to pick their way across on the stringers. No other Federal regiment would get across so lightly, as with the Confederate skirmishers still advanced, the full might of their comrades' firepower was not used on the advancing Federal troops.

As the brigade advanced across the ridge, one watching Confederate was full of admiration. "How beautifully they come on," he wrote, "Their bright bayonets glistening in the sunlight made the line look like a huge serpent of blue and steel."[22] Then the artillery opened on the advancing lines. Longstreet described the result as a "fearful carnage" as great gaps were torn in the ranks of the advancing troops.[23] With the Confederate cannoneers changing to canister shot, Kimball's lines staggered, but the men continued to advance with "invincible determination." Invincible until Cobb's command rose from behind the stone wall and "let loose a storm of lead into the faces of the advance brigade." The stone wall "seemed to blaze from end to end with one cracking sheet of flame." Kimball's men fell "like chaff before the wind."[24]

By the time the remaining two of French's brigades were similarly repulsed, the Confederates were four deep behind the stone wall. Cobb had been killed and was replaced by General Joseph Kershaw. When he arrived at the stone wall, Kershaw wrote that the reinforcements which had arrived could go into position only behind the lines already in the sunken road, and the combined firepower of these lines was "the most rapid and continuous I have ever witnessed."[25] The 1,200 men who lay dead or wounded on the slopes before the stone wall were bloody testament to its effectiveness. One member of French's brigade summed up the utter futility of the assault on such an impregnable position. "We might as well have tried to take hell," he later wrote.[26]

Any subsequent advance would find itself further impeded simply by the number of blue-coated bodies that were beginning to be so thickly strewn on the ground between the ridge and the wall. But no sooner had French's men began to melt

13. Visions of Hell

before the fire from the stone wall than Hancock was preparing his division to launch their assault. Early that morning Hancock had called a meeting of his officers to explain the orders for the day. They would be dispatched across the killing ground brigade by brigade, each formed in two lines, with 200 yards between each brigade. If one line stalled, the following one was to continue straight on until the position was carried. Hancock had been vociferous in his opposition to the plan from the start, and had been criticized by Burnside for so doing. As the meeting finished, he shook hands with all his officers, telling them to go into action on foot in order to make themselves tougher targets. The rifle fire, he believed, would be so hot "that scarcely a pigeon could live through it."[27]

"Desperate courage"

That morning, the men in the Irish Brigade had woken to find their blankets covered with a thick frost. After cooking their breakfast as best they could, the order to fall in was given at 9 a.m., after which they remained in line on one of the streets near the bank parallel to the river. It was an unnerving experience. At noon, as Kimball's regiments were starting to drive back the Confederate skirmishers, the order came to "Shoulder Arms, right face, forward, double quick march."[28] The division turned west into Hanover Street, and waited there for over another hour as the first assaults wrecked themselves against the stone wall. When their turn came, first off would be the brigade commanded by Samuel Zook, followed by Meagher's men, with Caldwell last in, as at Sharpsburg. As the battle began with shells flying overhead and some crashing into the town itself, "the smell of burning powder" was suffocating, even on the wharf, "half a mile distant from the place of conflict." As the first waves of attackers were repulsed, the sounds of "taunting cheers and yells" from the defenders in the sunken road drifted down to the waiting men.[29] Wounded men started to be carried past their position. One of these, a German, was long remembered by the men of the brigade. He had one foot shot off and was being wheeled in a barrow with his legs dangling over the side, a pipe in his mouth, and blood dripping from the exposed stump. When the barrow would tip to one side he would remove the pipe and call out, "Ach, make right." Some of the men smiled at this extraordinary sight. Another was seen to faint.[30]

Just before 2 p.m. the order eventually came to move out, Zook's brigade leading the way. "We marched rapidly forward," one of Zook's men wrote, "passing a huge pile of bricks, which the round shot was scattering in every direction, then came a mill-race [the canal], and on the other side of it a high board fence." Once past these, they formed behind the ridge before once again renewing the assault. As Zook's men went forward "with bated breath and heads bowed down ... the rebel guns ploughing great furrows in our ranks at every step; all we could do was close up gaps and press forward."³¹ Such "desperate courage" as Longstreet described it, gave heart to others. A wounded man was seen to prop himself on one elbow and swing his cap in welcome to the advancing lines. Other men from French's earlier attack, scattered on the slopes, got up to join in Zook's advance. Three hundred yards from the wall the Federals burst into a cheer and charged.

Their momentum carried them up to the furthest point of French's advance, far enough so that at least the Confederates could no longer hit them with flanking artillery fire. But what the cannons could not do, the rifles behind the stone wall did. As the deadly fire once again poured from the lines of guns behind the wall and on the heights, Zook's men bent forward "as men who breast a furious gale of wind." Some managed to reach the final rail fence, about 60 yards from the stone wall, but as they tried to clear it, they were simply mowed down. The brigade had taken 1,532 men into action. Within the space of half an hour it had lost 527.³²

But the supply of bravery and bodies appeared endless. Hancock's second brigade, Meagher's men, were following closely behind Zook's lines, ready to join the assault, with more columns appearing out of the town. Even Lee was uneasy that the persistence of the Federals might somehow result in breaking his lines. He approached Longstreet. "General, they are massing very heavily and will break your line. I am afraid," he said. Longstreet, now echoing the confidence displayed earlier by his chief of artillery, had no such doubts. "If you put every man on the other side of the Potomac on that field to approach me over the same line, and give me plenty of ammunition," he replied, "I will kill them all."³³

"Poor fellows, poor glorious fellows"

As the Irish Brigade had waited in the streets of Fredericksburg, the men could hear the sounds of battle rolling in from the outskirts of the town. One member of the Brigade remembered how, "Noonday was turned to dusk by the smoke and storm of battle."³⁴ At Fredericksburg, all the regiments would carry the Stars and Stripes. But for the first time, the three New York regiments would be going into battle without their green flags, the new ones not yet having arrived from New York. The more cosmopolitan 116th Pennsylvania did not have a green flag, which left the 28th Massachusetts as the only unit possessing the harp and sunburst that day. They were to be given pride of place in the center of the line.

To replace the symbolism of the missing flags, Meagher appeared on horseback with two orderlies "bearing on their arms large bunches of green boxwood" and requested that the officers present "in his [Meagher's] name a green sprig to each man in the ranks."³⁵ Meagher himself, wearing a nonregulation uniform of dark green with assorted adornments, set the standard, placing a sprig in the side of his cap. "Every officer and man followed his example," wrote one soldier, "and

13. Visions of Hell

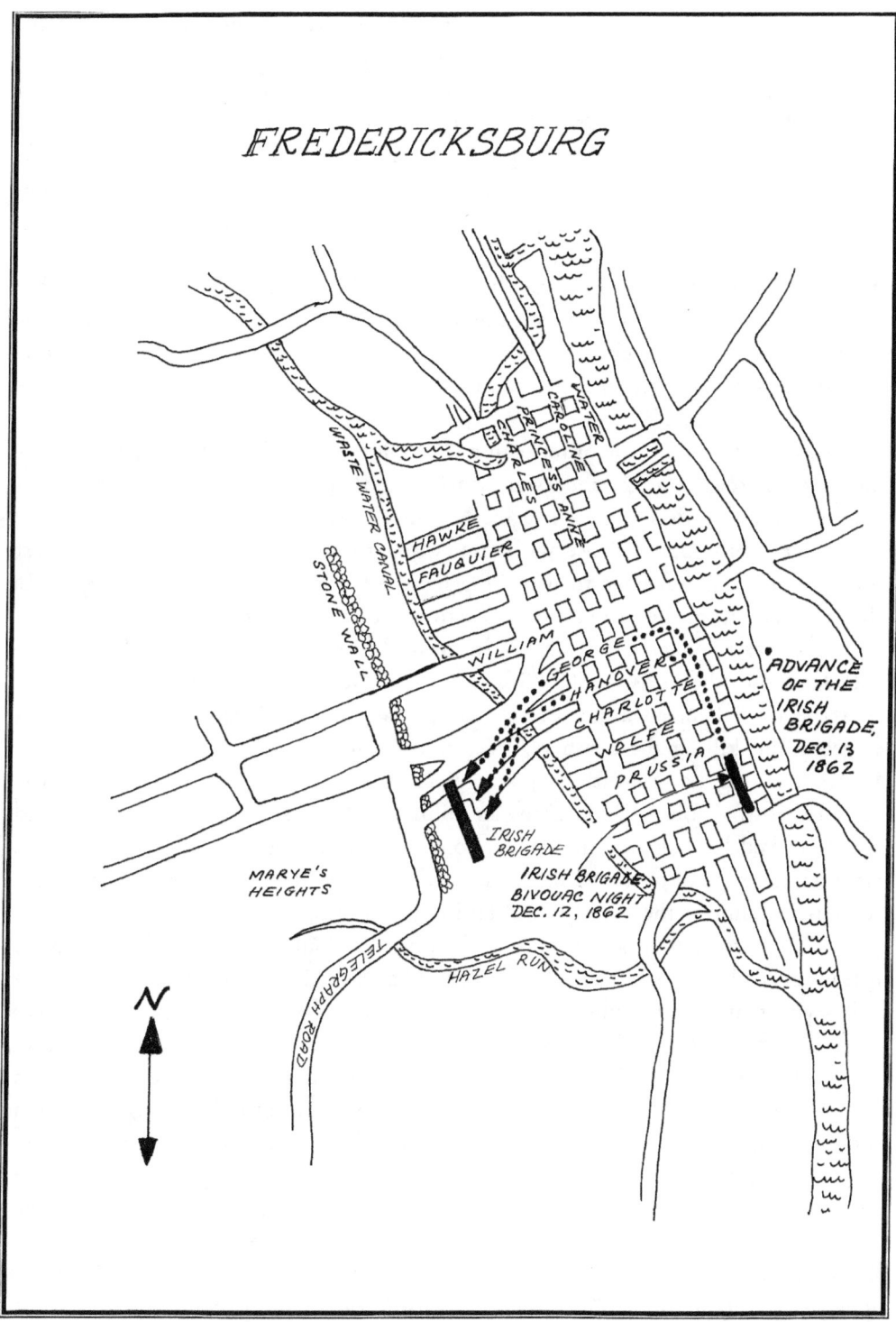

soon great bunches of the fragrant shrub adorned the caps of everyone. Wreaths were made and hung upon the tattered [U.S.] flags."[36] Father Ouellet asked Colonel Nugent if he could walk along the lines of the 69th New York and say a word to each man. Nugent concurred. "Although not a Catholic myself," he later wrote, "I was the first man to receive the good Father's blessing. He [Ouellet] then went along the lines blessing each man, Catholic and Protestant alike." When Ouellet had finished, Nugent decided he could do something to return the compliment. A sprig of green was placed in the chaplain's hat. If the colonel was going to be an honorary Catholic for the day, then he would "make an Irishman out of the Father that day—the good Father being a French Canadian."[37] As Meagher was addressing his men, a shell knocked over three men of the 63rd New York. Meagher continued his speech as "the mangled remains–mere masses of blood and rags—were borne along the line."[38]

Just before 2 p.m. the orders came, "Shoulder arms, right face, forward, double quick march," and the men started to make their way out on Hanover Street. There was none of the "finest fun in the world" about this advance. Most of the men were tight-lipped; those with something to say "spoke in low and earnest tones." They did not have to wait long for the work of destruction to begin. As they emerged from the protection of the town houses, solid shot from the Confederate artillery ricocheted off the frozen ground, tearing into flesh and bone. One shell landed in the midst of the 88th New York, wounding 18 men. Another burst over the 116th Pennsylvania, severely wounding Colonel Heenan, decapitating a sergeant and killing three others.[39] Captain Condon of the 69th New York saw Hancock riding along hunting up stragglers who were trying to see out the battle in some nearby houses.[40] Marching in columns of fours, the brigade approached the destroyed bridge over the canal. Some men plunged into the icy water and clambered up the opposite bank. Most tried to make their way across the stringers, some being shot in the attempt and falling into the canal.

Once across, they were sheltered behind the shallow ridge as they began to line up behind Zook's brigade. Blankets and haversacks were discarded. As was the habit with many men going into battle, some checked whether the paper they had pinned to the back of their jackets with details of their next of kin was still in place. Even behind the ridge, Confederate fire was so heavy that the men were ordered to lie down until it was their turn to charge. Zook's brigade crested the ridge and soon the sound of rifle fire rose again to a crescendo. The order came to "Fix bayonets" and "the clink, clink, clink of the cold glittering steel being placed in position sounded down the long rows of soldiers."[41] "Damn them," said one of the Irishmen to no one in particular as he fixed his bayonet in place, "That's the thing to fetch the sons of bitches."[42] Ten minutes later the order came. "Irish Brigade, advance. Right shoulder, shift arms, battalion forward, guide center, march."

13. Visions of Hell

As the men emerged over the ridge, they were met by a "blizzard of shot, shell and fire." Gaps in their ranks began to open up immediately with men having to march over dead and wounded bodies. Once again, men were described as advancing "with heads bowed as when walking against a hailstorm."[43] From his position in the grocery store near the stone wall, Thomas Galwey could see the tragedy unfold. As the men from the Irish Brigade passed his position, he could see that "Every man has a sprig of green in his cap, and a half-murderous look in his eye. They pass just to our left, poor fellows, poor glorious fellows, shaking good-bye to us with their hats! They reach a point within a stone's throw of the stone wall. No farther. They try and go beyond and are slaughtered. Nothing could advance that far and live."[44] A major in the 116th Pennsylvania, advancing on the left flank, described some of the scenes around him. "Officers and men fell in rapid succession. Lieutenant Garrett Nowlen fell with a ball through the thigh. Major Bardwell fell badly wounded, and a ball whistled through Lieutenant Bob McGuire's lungs. Lieutenant Christian Foltz fell dead with a ball through his brain. The orderly sergeant of Company H wheeled around, gazed up at Lieutenant Quinlan, and a great stream of blood poured form a hole in his forehead, splashing over the young officer, and the sergeant fell dead at his feet. Captain John O'Neill, Company K, was shot in the lungs, the ball passing completely through his body. But on, still onward, the line pressed steadily. The men dropping in twos or threes, in groups. No cheers or wild hurrahs as they moved toward the foe. They were not there to fight, only to die."[45]

In the center of the line was the 28th Massachusetts. A corporal in the regiment wrote that he had "seen some hot work at South Mountain and Antietam [Sharpsburg], but they were not to be compared to this." But they still "advanced boldly despite it all."[46] The green flag carried by the 28th made the Brigade recognizable to many of the opposing Confederates. As the many Irish behind the stonewall with Cobb's brigade saw the harp and sunburst making its way up the slope, a cry was reportedly heard, "Oh, God, what a pity! Here comes Meagher's fellows!" But they too did their duty, and an almost continuous sheet of flame poured forth from behind the stone wall. A Confederate soldier looking down from the heights saw the advance of the Irish Brigade into the hail of fire. Their lines "bent as it moved until it was the shape of a half moon, with the concave toward the town," he wrote, "Batteries opened upon them; and then broke out murderous musketry. Men staggered, reeled and fell, but still the Irish rushed forward." "I was amazed it [the rebel fire] did not absolutely sweep them from the face of the earth," wrote one watching newspaper correspondent.[47]

A Mississippi defender behind the stone wall would later report matter-of-factly how "We almost anihilated general Megearks Ireish Brigade."[48] While each volley would stagger the ranks of the Irishmen and leave more bodies as markers

As they approached the stone wall at Fredericksburg, the waiting Confederates from Cobb's and Kershaw's brigades, two or three deep, cut loose with a "murderous musketry," which Kershaw described as "the most rapid and continuous I have ever witnessed." "I was amazed it [the rebel fire] did not absolutely sweep them [the Irish Brigade] from the face of the earth," wrote one watching newspaper correspondent (Library of Congress).

as to where it struck, their advance would carry them past the flags stuck in the ground which marked the limit of previous charges, up past that last rise in the ground which was the last of any sort of cover, with still another fence remaining. "It was simply madness to advance as far as we did," wrote one soldier, "and an utter impossibility to go further."[49] Colonels Nugent and Kelly were to be found "at the front; with their own hands they undertake to tear down the fences and make a way to the stone wall."[50] As they reached the last fence, a captain in the 69th New York later described how the men were "met by a most disastrous enfilade and direct fire from the rebel artillery and infantry.... It was impossible for human nature to withstand this." Private William McCleland of the 88th New York wrote how "Our men were mown down like grass before the scythe of the reaper."[51]

As Nugent went down with a bullet in his side, some men passed through the fence, but for most, "Flesh and blood will not stand it longer."[52] A major in the 69th New York shouted out, "Blaze away and stand it boys."[53] The "boys" laid down to take whatever cover they could, loading their muskets on their backs, rolling over

13. Visions of Hell

to fire. Some soldiers in the 63rd Regiment tried to hold on by piling some of the bits of scattered wood to give some sort of cover. William McCarter of the 116th Pennsylvania felt his clothing "was being literally torn from my back by the constant and furious musketry fire." McCarter pulled his blanket roll off his shoulder to use it for cover. When he shook out his roll the following morning 32 spent bullets fell from it.[54]

Pinned down, and with hardly any cover, Nugent later called the scene in front of the stone wall as "a living hell from which escape scarcely seemed possible."[55] Some did escape. At that final fence, Colonel Byrnes of the 28th Massachusetts and Kelly of the 88th New York decided to try to get as many of their men as they could back down the slope and regroup near the town.[56] Byrnes could locate only 10 of his men as he reached the outskirts of Fredericksburg. There he met Captain Condon of the 63rd New York with nine men. "We shook hands," Condon wrote in his report, "he [Byrnes] remarking that our brigade was gone, meaning cut up."[57] In the town Father Corby was giving thanks with another officer of the brigade that at least a few men had survived. As Captain Sullivan of the 63rd New York was crossing the street he was struck by a solid shot which cut away his leg. Corby heard his confession on the spot. Sullivan died later that night.[58]

Following the Irish Brigade was that of Caldwell's, the same sequence of attacks that had broken the Confederate line at Sharpsburg. But history was not to repeat itself on the banks of the Rappahannock. Caldwell's men came up and advanced into the same maelstrom. They managed to get as far as most before inevitably wilting before the stone wall. Couch and his remaining division commander, General Howard, climbed into the cupola of the courthouse in the town to try to get a clear view of the field. Watching the charge of French and Hancock's men, Howard exclaimed, "Oh, great God! See how our men, our poor fellows, are falling."[59] A disgusted Couch, who had been opposed to Burnside's plan from the start, concluded by saying, "It is only murder now."[60]

Which is exactly what it was in front of the stone wall. The dead were piled in heaps. The living still trying to hide behind whatever cover they could get, some lying flat behind the slight rise in the ground in front of the wall, many crowding in behind the brick house, others using the bodies of their dead comrades. An officer in the 116th Pennsylvania described the scene. "What a cosmopolitan crowd these dead and wounded were," he wrote, "Americans from the Atlantic Coast and the Pacific States, from the prairies, from the great valleys of the Mississippi and the Ohio; Irishmen from the banks of the Shannon and Germans from the Rhine and the Blue Danube; Frenchmen from the Seine and Italians from the classic Tiber mingled their blood together and went down in death together that the cause and that the Union might live."[61]

More were about to join them. A wounded member of the Irish Brigade, lying amongst the dead and other wounded in front of the stone wall watched as more divisions charged continued up the slopes. The fire from the Confederates was merciless, and each new charge was "blown back in terrible confusion ... as if by the breath of hell."[62] As darkness began to fall, a captain in the 69th New York gave the command to fall back to anyone from his regiment within hearing distance. No more than a dozen men rose from among the bodies surrounding him to make their way back down toward the town. As the command to fall back passed along the line, Lieutenant Quinlan of the 116th ran forward to retrieve the regimental flag from the dead color bearer. "A hundred fired at him," wrote one of his comrades, "but quickly seizing the broken flagstaff he threw himself on the ground and, with the flag tightly clasped to his breast, rolled back to where the command had halted, a noble deed, well done."[63] The harp and sunburst carried into the fight by the 63rd was nowhere to be seen. Back up the slope the two bodies nearest the wall were Major William Horgan and Adjutant John R. Young of the 88th New York. It was not long after 2 p.m. on the day when they fell, scarcely 10 minutes since they commenced their charge. By the end of the day, the proud Second Corps of the Army of the Potomac, including the Second Brigade of the First Division, commanded by Brigadier General Thomas Francis Meagher, lay wrecked on the slopes outside Fredericksburg.

CHAPTER 14

"Our Noble Little Brigade Has Almost Disappeared"

What manner of men

As the fighting died down, darkness began to fall. With the heavy pall of smoke from the battle hanging over the field, Couch decided to ride forward to see for himself the situation to his front. When he and his staff reached the brick house they found it packed with men, "and behind it the dead and the living were as thick as they could be, crowded together. The dead were rolled out for shelter, and the dead horses were used for breastworks."[1] Despite the carnage, Burnside was still reluctant to withdraw entirely across the river. While he pondered his next move during December 14, the dying and wounded remained where they had fallen on the slopes. Burnside was clearly near breaking point. One visitor to his tent during the day found him alone, pacing up and down, "apparently in great distress of mind." "Oh! Those men! Oh! Those men!" he said, pointing across the river where so many thousands lay dead and wounded, "I am thinking of them all the time."[2] It was not until the following day, December 15, after the dying and wounded had spent two days and nights where they lay on the slopes, that Burnside asked for a truce to recover the dead and wounded. "Here was a sight to behold," wrote one member of the 28th Massachusetts, "men were shot and blown to pieces in every imaginable way. The majority of our dead were destitute of their clothing, it being taken off by the Confederates for their own use."[3] Then, on December 15, Burnside decided to abandon the town entirely. That night the Army of the Potomac recrossed the Rappahannock, taking their pontoon bridges up behind them.

The most suitable epitaph for the battle of Fredericksburg was penned by the correspondent of the *Cincinnati Commercial*. "It can hardly be in human nature," he wrote, "for men to show more valor, or generals to manifest less judgment, than was perceptible on our side that day."[4] The casualty figures for both sides told the story of the battle. Against a total of over 12,000 killed, wounded or missing for the Army of the Potomac, Lee's army suffered just over 5,000 casualties. They were the most lopsided casualty figures for any major engagement during the war. The

Thomas Francis Meagher and the Irish Brigade

Second Corps alone lost over 4,000 men, with Hancock's division contributing over half that total. "It will be observed," wrote a despondent Hancock in his report, "that the losses in some regiments were of unusual severity, such as is seldom seen in any battle, no matter how prolonged." Not only that, he continued, but "These were veteran regiments, led by able and tried commanders, and I regret to say that their places cannot soon be filled."[5] Such an outcome was particularly acute for the Irish Brigade. The story is told that while on parade soon after the battle, Hancock saw three men of the brigade standing off by themselves. "God damn you," he shouted, "why don't you close up on your company?" One of the men saluted and replied, "General, we are a company." "The devil you are," replied a stunned Hancock, "As you were."[6] Although often embellished in the retelling, the story is nonetheless indicative of the plight of the brigade post–Fredericksburg. Captain Nagle of the 88th New York wrote to his father in the weeks after the battle. "The destruction of life has been fearful," wrote Nagle, "Irish blood and Irish bones cover that terrible field.... We were slaughtered like sheep and no result but defeat.... All I can find of my once fine company of brave men is two Sergeants and three men."[7]

Following the Peninsula and Maryland campaigns, the Irish Brigade was only able to bring just over 1,200 men to the battle at Fredericksburg, less than a third of what the three New York regiments alone totaled at the start of their service. On December 14, Meagher reported that less than 300 men could be accounted for. Although this figure would rise to over 500 as stragglers and wounded men returned, the brigade was really no more than a small-sized regiment, and in serious danger of being disbanded if new recruits were not forthcoming in significant numbers. The omens were not good. The structural problems of recruitment remained, in that new volunteers generally ended up in entirely new companies and regiments, organized by ambitious men who were always eager to scoop the new commissions which came with new outfits. On the battlefield, the result was that while old regiments wasted away to skeletons, the new ones had to learn for themselves much that could have been taught by veterans. Despite this, politics continued to preclude common sense, and the system remained intact.

Yet there still was the possibility that the regiments might garner new recruits, if, as with other outfits, the survivors were allowed to go home in person to spearhead a recruiting drive. Meagher himself felt that a triumphal return of the heroes would be of immense benefit in the drive to recruit more volunteers. It was a request the War Department could grant, if it so wished. Many would have argued it was the least that could be granted given their conduct on the field at Fredericksburg. In his official report, Colonel Kelly of the 88th New York described the conduct of the brigade in simple and elegiac tones: "I cannot close this report without saying a few words with regard to the officers and men.... The gallantry and bravery of the men is too plainly visible in their now shattered and broken ranks...."[8] By

14. "Our Noble Little Brigade Has Almost Disappeared"

common consent the charge of the Irishmen toward the stone wall was a scene of almost unparalleled heroism. Confederate general George Pickett, who would give his name to the most famous charge of the war, recounted the scene in a letter to his wife on December 14. "Yours soldier's heart almost stood still as he watched those sons of Erin fearlessly rush to their death," he wrote, "The brilliant assault ... was beyond description. Why, my darling, we forgot they were fighting us, and cheer after cheer at their fearlessness went up all along the lines." Longstreet would later describe the charge as "the handsomest thing in the whole war," while the correspondent of the *London Times*, resolutely prosouthern in his sympathies and no great friend of the Irish, was perhaps the most eloquent in his encomium. "Never at Fontenoy, Albuera, or at Waterloo was more undoubted courage displayed by the sons of Erin than during those six frantic dashes which they directed against the almost impregnable position of their foe ... the bodies which lie in dense masses within forty yards of the muzzles of Col. Walton's guns are the best evidence what manner of men they were who pressed onto death with the dauntlessness of a race which has gained glory on a thousand battlefields, and never more richly deserved it than at the foot of Marye's Heights on the thirteenth day of December, 1862."[9]

If they were not allowed home to recruit, no fault could lie with the men who charged up the frozen slopes outside Fredericksburg. The same could not be said for their commander, Meagher. Perhaps no amount of heroism would have swayed the War Department from its chosen course, but Meagher's record, both on and off the field of battle since the start of the war, was not one to convince the War Department that he could be or should be trusted with the command of men in battle. His actions during and after Fredericksburg could merely have confirmed people's worst suspicions.

"Strange, unaccountable ways"

Meagher was nothing if not consistent in courting controversy when his brigade went into battle. He addressed his men on the streets of Fredericksburg before they advanced, in his own words, "reminding it of its duty and exhorting it to acquit itself of that duty bravely and nobly to the last." Meagher then accompanied the brigade to the shelter of the ridge outside the town where they formed into lines of battle, but he himself got no further. As described in his official report, owing to "a most painful ulcer in the knee-joint," which he had "concealed and borne up against for days," Meagher was obliged to turn back for his horse. And back is where he stayed. He was still there when he met the remnants of the 63rd New York and 69th New York, who had pulled back from the slopes. Worse was to follow. He and his men then withdrew back across the river without orders, before being peremptorily ordered by Hancock to cross over again into Fredericksburg.[10]

Thomas Francis Meagher and the Irish Brigade

Writing soon after the battle, Colonel Edward Cross of the 5th New Hampshire Regiment, who was in a position to have seen Meagher in action throughout the Peninsula campaign and later at Sharpsburg as well as at Fredericksburg, echoed Colonel John Brooke's later comments to Francis Walker in 1884. "After more than one year's observation in the field," wrote Cross, "there is not in the United States, certainly not in the Army of the Potomac, another such a consummate humbug, charlatan, impostor, pretending to be a soldier as Thos Francis Meagher! Nor do I believe him to be a *brave* man since in every battlefield he has been *drunk* and not with his Brigade ... [the] drunkenness & incompetence of Gen Meagher will sooner or later be exposed."[11] Another forthright critic was the correspondent Henry Villard, who had already criticized Meagher's conduct during the First Battle of Bull Run. During Fredericksburg, Villiard had come across Meagher next to a hospital behind the lines. "His [Meagher's] retreat across the river without orders was nothing but a piece of arrant cowardice," wrote Villiard, "for which, however, he never received punishment on account of his popularity among the Irish."[12] Meagher himself claimed that he thought he had permission from Hancock to cross the river and that he "was solely actuated by an affectionate and intense concern for the wounded officers and soldiers of my command," an explanation which he told to anyone he could find to listen. This included the commanding general himself, whom Meagher said he went to see on the afternoon of the battle to explain his actions. Just how the distracted Burnside, trying unsuccessfully to coordinate the action of over 100,000 troops, received this rather lowly brigadier and his entreaties as to why he had retired across one of the bridges with a few dozen men is not recorded. "The circumstance of the retiring of this brigade [Meagher's] across the river, after it had been withdrawn from the battle ... I very much regretted at the time" was Hancock's terse comment, who also added that their leader's actions "in no wise affecting the conduct of the brigade in action (it behaved with great spirit)."[13]

No doubt aware of how his absence from the charge to Marye's Heights would be perceived, two days after the battle Meagher had one of the brigade surgeons furnish him with a medical certificate stating that he had been suffering from a "'Furunculous Abscess' of the left knee, which quite disables him for active duty in the field."[14] Yet even normally sympathetic publications remained silent on Meagher's conduct at Fredericksburg, while perhaps the most damning criticism of the commander of the Irish Brigade was made implicitly by the historian of the Second Corps, Francis Walker. At the time of Fredericksburg, Walker was a colonel on the staff of General Couch. Reflecting what must have been the feeling of his fellow officers regarding Meagher's role and his subsequent excuse for his actions, Walker was scathing. Meagher, "in his strange, unaccountable way, [had] been separated from his command during its charge," he wrote, "eventually finding his way into the city ... and even across the river." During the charge, it was Nugent and

14. "Our Noble Little Brigade Has Almost Disappeared"

Kelly who were "at the front" and "to whom the Irish Brigade has been accustomed to look for examples of courage and devotion."[15]

Walker's use of the phrase "courage and devotion" is interesting in that he could be alluding to something other than straightforward accusations of cowardice or incompetence, such as Villiard printed, the latter of which is certainly difficult to sustain against Meagher at Fredericksburg. If anything, he was at his inspirational best before the assault. For the assault itself, like other commands that day, there was little any of them could do given Burnside's plan of attack. Following Hancock's and French's attacks, in desperation, Couch had ordered Howard to try to launch his assault on the right flank of the Confederate line rather than straight up the slope toward the stone wall. Howard's men found that they could not swing around because the ground was marshy and impassable, and like toward the sirens' rocks, they were inexorably drawn back toward the killing ground over which Hancock and French had watched their lines disintegrate.

It is also difficult to accept that personal cowardice played a part in Meagher's actions. As far back as 1847, when the Young Irelanders attempted to hold their first meeting in Belfast, Meagher was set upon by "a gang of ruffians." One of his comrades recorded how "He [Meagher] set his back to the wall, his face pale with excitement and rage — 'You may be able to kill me,' he said, 'but I do not leave this place except as a corpse.' I admired him at that moment, and felt that at any rate the Irish cause would never be disgraced by any lack of manhood in that man."[16] At Sharpsburg, where his courage was again questioned, Francis Barlow, who was unsparing in his criticism when he felt it was warranted, later recounted to a skeptical Maria Daly Meagher's bravery in riding "before his troops during fire."[17]

While lack of personal courage is perhaps the least sustainable of the charges against Meagher, maybe there is probably a larger question mark over his devotion, or a fourth "C," commitment. Meagher was an intelligent man. One could convince oneself that the experience of First Bull Run had been something of a learning curve for all concerned. Things could only get better. The Peninsula campaign started off well with Fair Oaks, only to deteriorate into arrest, farce and mayhem. Sharpsburg was a chance for redemption, but was a very bloody affair that ended in disaster for the brigade and almost personal disaster for Meagher himself. After his experiences during the Seven Days' and Sharpsburg, maybe he had realized that he was simply out of his depth trying to lead troops in battle. Like many others, he certainly would have realized that the military adventure he had been so keen to pursue in 1861 was not the quick path to fame and fortune. Did his commitment to the Union include being killed in some god-forsaken swamp or frozen hillside in Virginia? Did he feel that he was meant for better things? Maybe returning to Ireland some day? Maybe he felt that he was too important to the cause to become just another name on the casualty list? Maybe it wasn't the cause of Ireland that led him to hold back, but the vision of some new political career in his adopted country should he survive the war?

There were other, more explicit questions regarding Meagher that hung in the air after the battle. One was in regard to his drinking. The *Times* correspondent, in the same article in which the men who charged the stone wall were eulogized, also recorded stories doing the rounds of drinking on the morning of the battle. Meagher had "harangued his troops in impassioned language ... and plied them extensively with the whiskey found in the cellars of Fredericksburg." The other was regarding his judgment. During the day, the new flags had arrived from New York accompanied by members of the civilian committee. The flags had the names of the previous battles proudly emblazoned upon them, but with the armies still drawn up ready to do battle along the Rappahannock, one would have thought that their presentation would have had to wait for a more propitious moment. Not so. On Sunday, December 14, Meagher decided to carry on with the banquet that had originally been scheduled to take place on the day of the battle. The hall which had been prepared across the river was no longer an option, so the small theater within Fredericksburg itself was to be used. The Irish Brigade, or what was left of it, was assembled and marched up to the theater. Inside, the tables were laid out with the food and drink which had been especially brought from Washington. Invitations were sent out, and at midday, about 300 officers, including 22 generals, arrived for what has been described as the "death feast." With the conduct of the commander of the brigade on the previous day open to question, with Confederate shells still hitting the town, and the dead and wounded of the regiments whose new flags were to be presented still laid out on the slopes before the stone wall, well could Hancock be heard to remark that "Only Irishmen could enjoy themselves thus."[18]

After the new colors were presented "to those commanding officers of the separate regiments who were able to be present," the flags were taken outside and given to the much-depleted regiments. "The brigade gave three cheers," wrote one soldier in the 28th Massachusetts, "which caused the Confederates to open a terrific cannonading."[19] Before the assembled guests hastily departed, Meagher had managed to court further controversy with the War Department. He told the assembled guests there were not enough men left in the brigade to guarantee the safety of the flags. Therefore, he could not accept them and rather melodramatically asked the members of the committee to take them back to New York, until such time as the brigade was up to strength. He then went on to denounce, rather precariously for a man in his position, what he saw as the political partisanship and the criminal incapability which had caused the Army of the Potomac to suffer so many costly defeats. For this most acutely "political general" with, to say the least, a highly suspect record in battle, to be publicly denouncing the Republican administration over the appointment of other "political generals," whom he in turn accused of incompetence, was not the way to win friends and influence people, especially if he hoped to enlist the support of the War Department to try to get his brigade back up to strength.

Maria Daly, although, as described by the editor of her diaries, someone who could express "her many prejudices with great poignancy," perfectly captures the cloud of miasma surrounding Meagher following Fredericksburg. Writing in her diary at the end of December she described Meagher as "cautiously frank, prudently reckless, and brave enough to risk his life when reputation actually requires it. He wears a swashing and martial outside with an appearance of whole-soulness. His generosity and liberality are very taking, but he pays no one. He is the fox all over, as anyone might see by watching his small bright eye. I confess I do not want him to come near us. In his neighborhood, there can be no luck for others"[20] In all likelihood, the Irish Brigade in its original form had effectively perished as an effective fighting unit at Fredericksburg, while its commanding general hammered the nails into its coffin.

Exit Burnside and Sumner

After recrossing the Rappahannock on the night of December 15, the brigade went back into the same camp as they had vacated on December 11. Corby noted that at mass "he had a very small congregation compared with former ones." Father Ouellet was unable to find enough off-duty men in the 69th to help him rebuild his hut.[21] One private in the 88th New York wrote to a friend describing how walking through his old camp, "You feel as if you are going through a grave yard alone; all is dark, and lonesome, and sorrow hangs as a shroud over us all."[22] Some soldiers remembered the winter camp under Burnside at Falmouth as the nadir of their experiences, the "Valley Forge" of the war. "I have never seen the army so dejected after any engagement," wrote one officer. "As for the remnant of the Brigade," he continued, "they were the most dejected set of Irishmen you ever saw or heard of."[23] Apart from their missing comrades, Burnside's regime on the banks of the Rappahannock was slack and inefficient. In the month of January, men in the ranks were deserting at the rate of 100 a day or more. By the end of the month, over 85,000 men were officially listed as missing. Among those that remained, the sicklist became swollen because of slack discipline in regimental camps and corruption in the commissary which had produced health and dietary deficiencies. Scurvy, normally associated with sailors, was common due to the lack of fresh vegetables, although there were warehouses full of them at Aquia Creek. "I do not believe," wrote a medical inspector, "that I have ever seen greater misery from sickness than exists now in the Army of the Potomac."[24]

It was not just the men in the ranks who were disgruntled for the Army of the

Potomac was riven by dissension and ill-will from top to bottom. Four generals from the Sixth Corps, led by Franklin, who rarely displayed as much energy in the face of the Confederates, went directly to Lincoln with complaints about Burnside. The criticism reached a crescendo following the infamous "Mud March" of January, when an attempted flanking movement by Burnside turned into a complete farce. Poor weather turned the roads into quagmires forcing the whole enterprise to be abandoned. Burnside had followed up his defeat at Fredericksburg by "a ridiculous campaign," wrote one member of the Irish Brigade, "in which one half of the army had to be employed to dig the other half out of the mud."[25] On January 24, Burnside was relieved of command and Major General Joseph Hooker was named as his successor.

The main cause of sadness was that the same orders which contained Burnside's removal and Hooker's appointment also contained the news that Sumner was also relieved of command. "Old Bull" had been connected with the brigade since the days at Camp California, and was a favorite with the men as they were with him. But after the debacle at Sharpsburg, he played little active part in the proceedings at Fredericksburg, Burnside keeping him across the river at Falmouth because of what Couch described diplomatically as his "supposed rashness."[26] When he left, it was the end of an era for the Second Corps, just as another one was drawing to a close for the brigade on which he had once said he would stake his stars in battle.

Setting the stage

To almost the surprise of everyone, the man with the reputation for hard drinking and hard fighting was to prove adept at running an army. Everything that Burnside had lacked, "Fighting" Joe Hooker appeared full of. He was brash and confident, and unexpectedly proved to be an excellent administrator. As army numbers and morale increased dramatically during the spring months, Hooker declared that he had "the finest army on the planet," and "may God have mercy on General Lee, for I will have none."[27] Yet there were doubts about Hooker. Nothing definable, but loosely centered on the question of character. He had schemed mercilessly and openly to replace Burnside, and even as Lincoln appointed him, he felt the need to chastise Hooker for having "taken counsel on your ambition ... in which you did great wrong to the country, and to a most meritorious and honorable brother officer." His camp and his staff had a poor reputation. One cavalry officer described army headquarters as "a place no self respecting man liked to go, and no decent woman could go. It was a combination of barroom and brothel." Nor did Hooker's braggadocio help. When Lincoln visited the army at Falmouth, he winced as Hooker's constant refrain was not whether he would take Richmond, but when he would take Richmond. "That is the most depressing thing about Hooker," Lincoln later remarked to a friend, "It seems to me that he is overconfident."[28]

For the moment, Hooker's appointment and administrative abilities helped raise the morale of the army. Besides being kept occupied under the new army regime, the men had time for other diversions. In the Irish Brigade, one such diversion was the monthly meeting of the "Potomac Circle" of the Fenian Brotherhood in the hospital tent of the brigade, Dr. Reynolds being the center or leader of the circle. The meetings began at 8 p.m. and, according to one member, with only a few minutes needed "for the dispatch of routine business," the participants could soon partake of the good doctor's punch. During the course of the evening, "the doctor perhaps recites an original poem, or some of the gentlemen tell stories of the dear old land, 'the Ould Dart,' as they delight to call it." "Whiskey is a great thing in the army," recorded the same writer, "At times we have 'lashins' of it ... and then it is sometimes hard to find."[29] There was no such difficulty at the major social occasion during the brigade's stay in Falmouth that winter, St. Patrick's Day 1863, which looms larger in many accounts than some of the battles.

Preparations for the day had been elaborate. A special church was constructed for the saying of mass. As described by Father Corby, "Posts, about fifteen feet long, were cut in the pine forest, and planted in the ground two feet apart. Along the tops of these were fastened beams, on which rafters rested.... Then the upright poles ... were interwoven, basket like, with green pine branches, and in the same way the roof was formed.... When the whole was finished it presented a delightful picture, and was in fine contrast with the surrounding white tents." For the material needs of the men, the quartermaster of the brigade had been sent to Washington "for liquors and meats" returning with, among other items, "thirty five hams, and a side of ox roasted; an entire pig, stuffed with boiled turkeys ... eight baskets of champagne, ten gallons of rum, and twenty two of whiskey." Most of these were laid out in front of Meagher's headquarters in two Sibley tents, "separated by a space of ten yards, which space was inclosed by an awning." The center piece of the display, "elevated on a pedestal, is a huge tub made of pork barrels and painted green." This contained the punch which Captains Gossen and Hogan had originally been responsible for making. However, "they labored so diligently that before the mixture was complete both felt overpowered by their labors and had to be relieved from duty."

The highlight of the day was to be the horse racing for which a course had been laid out, with a grandstand constructed at the finish line for the judges and guests. These were to be followed by footraces, wheelbarrow races and a greased pig chase. After Father Corby had celebrated mass in the morning, the guests began to arrive. By 11 a.m. the grandstand was packed, for a general invitation had been sent out to all the officers in the Army of the Potomac. Several generals, including

Meagher had to warn junior officers and enlisted men not to sit under the grandstand erected for the St. Patrick's Day celebrations in March 1863. "If that thing should ever collapse," he said, "you'd be crushed under four tons of generals" (Library of Congress).

Hooker himself, attended, while some thought as many as twenty thousand soldiers were spread around the camp for the day. Meagher, directing the events, was "conspicuous in his Irish sporting gentleman's dress ... a white hat, blue swallow tail coat with immense metal buttons, buckskin knee breeches and top boots, and he carried a heavy dog whip, with the air of one used to the sport."

The evening finished rather prematurely for some with a hurried order to "fall in" over a false report that the Confederates were preparing to attack. Nobody was able to discover whether it was some New England troops who spread the rumor, although one member of the brigade, whose memory might have been rather hazy, claimed that "the Brigade was in line in light marching order in five minutes and ready to march." By all accounts, the event was adjudged a great success and a good time was had by all. During the day, Hooker, "when a fitting opportunity offered ... proposed three cheers for 'General Meagher and his Irish Brigade, God Bless them.'" As well he might. Barely a fortnight before he had told Meagher that his small band was so indispensable they could not be allowed home to try to recruit new men, a decision which made it highly unlikely that the festivities of March 17, 1863, would be repeated in the future.[30]

"Our noble little brigade has almost disappeared"

As the men once more settled back into the camp routine of drill and picket duty, the final efforts were being made to try to prevent the regiments in the brigade from being either consolidated or disbanded. Reports were circulating that some veteran regiments, particularly those in the Irish Brigade, "which have been reduced to mere skeletons," were likely to come under the axe. The *Irish American* could "hardly believe that such a step can be contemplated by the War Department," given the service such units had given to the Union.[31] But already after Fredericksburg, the 116th Pennsylvania had been consolidated into a battalion of two companies.[32] On December 15, as the Army of the Potomac pulled back across the Rappahannock, Meagher had asked Dr. Reynolds to supply him with a certificate describing and authenticating his knee injury in order that he might apply for leave. Not for the last time, Reynolds obliged and stated that unless Meagher had 20 days' leave immediately he would suffer permanent disability. The leave was granted and Meagher left for New York at the start of the new year.[33]

Once there, he began what was effectively a public lobbying campaign of the War Department in order to try to get the remainder of the brigade back to New York en masse to help in attracting new recruits. Assisting him in this was the main Irish newspaper in the city, the *Irish American*. But the paper itself only too well reflected Meagher's own self-destructive tendencies in that demands for the brigade to be allowed back to New York to recruit were invariably accompanied by criticism of the administration, whose support was crucial if men were to be allowed to return. "Think of the regiments, of our Brigade, of old Sumner's corps," it railed at the end of December following the debacle at Fredericksburg, "may God as he will with a just judgment, the man or men who caused so much good, true, loyal blood to be shed in vain; so many brave children ... to be led up to slaughter, to destruction, to the coldest blooded murder ... this little Brigade was going off to death." It concluded by calling upon the government to allow the Irish Brigade to return to New York to recruit, albeit saying that "if men can yet be found to volunteer in a war — the conduct of which reflects anything but credit on those who have undertaken its management."[34]

With little response from the War Department, the paper later blustered, "We trust the matter will be taken up by the state authorities, who cannot be indifferent to the welfare of our brave troops."[35] But by early 1863, the war had taken on a life of its own. To a great extent it had outgrown the influence and demands which state officials had once placed on the government and the War Department in particular, during the early stages of the conflict. Gone was the time when the same paper reported in May 1861, how "the personal application of Mr. Meagher at the War Department," no doubt bludgeoning the officials with the names of several influential political friends, had secured his place and that of his company of Zouaves with the 69th New York State Militia as they prepared to fight at the First Bull Run. It was not so much that outside influence had entirely disappeared. Rather, the War Department, with the support of the administration, or at least without the active intervention of the administration on someone's behalf, was in a better position to resist demands that it did not wish to meet.

In that same month of January, it was reported that some New England regiments had been allowed home to do exactly what Meagher was requesting the Irish Brigade be allowed to do, something which caused great ire in the Irish camp. But once again when arguing its case, the *Irish American* returned to the theme that had certainly been one of the major causes of Meagher's fall from grace. After complaining that the Irish were the victims of "discrimination" for "political reasons," which may have been quite true, it again continued to assert "that the 'political reasons' to which may be traced so many of the wretched blunders which have well nigh ruined the cause for the Union." As a lobbying campaign, it was not best designed to win over the very people that mattered most.[36]

With only three months separating the horrors of Sharpsburg and Fredericksburg, it is also arguable how successful the brigade might have been had they been allowed back to New York to recruit. The same factors that had worked against Meagher's previous attempts at recruiting for much of the second half of 1862 remained, with probably even greater force. The economic boom in the North continued, while the Emancipation Proclamation freeing the slaves came into force on January 1, and was unlikely to be of any assistance in helping recruit the Irish, who remained implacable enemies of the blacks. "The feeling against niggers is intensely strong," one soldier in the brigade wrote his wife in February, "They are looked upon as the principal cause of this war and this feeling is especially strong in the Irish regiments."[37] Combined with opposition to the draft which began to operate in July, the intensity of feeling would eventually erupt with the New York Draft Riots of that month.

Reinforcing and entwined with these factors was the whole general attitude of the Irish to the war and the fighting itself. In the immediate aftermath of Fredericksburg, as with other battles, many men wrote home giving accounts of their experiences. The *Irish American* itself would contain some of these letters, and one in particular was a bitter account from an officer in the 88th New York in which he wrote, "May the Lord pity and protect the widows and orphans.... It will be a sad, sad Christmas by many an Irish hearthstone in New York, Pennsylvania, and Massachusetts." As Burnside had prevaricated over his next move, and Meagher had arranged his banquet in the theater in Fredericksburg, "The lying government papers state that all the wounded have been cared for!" the letter continued. "There are hundreds yet who have never had the blood washed off their wounds, and their gunpowdery hands and faces crusted with the clotted blood are meeting you at every

14. "Our Noble Little Brigade Has Almost Disappeared"

turn.... The men appear like a few ghosts among the huts." Another young Irish soldier from Jersey echoed these sentiments, concluding that, "the Irish Brigade is completely used up ... slaughtered like sheep."[38]

Another barometer of Irish opinion was the hostile reaction to the accounts of Fredericksburg in contemporary Ireland, also fueled by letters home by some of the men themselves. Meagher's men, wrote one journal, were "driven to mere slaughter" on the heights outside Fredericksburg, while even the period's popular ballads displayed growing hostility to the "cursed Yankees" and "savage blacks," in whose cause Irish "blood in rivers ran ... / And wounded men did loudly cry in pain." By mid–1863, William West, the American consul at Galway, admitted that the Irish countryside was filled with thousands of bereaved households, bitterly "bewailing the loss of brothers, sons and Husbands in our disastrous war."[39] In May, Father Corby had sent a letter to Archbishop Hughes in New York which contained $1,240 he had collected from the men of the brigade for the "relief of the suffering poor of Ireland." The list of donations enclosed by Corby showed a large amount of the almost heartrending donations of single dollars and upward from many of the enlisted men, many of whom had their own families to support in America. Corby felt the need to apologize to the bishop for the numerous small amounts donated, noting, with unintended poignancy, that "the amount would have been far greater had not our ranks been so horribly thinned by deaths, wounds and sickness."[40] At the same time, the *Boston Pilot*, in effect the national voice of the Irish in America, which in January 1861 had exhorted its readers to "Stand by the Union; fight for the Union; die by the Union," had tired of the war. When the Emancipation Proclamation was issued, one writer declaimed the fact that "We find ourselves after nearly two years ... engaged in an abolition war." This was not something which should be allowed to claim the lives of thousands more Irishmen. "How many brave Irishmen have been mutilated in the war? How many of them have been killed in it? How much Irish blood shed in all our bloody fields? How many widows and orphans has it made? ... What has their blood, their valor, their patriotism achieved? We blame the inability and the dishonesty of the politicians, statesmen, and county attorney warriors at Washington. There were once ample reasons for holding that they [the Irish] did not enlist in vain ... these reasons now exist only in the shadows."[41]

Lincoln himself appears in one of the two defining scenes of this period in the life and demise of the original Irish Brigade. The first of these scenes was a requiem mass which was held in St. Patrick's Cathedral in New York on January 16, "for the repose of the souls of all the dead" of the Irish Brigade. The congregation included "some of the highest citizens of New York, connected with Ireland by birth or descent," a number of widows, orphans and relatives of the dead; General and Mrs. Meagher; Colonel Nugent; and a number of serving members of the brigade. The latter were distinguished from other soldiers present by sprigs of evergreen worn in

One newspaper correspondent who witnessed the grand requiem mass at St. Patrick's Cathedral in New York, January 16, 1863, held "for the repose of the souls of all the dead" of the Irish Brigade, caught the sense of elegy of the occasion: "They loved their adopted country even unto death," he wrote. "They fought, and bled, and died to save her from disruption.... Our noble little brigade has almost disappeared" (Library of Congress).

14. "Our Noble Little Brigade Has Almost Disappeared"

their hats.[42] "The dark bier," wrote one soldier who was present, "surrounded by its military escort, the sable vestments of the officiating clergy, the vast congregation uniting their prayers with the service of the altar, and the solemn tones of the organ pealing the *Dies Irae*— all combined to produce a sensation of awe and devotion to which no heart susceptible to the finer emotions of our nature could be indifferent." No doubt partly intended by some as a very public display by the Irish Brigade in the midst of the attempts to have them released for recruiting, one newspaper correspondent who witnessed the service caught the mood, not of an ongoing crusade, but rather the sense of elegy of the occasion. "They loved their adopted country even unto death," he wrote, "They fought, and bled, and died to save her from disruption.... Our noble little brigade has almost disappeared."[43]

The second scene took place in the White House in mid–February. On January 21, as Franklin's and Hooker's men were knee deep in mud, and his men waited in readiness to cross the Rappahannock for another battle, Meagher's leave officially expired. The "Mud March" was called off and the men settled back into their camps again. But there was still neither sight nor sound of Meagher back in Falmouth. Finally, on February 3, Meagher wrote to the adjutant general explaining that as he had not yet fully recovered from his knee injury, he was unable to return to the front, but, as if in private employment, he did promise to report to Washington on February 11. Meagher had obviously another tack in mind in his quest to have the brigade relieved, for while in Washington, he went to see President Lincoln in person with his request, according to his biographer, "studiously ignoring official channels."[44] The photo album of the Irish in America is all the poorer for no camera was there to record this meeting. It would also be interesting to know whether Lincoln appreciated the incongruity of the occasion. Here was Meagher, one of his own political appointees, currently absent without leave from the army, who had consistently and publicly forsworn practically all the actions of Lincoln since before and after his inauguration, who only three months previously on the occasion of McClellan's dismissal had publicly warned "the gentlemen of the White House" that they would never be forgiven by the Army of the Union, presenting himself, cap in hand, to politely request a favor of the chief gentleman in the White House. According to one report, "The President received him kindly ... and promised to take his request into consideration," which is where it remained.[45]

On returning to Falmouth, the commander of the Irish Brigade found himself brought before a military commission, headed by Major General Howard, to explain his unofficial absence. This he was somehow able to do although it was probably lucky for Meagher that the rain and the mud had halted Burnside's campaign the previous month. Then, following up his visit to Lincoln, he wrote a long letter directly to Secretary of War Stanton, again ignoring official channels, requesting that the three New York regiments "be temporarily relieved from duty in the field; and, being so relieved, have the opportunity of restoring, in some serviceable measure their exhausted ranks."[46] The following week Meagher then tried to go through channels, writing to his immediate superior, Hancock, making the same request as he did to Stanton, but with a greater degree of boldness. He asked for three or four days' leave in Washington to "facilitate" the action; he reminded Hancock that Congress was due to adjourn shortly and he wanted to see some of his "influential and active friends" before they left. Hancock passed the letter on through channels. In early March, Meagher received his answer from the new commanding general, Hooker. "The Commanding General cannot entertain the proposition for the temporary withdrawal of the Irish Brigade from the Army, without positive assurances, that it will be immediately replaced by an equal body of troops. By Command of General Hooker." At that time Hooker was in the process of amassing over 100,000 troops under his command. The less than 600 of the Irish Brigade might not have been missed.

Lacking the necessary political backing, Meagher had come to a dead end. His biographer wrote how the "Regular Army officers in the War Department were resentful of the legion of political generals with whom they constantly had to contend and were thoroughly tired of the multitude of pressures which were continually brought to bear. The outspoken orator-general was not popular with them, and they were fully aware that to keep him out of New York was to prevent any further independent promotion or commotion on his part." The next time Meagher would visit Washington would be as a private citizen.

After a busy term of campaigning in Washington and New York, and organizing the St. Patrick's Day hoolie, Meagher concluded that he needed some more leave. On March 24 he again wrote to Hancock, informing him that he was suffering from a severe attack of rheumatism which prevented him from attending his duties. "The treatment absolutely necessary to my recovery from this attack is such as to necessitate my going to Baltimore or Philadelphia," he wrote, "it not being possible to procure hot or vapor baths at any point nearer." As a sign of the changed times in the capital, he also added that he would not venture near Washington, "as I understand, there is a decided objection to officers visiting that city, unless there on duty." Dr. Reynolds again diagnosed Meagher as being in great need of expert attention and supplied another medical certificate to that effect. Meagher's leave was granted. Taking a break from the hot baths, he addressed a fund-raising gathering in New York on April 11, in aid of the famine-threatened Irish back home, during which he told his audience that he was not there in any public capacity, but rather was in New York for the purpose of mending "a sprain I lately received, which compelled me to leave camp for a few days."[47] Somewhat chastened by his past experiences when on leave, Meagher returned to Falmouth when his leave expired, just in time to join in Hooker's first and last ill-fated attempt to best Robert E. Lee.

CHAPTER 15

A Sideshow of the Big Show

"A whipped man"

Hooker's plan to defeat Lee, like so many others, was a good one. He proposed to take part of his force and outflank Lee's army at Fredericksburg by crossing the Rappahannock farther upriver before descending on Fredericksburg from the rear. Just where any actual fighting would take place would depend on how Lee would respond to the move, and whether he would wish to give battle knowing that he was caught between two Federal forces. The initial stages of his campaign were carried out with speed and efficiency. There were no missing pontoons, no mix up on the marches. On April 30, he had approximately 50,000 men at a crossroads clearing of Chancellorsville, with another 22,000 on the way. And all this before Lee realized that the main danger was not in his front, but to his rear. Hooker seemed to think the campaign was as good as won, issuing General Order No. 47 in which he stated his belief that "the operation of the last three days have determined that our enemy must either ingloriously fly or come out from behind his entrenchments and give us battle on our own ground, where certain destruction awaits him."[1] With these words, apart from tempting fate, already it appeared as if Hooker was passing the initiative over to Lee rather than maintaining the decisiveness and control which he had maintained over the campaign so far.

The battle of Chancellorsville, Hooker's downfall, was Lee's masterpiece. Having been caught on the hop, the outnumbered Lee divided his forces, leaving some on the heights at Fredericksburg while setting the remainder off toward Chancellorsville. At noon on May 1, Lee's advance skirmishers ran into the Federals in the Wilderness just east of Chancellorsville. Hooker's nerve failed him. He ordered his advance to be halted; the troops were to return to defensive positions around Chancellorsville. A furious Darius Couch went to Hooker to find out why the advance had been halted. He later wrote that, on hearing "from his [Hooker's] lips that the advantages gained by successful marches of his lieutenants were to culminate in fighting a defensive battle in a nest of thickets ... I retired from his presence with the belief that my commanding general was a whipped man."[2]

The following morning, Lee again split his forces directly opposing Hooker, sending a force under Stonewall Jackson around the right of Hooker's line. It took

Jackson until 5 p.m. to finally get his men into position, but when they launched their attack, it was irresistible. The Federal line collapsed and was driven back for a good two miles before the jubilant Confederates were brought to a halt by a new defensive line. In the darkness, the ever-aggressive Jackson had gone ahead with some of his staff to see if there was any way of further pressing the Federals. When returning to his lines, he was accidentally fired on by his own men. Jackson fell, mortally wounded. He was taken to the rear, eventually having his left arm amputated before finally succumbing to new pneumonia.

The following day, on May 3, the bloodiest fighting of the campaign took place as both wings of Lee's force began to press the Federals back, while also desperately trying to unite with each other. At 10 a.m. the two wings of Lee's force united and began the final drive for the Chancellorsville clearing. As the Federals pulled back to a new defensive position, Hancock's division was left to cover the retreat, with the encircling Confederates now closing in on three sides. Hancock brought a battery into the open space around the clearing in a desperate attempt to stem the Confederate advance. Within 20 minutes most of the gunners and horses of the battery had been killed. As the Confederate skirmishers now advanced to within 150 yards of their position, they could see guns being manhandled back into the forest by some Federal troops.

"The regiment that saved the guns"

The battle of Chancellorsville would be the last engagement in which Meagher would lead the Irish Brigade. By now it was so reduced in numbers that it would spend much of its time away from the main bodies of troops on picket or guard duty. The brigade broke camp along with the rest on the Second Corps at dawn on April 28 and made their way through the woods along the north bank of the Rappahannock. The weather was fine and the men were in good spirits. The 63rd and 88th New York went into bivouac at Bank's Ford under the command of Colonel Kelly, while the 116th Pennsylvania, the 69th New York and the 28th Massachusetts continued up to United States Ford.[3] "We will be safe enough and do not expect to have anything but picket duty to do," wrote one soldier to his wife.[4] They remained there for two peaceful days in full view of the Confederate pickets on the far side of the river, who were as puzzled as the Irishmen were as to "why they had been sent to this lonely spot."[5] Then, early on April 30, Hancock and the rest of the division came up, after which the men had their first inkling that a number of the other corps had made a crossing farther upriver and were now advancing down the opposite side of the river.

The following morning, pontoons began to be laid. It was after dark when the brigade crossed the river. Once across, they were put in position covering a road

15. A Sideshow of the Big Show

leading to the ford. During the afternoon they could hear the sound of musketry fire off to the south as Hooker's men advancing from Chancellorsville came into contact with Lee's advancing columns from Fredericksburg. The following morning, May 2, they moved farther to the right to a place called Scott's Mills, covering the extreme right of the Union line nearest the river. Trees were cut down and an abatis constructed to their front, while loopholes were cut in the nearby buildings, turning them into blockhouses. Some must have been feeling the first twinges that something was not quite right with the campaign. The army had been marching for three days to outflank Lee's army, presumably so that they could attack the Confederates. Now, after having successfully maneuvered into the right position, but without apparently having fought a battle, they were digging in.[6]

They could hear the intermittent roll of musketry and cannonades as the skirmishing continued across Hooker's front during the day. Toward early evening, the volume and intensity suddenly increased off to the west, which was strange, as Lee should have been advancing east from Fredericksburg. Meagher was talking to the men on the right of the line when one of the pickets came hurtling back to the line, telling anyone who would listen that the Confederates were advancing toward them. As the men stood ready, they were astounded to see a deer come crashing through their woods, leaping the abatis and continuing onto their rear. Hot on the heels of the deer came some of their own troops, fleeing Jackson's furies. First in ones and twos, and then in 10s and 20s, until hundreds of demoralized and frightened troops were milling around the Irish line.[7] Meagher would not let them go farther and the brigade was ordered to form line and stop the flight at the point of bayonet. Not knowing what might follow the Eleventh Corps out of the woods, the fugitives were quickly gathered into squads and forced to the rear, from where, once the initial panic subsided, many would eventually rejoin their units. No Confederates appeared that night, and despite the melee, the brigade didn't fire a shot. After dark, arms were stacked, coffee was made, and the men settled down quite peaceably for the night.[8]

At daylight the following morning, May 3, as the men were cooking breakfast, heavy firing began off to the west as Lee continued his assault on Hooker's position. The firing was closer now as Hooker began withdrawing his men to a new defensive line closer to the river. The new line swung around to cover the position where the Irish Brigade had been placed, leaving the brigade free to go forward toward the Chancellorsville clearing where the rest of Hancock's division was engaged. As the brigade was recognized on its way, cheers would break out from other units. For those who were still there to remember it, it was like some of the advances on the Peninsula all over again as the brigade made their way to the front through streams of wounded and retreating men. The brigade was deployed in the woods at the edge of the clearing in support of a battery from the First Corps that was in position in

The much-reduced Irish Brigade spent much of the battle of Chancellorsville guarding the fords on the Rappahannock River, when in the late evening on April 30, they found themselves attempting to stem the tide of Eleventh Corps soldiers fleeing for the river after they were flanked by Stonewall Jackson. The scene was captured by the war artist Edwin Forbes (Library of Congress).

the clearing. The men were under heavy fire from the Confederates, now advanced to the edge of the woods on the opposite side of the clearing. Many felt they were in another tight spot, as only some of Hancock's men were left holding the clearing, while the other corps were retreating to the new defensive line.

The battery in the clearing, the 5th Maine, was that sent forward by Hancock to help cover the withdrawal. It was off to the left of the brigade, positioned in an orchard behind the Chancellorsville House. It was a desperate position for a lone battery to find itself, and the pounding which it took probably made some of the Irishmen feel a whole lot better about the pounding they were taking in the woods. One of the watching soldiers described the scene as one "of wild grandeur.... The shells from the Confederate batteries seemed to fill the air, tearing up the ground, rending the men and horses limb from limb.... The orchard was a very hell of fire." Within 20 minutes after deploying, the battery had nearly been silenced. "All the officers and [men] belonging to it had either been killed, wounded, or had

15. A Sideshow of the Big Show

abandoned their pieces," wrote Major St. Clair Mulholland of the 116th Pennsylvania, "with the exception of one man (Corpl. James H. Lebroke), and all the guns were silenced except one."

By this time there was not much left around the clearing excepting the Irish Brigade, the remnants of the battery, and some men were trying to drag the wounded from the Chancellorsville House which was now in flames. When the order came to withdraw, with all the horses from the battery also *hors de combat*, it fell to the 116th Pennsylvania regiment to try to save the guns of the 5th Maine. Corporal Lebroke fired a final round, and under covering fire from the rest of the brigade, ropes were fastened to the trails of the gun carriages and the men started to haul them out of the clearing. A shell burst among one of the human teams, wounding a number of men, but the remainder took the strain again and hauled the gun off. The men of the 116th Pennsylvania were the last to leave the clearing as the Confederates swarmed forward to take possession of the prize.[9]

St. Clair Mulholland would receive the Congressional Medal of Honor for his bravery in the Chancellorsville clearing. "Too much praise cannot be bestowed on him [Mulholland]," wrote a watching Lieutenant Whiteford of the 88th New York, "for his own cool bravery, and that of the men under his command, having to take them out of stiff yellow clay, where the guns were stuck, and under a galling fire of the enemy."[10] As the men of the 116th Pennsylvania made their way back to the new line, they passed General Sickles, who, rising in his stirrups, called for three cheers "for the regiment that saved the guns." The following day, May 4, the men rested on their arms, expecting a renewal of the Confederate assault, which never came. After corralling Hooker against the river, Lee now had to head off more Federal columns that Hooker had ordered to advance from Fredericksburg. On May 5, the men heard the sound of trees being felled as paths were being cut through the woods to their rear to facilitate the withdrawal of Hooker's force to the river. In the middle of a torrential downpour that night, with the rest of Hooker's army they recrossed the Rappahannock. On May 8, the brigade was back in their camps at Falmouth.

Taking leave

The Irish had once again given as much as they could give, and the action around the Chancellorsville House was yet another proud deed to be recounted around the campfires. A gallant episode. But only an episode, a small footnote among thousands of a great battle. The Irish Brigade would never be center stage again. It might not exist to become even a footnote in future battles. Chancellorsville cost the brigade another 100 casualties, which, by that time, was 20 percent of Meagher's force. Even without this loss, with no hope of getting his men back home to recruit, or of being given any other units to bolster his brigade, Meagher was in an invidious position: a brigadier general in charge of no more than a corporal's guard. If the regiments were to be disbanded, he would be forced, to use Hooker's injudicious phrase, to "ingloriously fly." Meagher didn't wait. On May 8, he wrote to divisional headquarters, tendering his resignation. He could no longer in all conscience remain in command of the Irish Brigade, because "That brigade no longer exists." But he didn't want to close the door completely. "In tendering my resignation, however, as the Brigadier-General in command of this poor vestige and relic of the Irish Brigade," he continued, "I beg sincerely to assure you that my services, in any capacity that can prove useful, are freely at the summons and disposition of the Government of the United States."[11] Meagher's forlorn offer was unlikely to be met with much enthusiasm. In a dispatch from Chancellorsville on May 3, one of Lincoln's correspondents mentioned how "Gen. Meagher is *again* wounded."[12] Colonel Cross of the 5th New Hampshire, with an already low opinion of Meagher, described how, at Chancellorsville, he saw Meagher lying on the ground among Company G of the 5th New Hampshire, "evidently badly scared.... As soon as the firing ceased, he ran as fast as possible to the left rear where he had a private fortification constructed."[13] While the former report was incorrect as to Meagher's wounding, the underlining of "*again*" tended to suggest the cynicism and wariness with which he was regarded in high places. The latter report, while recorded almost jokingly and unlikely to be true, further demonstrated how Meagher's reputation was irretrievably sullied and he himself close to becoming a figure of fun. On May 14, a terse, one-sentence reply from the War Department was sent to Meagher. "Your resignation has been accepted by the President of the United States, to take effect this day." No other comment was appended.

On May 19, the remnants of the Irish Brigade, no more than 400, formed into a hollow square inside of which stood the brigade's first and only brigadier general. After "some excellent music had been discoursed by the fine band of the Fourteenth Connecticut Volunteers," Meagher addressed the veterans, before passing along the lines, shaking hands with each man and wishing them "God Bless." Command was then passed over to Colonel Patrick Kelly of the 88th New York, "who promptly dismissed his little column."[14]

Chapter 16

Gettysburg — The "terifick battle"

To a last grand hurrah

His brilliant victory at Chancellorsville only further cemented Robert E. Lee's reputation and his daring. He decided upon another invasion of the North. As the Army of Northern Virginia went splashing across the Potomac that June, here was seen to be the supreme Confederate opportunity, the Confederate "high tide." Independence was glimpsed, however fleetingly, in that summer of 1863, as Lee's myrmidons once more crossed the shallows of the Potomac. The men were in much better shape than when they last headed northward on their way to Sharpsburg, and their commander had complete faith in them. "There were never such men in an army before," Lee said. "They will go anywhere and do anything if properly led."[1]

While the leadership of the Army of Northern Virginia was not in question, the same could not be said for the Army of the Potomac. Following the defeat at Chancellorsville and Lee's aggressive follow-up, Hooker got to arguing with Lincoln over the best response. On June 27, following a further argument over reinforcements, Hooker finally requested that he be relieved from his post.[2] On June 28, Lincoln granted Hooker his request, naming Major General George Meade from the Fifth Corps, in his place. Three days later on July 1, the armies clashed at the crossroads town of Gettysburg in Pennsylvania.

The Irish Brigade which marched north that June was only a shadow of its former self, even if it had not quite come to pass that, as one officer in the 88th New York wrote, "The history of the Irish brigade in the United States army is closed!"[3] But it was close. With barely 500 men, there was not enough to fill even a small-sized regiment. The five regiments in the brigade remained so in name only. The three New York regiments were reduced to battalions of two companies, commanded by company officers, and numbering 240 men. The 116th Pennsylvania was reduced to four companies totaling 66 men, while the 28th Massachusetts numbered 224.[4] The same day as Meagher had departed, the remnants of these regiments had requested from the War Department that they should be merged into a single new regiment, with the old regimental numbers retired so as to remain memorials to their dead. Although every officer in the brigade signed the request, nothing ever came of it.

Indeed, when Meagher himself was attempting to obtain another command following his resignation from the Irish Brigade, apart from his own personal record of past indiscretions and indecorum, and despite "the importunities of his friends" in Congress and elsewhere, he found his path frustrated by "the indisposition of Regular Army officers" in the War Department. His biographer has written that, "The War Department seemed to regard the Irish general as a communicable disease — something which ought to be isolated for the protection of other members of the organization."[5] Ethnic regiments and all the politicking that accompanied them had always been anathema to the professionals in the War Department. By 1863 they increasingly felt they no longer had to pander to the wishes of ethnic groups. In this respect, 1863 was a turning point in the sense that it marked the end of the first, almost romantic or naive phase of the war, after which hard-headed logistics and even harder headed generalship would eventually grind the Confederacy into submission. Gettysburg would in many ways be a last glorious hurrah for the volunteer soldiers of 1861 and 1862 in both armies, before they became subsumed into a military juggernaut.

Meagher's successor as brigade commander was Galway-born Colonel Patrick Kelly of the 88th New York. As well as a new brigade commander, the men also had new corps and division commanders. Hancock had been promoted as the new commander of the Second Corps after Darius Couch had resigned, refusing to serve under Hooker following the debacle at Chancellorsville, while Caldwell had been promoted in Hancock's place as commander of the First Division of the Corps. On the night of June 13–14, the Second Corps withdrew from its camp at Falmouth and joined in the northward pursuit of Lee's army. The first few days' march were made in oppressive heat, with "the dust rising in clouds.... Water was not to be had. Hundreds of men fell by the way." On June 17, the Irish Brigade went into camp near Fairfax Station. Here, in the usual precursor of a battle, all surplus baggage was sent to the rear. By June 19, the corps was at Centreville, and bivouacked inside the Washington fortifications, where, mercifully it started to rain. The following day, in steady rain, they passed over the old Bull Run battlefield where "the bodies, or rather the skeletons of the dead of the battle were exposed," leaving some of the men "evidently affected and depressed at the sight."[6] Others were obviously not so affected. Spying a dead hand reaching out from a shallow grave, one New Jersey soldier called out, "Look, boys! See the soldier putting out his hand for back pay."[7]

They crossed the Potomac at Edward's Ferry on a drizzly June 25, marching across Maryland and into Pennsylvania. Once there, the men's spirits noticeably perked up as they found themselves marching on "home soil," rich, abundant farm country, untouched by the war. Cheering crowds greeted them as they marched through the small hamlets, with drinks and food left on tables by the roadside. On

16. Gettysburg—The "terifick battle"

June 27, the corps marched as far as Sugar Loaf Mountain. The following day it marched 25 miles, according to one officer, "with few stragglers and in excellent condition." To Michael MacNamara in the 9th Massachusetts, the "Irish 9th," the landscape was almost lyrical. "The picturesque farmhouses and granaries appeared under the bright sunlight as white as driven snow," wrote MacNamara, "The undulating farming lands were covered with their rich nodding plumes of yellow grain which rose and fell in the breeze.... The scenery of it all, in its greatness, when viewed from a vantage ground, was a magnificent spectacle."[8]

On June 29, the corps did not begin their march until 8 a.m., but the leisurely start to the day was only a precursor to what an officer in the 116th Pennsylvania regarded as "the longest march the regiment was ever called upon to perform." Unknown to the men, the corps had been ordered to march at 4 a.m. Because of a mix-up, Hancock did not learn of the order until 6 a.m., and was determined that his corps would make up for the lost time. This they did handsomely. They covered 34 miles that day, not stopping until they reached Uniontown at 10 p.m., with the men collapsing to sleep as soon as they halted. On the march, the brigade chaplain described how "the click of a large spur, the occasional rattle of a sword, and other mechanical movements are the only sounds heard above the slow, steady tramp of the line ... mounted officers frequently dismount and walk to avoid being overpowered by sleep and to save themselves from falling from the horses.... How men live through all this is a mystery."[9] When one regiment finally halted for the night, there were less than 40 men in the ranks while the major in another regiment apparently "turned round to give orders to his men and found he had but one man to command."

At 8 a.m. on July 1, the Second Corps started for Taneytown, going into bivouac at about 11 a.m. Less than three miles away was the town of Gettysburg "from which no less than ten roads ran to as many disparate points of the compass, as if it were probing for trouble in all directions."[10] And trouble had indeed found the town. At 1 p.m., the new commanding general of the Army of the Potomac arrived at Hancock's tent. Fighting had broken out at Gettysburg involving at least two of the Union corps. The general on the spot, John Reynolds, had been either killed or mortally wounded. Meade wanted Hancock to go to the town at once and take command of the fighting. At about 1.30 p.m. an army ambulance went bouncing out of the Second Corps bivouac, heading north. In the back was Hancock, studying all the available maps of the area.[11] Up ahead the greatest battle ever fought on the North American continent had been under way since early morning.

The first day's fighting, a battle in its own right, had taken place off to the northwest of Gettysburg. The result was a resounding defeat for the Federal forces, who were forced to retreat through the town, eventually taking up defensive positions southeast of Gettysburg. The ground which the Union army occupied has most often been described as resembling the shape of a fishhook. To the northeast was Culp's Hill, rocky and heavily wooded; to its west was Cemetery Hill, and running south from the hill for about a mile was a lower ridge known as Cemetery Ridge, which leveled off as it reached another hill known locally as Little Round Top. South of this hill was another, higher, steeper and more inaccessible hill called Big Round Top. In front of the lower end of Cemetery Ridge and Little Round Top, other features of the terrain included a jumbled mass of rock outcroppings with huge boulders here and there, known as the Devil's Den. There was also a wheatfield and a peach orchard, known ever after as *the* Wheatfield and *the* Peach Orchard.[12]

Early on the morning of July 2, the Irish Brigade and the rest of the Second Corps made their way to Gettysburg, resting to the southeast of Big Round Top before eventually taking position along the center of the Union line along Cemetery Ridge.[13] On the left of the brigade was the Third Corps under General Daniel Sickles, who were to extend the line down to the Round Tops. The morning of July 2 passed quietly, as the Confederates, under cover of local ridges and woods, attempted to get into position for an attack on the this extreme left flank of the Union line. The waiting was tense. Too tense for Sickles, who, believing his present position was vulnerable to Confederate artillery fire, advanced his entire Third Corps forward about three-quarters of a mile to a position he believed was much more tenable in the event of being attacked. His new line was longer than the one he had abandoned, leaving his men stretched very thin, and both flanks were "in the air," one of which had to bend back at a 90-degree angle at the Peach Orchard to cover his southern flank.

Just before 4 p.m., Meade rode along the line to inspect the positions and was appalled to see what Sickles had done. Sickles offered to pull his men back to their original position. "I wish to God you could," Meade replied, "but those people will not permit it." Accompanied by a crash of artillery, "those people," in the form of John Bell Hood's Confederate division had just emerged from the woods to the southwest and advanced toward Sickles exposed left flank. Before long, the entire Union left flank was in trouble as the line along the Wheatfield and the Peach Orchard was breached by the Confederates. As the elated Confederates streamed across the Wheatfield, it appeared that nothing could stop them from then turning northward to sweep up along the rear and left flank of Sickles line, when they were met by a volley from fresh Federal reinforcements, advancing at the double quick. It was Caldwell's division, and the manner of their arrival on the scene of the fighting, advancing pell-mell through retreating comrades to plug a gap in the line, must have felt very familiar, perhaps too familiar, to many of the men in the ranks.[14]

16. Gettysburg—The "terifick battle"

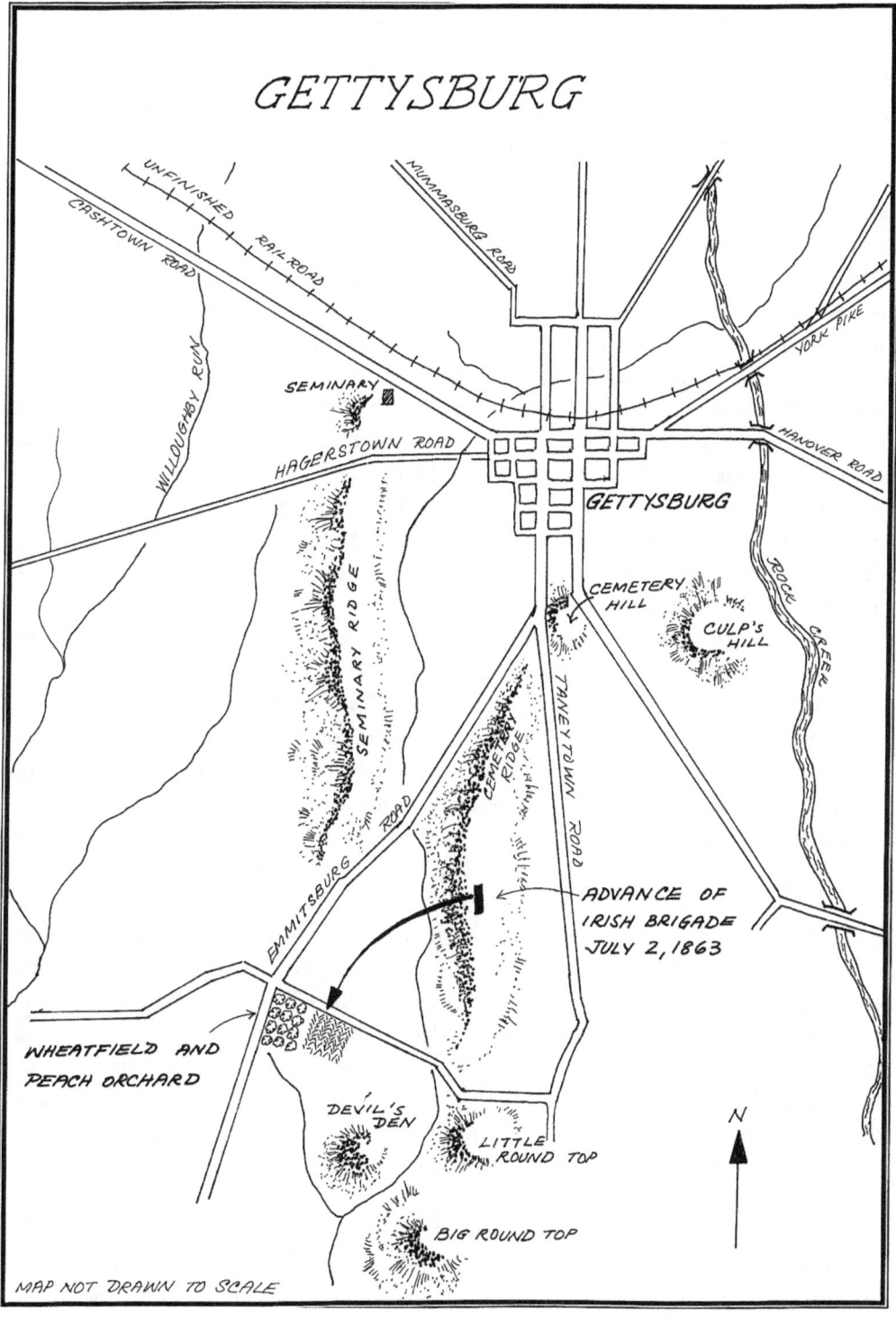

Slaughter in the Wheatfield

The contribution of the Irish Brigade to what one of its members described as this "terifick battle" was nasty, brutish and short, but tempered as always by episodes of nobility and pathos.[15] From their position on Cemetery Ridge, they had waited for most of the day in the July sun, observing the movement of Confederate troops off to their right, from where Meade himself expected the Confederate attack would be launched. Just after 3 p.m., as Sickles moved his corps forward, they were as "deeply interested and full of admiration at the splendid spectacle," if no less perplexed as other spectators on Cemetery Ridge. Watching the movement were a number of officers from the Irish Brigade, along with Caldwell and Hancock. "It looks like a dress parade, a review," someone said. Indeed, Sickles' advance was so deliberate and so methodical in its execution that one of the watching division commanders, Major General Gibbon, almost believed that he had somehow missed a general order to advance the line. Hancock, leaning on one knee and resting his sword on the ground, knew better. "Wait a moment," he said to the watching officers, with equal amounts of calculation and trepidation, "You will soon see them come tumbling back."[16] An hour later, the ferocious assault of Hood's was just about to accomplish this.

As the position of the Third Corps was so precarious, Hancock had little option but to send some of his corps forward. The nearest division was that of Caldwell's on the left of the line. At about 5 p.m., Caldwell was ordered to get his men ready to advance. As the brigades readied themselves, there occurred another of the celebrated scenes which characterized the history of the Irish Brigade. With the rising noise of the battle coming from below among the rocks of Devil's Den, the Wheatfield and the Peach Orchard as accompaniment, Father Corby mounted a rock and pronounced that he was going to give a general absolution to all men going into the fight. As he raised his right hand the men of the brigade "knelt with their heads bowed to recite the Act of Contrition, each man holding his cap in one hand while the other hand cradled his musket." According to one witness, as Hancock and a group of mounted officers nearby removed their hats, "every man, Catholic and non–Catholic, fell on his knees with his head bowed down.... The scene was more than impressive. It was awe inspiring ... the roar of battle rose and swelled and re-echoed through the woods making music more sublime than ever sounded through cathedral aisle.... I do not think there was a man in the Brigade who did not offer up a heartfelt prayer. For some it was their last; they knelt in their grave clothes." Corby himself later wrote, "The general absolution was intended for all— not only for our brigade, but for all, North and South, who were susceptible for it and who were about to appear before their Judge. Let us hope that many thousands of souls, purified by hardships, fasting, prayer and blood, met a favorable sentence

16. Gettysburg—The "terifick battle"

on the ever memorable battlefield of Gettysburg."[17] The ceremony finished, the Irish Brigade moved off by the left flank in the direction of Little Round Top.

Caldwell had the division in a column of four brigades, with that of Colonel Cross in the lead, followed by Colonel Brooke, then Kelly's, and lastly Colonel Zook.[18] As they passed through a plowed field, solid shot from the Confederate batteries positioned out by the Peach Orchard to their right showered the men with dirt as it burrowed into the soft soil. As they reached the foot of Little Round Top, Caldwell had little time for any elaborate tactics but had simply to try to deploy his men as quickly as possible and feed them into the fray. The Irish Brigade were sent countermarching across the right rear of where Cross had advanced. With arms at a "right shoulder shift," the Irishmen went forward through the Wheatfield at the double quick. Their advance had all the old élan of previous engagements. A wounded Confederate officer in the Wheatfield observed the advance of the Irish Brigade. "Is that not a magnificent sight?" he remarked to another colleague, "pointing to the line of gaily dressed Union forces [Irish Brigade] in the wheatfield whose almost perfect line was preserved, though enfiladed by our fire from the woods, decimating the front line, whose gaps were promptly filled by each file-closer."[19] On clearing the other side, they found rising wooded ground, laced with boulders and trees. As they neared the crest of the rise, the waiting Confederates, the 3rd and 7th South Carolina regiments from Brigadier General Joseph Kershaw's brigade, rose from behind their cover and let loose a volley. Firing downhill, their aim was too high and many overshot. With the opposing lines only a few yards apart the Irishmen stopped to deliver their own fire. The result "was deadly in the extreme." "I have never been in a hotter place," Kershaw later wrote.[20] Led by Kelly, who according to Caldwell's report, "behaved with his wonted gallantry," they continued their advance to the crest.[21] Here there was some brief hand-to-hand fighting before the Confederates surrendered. Off to their left, Brooke's brigade, which Caldwell had held in reserve, went forward to support Cross's brigade, which had been engaged the longest. Soon the situation to the division's front, along the line of the Wheatfield and Devil's Den, appeared to have stabilized. After prisoners had been sent to the rear, regimental lines were quickly redressed in preparation for the next task. Off to their right, the sounds of heavy fighting could be heard beyond the Peach Orchard.

The firing off beyond the Peach Orchard was ominous. The Confederate plan was for their divisions to attack *en echelon*—a staggered pattern of attack, gradually bringing all the force to bear along the length of the opposing line. Hood's division had led off the Confederate attack, but it was the following Confederate division that was to finally break the shored-up Third Corps line at the Peach Orchard, just as Caldwell's brigades were regrouping. The Federal line angled off to the southeast from the Peach Orchard, and when the Confederates broke through, their advance put them in the rear and right flank of the Federal brigades. Apart from some soldiers in the 116th Pennsylvania holding the extreme right of the line beyond the edge of the Wheatfield and who could vaguely distinguish columns of men moving through the Peach Orchard to their right rear, Kelly's men were unaware of the disaster about to be visited upon them. The colonel of the 116th asked Kelly if he could make a reconnaissance of the Peach Orchard to see exactly whose troops were moving through it. It didn't take long to establish that they were rebels, and just as the officer arrived back to raise the alarm, another officer galloped up and called out that they were surrounded and to fall back.

With other Confederates also beginning to push forward again on the right flank of the line, the Irish Brigade and the rest of Caldwell's men were in a tight spot. "Finding myself in this very disagreeable position," Kelly later put it with some understatement, "I ordered the brigade to fall back."[22] Colors were quickly rolled up, with no option left but to make a run for it. The only escape was through the Wheatfield. With Confederates closing in on both sides, it would prove to be "an alley of death." The retreating men were trying to load and fire on the run to somehow slow the closing rebel vise. "It was impossible after falling back to rally the men," wrote Lieutenant Smith of the 69th New York, "as the enemy's line extended down to the wheatfield that we had to cross; also there was no line immediately in rear of us to rally on; also in consequence of the small number of men in our regiment falling back in double-quick time, and the great confusion that prevailed at the time we crossed the wheatfield."[23] By the time the men were halfway through the Wheatfield, the Confederate lines were so close that they were almost in danger of hitting each other as they were of hitting the retreating Federals. "The slaughter was appalling," wrote one Irish soldier. "We encountered the full sweep of the enemy's fire," reported St. Clair Mulholland of the 116th Pennsylvania, "which at this point was most destructive."[24] The 28th Massachusetts, which was the farthest advanced on the stony hill, was the last regiment to get the order to retreat. "Finding all save this regiment were retiring from the hill," described Colonel Byrnes, "and that the enemy were on both our flanks, as well as in front, I brought my command from the field, losing many men from the concentrated fire of the rebels."[25]

In the entire advance and retreat which lasted no more than half an hour, Caldwell's division lost nearly 1,300 men, with the regiments in the Irish Brigade losing nearly 200, or 40 percent of their total. Most of the casualties were sustained in the retreat across the Wheatfield, with the 28th Massachusetts suffering the heaviest casualties, 100 men, or 45 percent of its total. The battered remnants finally rallied on the Taneytown Road at the base of Little Round Top. Fresh Federal reinforcements once again halted the Confederate advance, and the left flank of the line finally stabilized as the focus of the attacks shifted up toward Cemetery and Culp's

16. Gettysburg—The "terifick battle"

Confederate dead laid out on the Rose farm, just southwest of George Rose's wheat field. With the Confederates closing in on both sides, the wheat field would prove to be "an alley of death" for the retreating members of the Irish Brigade (Library of Congress).

Hills. Under cover of darkness, the brigade moved back to a position on Cemetery Ridge, once more forming on the left of the Second Corps.

The price of glory

The following day, against the advice of some of his commanders, Lee decided to assault the Federal position once again. Underestimating the strength of the position and the resolve of its defenders, while overestimating the capacity of his own veterans, Lee marshaled all the fresh troops he had left, about 15,000 in all, and sent them on a frontal assault on Cemetery Ridge at the center of the Union line. Having to march across a mile of open ground, under constant fire from the Union artillery, enfiladed from both flanks as they got nearer the Union position, the charge was glorious but doomed. Longstreet, who had endeavored to talk Lee out of the maneuver, told him that it was his belief "no 15,000 men ever arrayed for battle can take that position."[26] He was right. But Lee overruled him, and the repulse of Pickett's Charge, as it became known, was the final decisive encounter of the battle of Gettysburg.

Positioned on the extreme left of line on Cemetery Ridge, the Irish Brigade was not directly involved in the fight. Many of the Union troops were positioned behind a stone wall which ran along the crest of the ridge as the Confederates advanced toward them into the hail of shot and shell. One admiring member of the Irish Brigade later wrote that "the enemy continued to advance with a degree of ardor, coolness and bravery worthy of a better cause."[27] But there could also be heard cries of "Fredericksburg! Fredericksburg!" from the Union lines. It was sweet revenge. Perhaps some of the watching members of the brigade wished they could have taken their place behind the wall. They had certainly earned their place, in front of the stone wall at Fredericksburg, and the sunken road at Sharpsburg, and numerous other bloody encounters over the last two years. Following Gettysburg, the *Irish American* once more found itself having to put the words Irish Brigade in quotation marks as it "no longer exists in the army of the Potomac.... It has been literally 'wiped out.'"[28] For the 300 or so survivors, the ghost of the original Irish Brigade, they had to be content that they had already done their share of the fighting in yet another "hot place" where, once again, "[our] little Brigade fought like heroes."[29]

Chapter 17

Fire in the Rear

The riots

With the rest of the Army of the Potomac, the Irish Brigade rested on its arms during July 4, waiting to see whether Lee would try to attack again. In front of their position, following Pickett's Charge of the day before, "the dead lay in great heaps ... dead and mutilated men and horses were piled up together in every direction." In the heat "the stench from the dead became intolerable, and we tried to escape it by digging up the ground and burying our faces in the fresh earth." When Lee withdrew on July 5, the brigade went into camp at Two Taverns before joining in with Meade's hesitant pursuit of the Confederate army. On occasions like this, outside of the context of a battlefield, the men of the brigade would be more concerned with recuperating from their recent exertions than with harrying their foes, and if on picket duty would frequently reach an accommodation with the opposing rebel pickets. When asked about the absence of the usual potshots being fired on the picket line, one soldier replied that, "Arrah, the moment we go out, we stack our arms, and they does the same. What good would it do to kill a few of the poor devils? And sure it looks like murder." On July 15, after the Confederates had finally managed to cross the Potomac, the brigade retraced their steps before going into camp at Morrisville.

The camp at Morrisville was "a most happy one." The weather was good, supplies were abundant, and "never were the men in such health and spirits." Around the campfire, stories about the "terifick battle" were relished and no doubt embellished. One soldier recounted how in the march through Pennsylvania he had been so near his home that he left camp one evening, walked all night to see his wife and children, and rode back to camp in his farm wagon before he was missed.[1] Another story told how, on July 2, Brigadier General Alexander Hays requested an orderly to accompany him on a reconnaissance in front of the Union lines. When a small Irish private on a rather big white horse was detailed for the job, "The General looked at the diminutive son of the old sod and judged by his appearance that he might not be very reliable. 'Sir,' demanded Hays, 'are you sure you are brave enough to follow me on the skirmish line?' 'Gineral,' replied the by now indignant son of the old sod, touching his cap, 'go right on, sir; go right on to the line. If yiz

ENROLLMENT!

Office of the A. A. PROVOST-MARSHAL-GENERAL, SOUTHERN DIVISION OF NEW YORK,

NEW YORK, JUNE 23, 1863.

NOTICE IS HEREBY GIVEN to all persons whose names have been **ENROLLED** in Districts other than those in which they reside, that by calling upon the Provost Marshal in the District in which they have their residence, they can obtain a **CERTIFICATE** of the fact of their enrollment in such Dist., which, upon presentation, will entitle them to have their names taken from the lists where they may have been enrolled elsewhere.

By adopting this course the Provost Marshals will be enabled to perfect their lists and prevent the possibility of names appearing more than once in the enrollment.

APPLICATIONS SHOULD BE MADE TO THE PROVOST MARSHALS, AS FOLLOWS:

1st Congressional District	Jamaica, L. I.
2d " "	No. 26 Grand Street, Williamsburgh.
3d " "	No. 259 Washington St., Brooklyn.
4th " "	No. 271 Broadway.
5th " "	No. 429 Grand Street.
6th " "	No. 185 Sixth Avenue.
7th " "	No. 63 Third Avenue.
8th " "	No. 1184½ Broadway.
9th " "	No. 677 Third Avenue.

COL. ROB'T NUGENT,
A. A. PROVOST-MARSHAL-GENERAL.

BAKER & GODWIN, Printers, Printing-House Square, 1 Spruce St., N.Y.

17. Fire in the Rear

is killt out there, yiz won't be in hell five minutes until yiz'll hear me tappin' on the window to get in.'² The most startling stories, however, would be those which reached camp about the draft riots which erupted in New York on July 13.

The Draft Act, enacted by Congress on March 3, 1863, made all men between the ages of 20 and 35 and all unmarried men between 35 and 45 liable for military duty. A lottery among the eligible names in each congressional district would determine who would have to go to war. However, drafted men who presented an "acceptable substitute" or paid $300 were exempted. Although broader issues of social and political change were also involved, most accounts regard the riots as a straightforward episode of Irish Catholic violence. "The Irish," wrote one historian, "were ripe for revolt against this war waged by Yankee Protestants for black freedom," crowded as they were "into noisome tenements in a city with the worst disease mortality and the highest crime rate in the Western world, working in low skill jobs for marginal wages, fearful of competition from black workers, [and] hostile toward the Protestant middle and upper classes who often disdained and exploited them."³

Apart from the obvious inequity regarding the exemptions, and the general Irish hostility toward the war itself, there was also the suspicion that "anti-administration" or Democratic districts were given larger quotas to fill than their Republican counterparts. The subsequent "revolt" started in the Ninth Congressional District, one filled with Irish laborers. As the names began to be drawn on the Monday morning of July 13, a paving stone came through the window of the draft office. One of the worst riots in American history had begun.⁴ Four days later at least 150 people were dead and countless businesses and homes gutted by fire. Among these was the home of Colonel Nugent, who was serving as assistant provost marshal in charge of the draft in Manhattan while recovering from the wounds he received at Fredericksburg. The following week his sword of honor, presented for gallantry, was found in the hands of a small child on the Upper East Side. Its jewels were missing, having being prised from the hilt, and the blade broken.⁵ Meagher counted himself fortunate he had not been there. When he met the Fenian John O'Mahony later that year, O'Mahony said to Meagher, "Had you been in New York those days and shown yourself to the people, you would have stopped all the rioting." "Not

Opposite: Out of the frying pan...: After surviving the horrors of Fredericksburg, Nugent found himself amid the maelstrom of the draft riots in New York, as assistant provost marshal in charge of the draft in Manhattan. During the riots his home was burned down. It was later suggested to Meagher that he might have been able to stop the rioting had he been present. "Not at all," replied Meagher, "The people those days were in a mood of mind to tear me limb from limb if they caught hold of me" (collection of the New York Historical Society; Poster File, PR-055-3-105, digital i.d. ac 03106).

at all," replied Meagher, "The people those days were in a mood of mind to tear me limb from limb if they caught hold of me."[6] It was not until units from the Army of the Potomac were dispatched to New York that the violence began to ebb. As if to demonstrate the gulf which had grown between the volunteers and those who remained at home, one member of the Irish Brigade back in Morrisville wrote to his wife about the "disgraceful riots in New York," and hoped that with troops now in the city, the authorities would not hesitate to use artillery on the rioters to "bring the bloody cut-throats to their senses."[7]

Back in Virginia during August and September, Meade and Lee faced off to each other across the Rapidan River. At the start of October, a series of moves and countermoves began, as the opposing commanders tried to best each other. This was finally abandoned at the end of November, and by December 3 the Irish Brigade was building winter huts on the north bank of the Rapidan, about 20 miles upstream from Fredericksburg. The only campaigning left was to try to recruit new members to the ranks of the brigade.

More trouble than they were worth?

The news of July's riots certainly gave no cause for optimism regarding the immediate appearance of new recruits. Enforcement of the draft had been temporarily suspended and did not start up again until the following month. This time there was a brigade of veterans from the Army of the Potomac already in position in order to deal with any disturbances. There were none. One of the soldiers was Thomas Galwey of the 8th Ohio. "Generally the people treat us well," wrote Galwey, "That is to say the moneyed people, those who are able to buy substitutes.... But the poor, who have to fight in person ... look upon us with dislike, at least with suspicion, knowing that we were sent here to enforce the draft, which the riots in July had deferred."[8] Such attitudes did not bode well for possible recruitment to the much-depleted ranks of the Irish Brigade, and whose continued existence remained precarious, as for a variety of reasons there would be no rush to the colors by the Irish.

Exemption from the draft would be the cheapest method of avoiding the war. Every avenue was explored. There were the "Quaker Irish" who wore broad hats to support their claim to draft exemption on the grounds of religious belief.[9] Many more thronged the consulates of the old enemy, Britain, demanding citizenship to avoid the draft. One Chicago newspaper professed itself "shocked by the number of young Irishmen in St. Louis who insisted they be treated as subjects of Great Britain."[10] Others simply fled to Canada. In the end, conscription itself would prove to be merely a big sign outside a very small shop. Nationally, only 7 percent of the men whose names were drawn in the lottery, 46,000, actually served in the army,

17. Fire in the Rear

alongside 74,000 substitutes. Both of these figures are dwarfed by the 800,000 men who enlisted or reenlisted voluntarily during the two years after the passage of the Conscription Act. Conscription, or the threat of conscription, combined with the payment of bounties to volunteers, proved to be the successful carrot-and-stick approach by which the government was able to stimulate voluntary recruitment.[11]

Amongst these new recruits would be brand-new immigrants, newly arrived in America and swept up from the docks and seaports straight off to the recruiting offices. One such Irishman wrote home describing how he had been "the dupe of a Federal agent" who had been operating in Ireland. "I am not the only one," he added, "They are enlisting young men every day, and the moment they land they are drafted to the battlefield." Not all would necessarily be dupes. Another wrote that he had neither been fooled nor forced to enlist, but was enticed by the bounty of $700. This was several years' wages for an Irish laborer, and which, unsurprisingly, "was very tempting, and I enlisted the first day I came here." As with the early stages of the war, poverty would be an enormous stimulus to whatever Irish enlistment there was. With near-famine conditions in Ireland during the early 1860s, the American consulates in Ireland had to deal with hordes of poor Irish asking for free passage tickets to the States in return for enlisting in the Union forces. But many emigrants neither intended to fight nor in fact did fight in the war. The American consuls in Ireland were equally inundated with demands for draft-exemption certificates from would-be emigrants whose only intention was to find employment in the booming northern economy. "There is ... plenty of demand for working men," one such emigrant wrote home, "and they can easily earn from one to two dollars per day."[12] Despite protests from the British government, the Union consuls were not blind to the benefits of Irish immigration. "The current is now in our favour," the consul at Galway wrote to his superiors in 1863, "let us then seize the prize while it is within our grasp — it is our most effective recuperative power, and would, I believe, help materially to resuscitate our exhausted resources."[13]

The problem for the army, however, with regard to those who did enlist on the back of large bounties, would be that bounty-stimulated volunteering came to seem an even greater evil than the draft, given the quality of many of the recruits for which it was responsible. "Substitute brokers" appeared. For a price they would help find substitutes for someone whose name was drawn. They were none too bothered about the type of substitute they would furnish for the army, and "horrified medical officers of the Army of the Potomac were finding that new lots of recruits often included hopeless cripples, lunatics and men far along in incurable disease." Another type of broker to make an appearance was the "bounty broker," who, with local, regional and national bounties to be exploited, would seek the best deal for their clients, with a cut of the bounty for payment. More often than not, entrepreneurial individuals would simply become professional bounty jumpers, who "made a business of enlisting, collecting a bounty, deserting at the first chance, enlisting somewhere else for another bounty, deserting again, and keeping it up as long as they could get away with it."[14] One Connecticut soldier wrote of the 300 recruits his regiment got that winter as, "the most thorough-paced villains that the stews of New York and Baltimore could furnish — bounty jumpers thieves and cut-throats, who had deserted from regiment after regiment in which they had enlisted under fictitious names, and who now proposed to repeat the operation." And repeat it they did, with 250 of the 300 absconding within a few weeks.[15]

Lost a brigade and looking for a role

Offstage from all the brouhaha which was brewing over conscription and recruitment, Meagher soon regretted his resignation. Missing the salary, the status, or even yet, the possible opportunities his commission might provide, he had written to Lincoln early in June offering to renew his military service. With his version of the carrot-and-stick approach, Meagher promised that he could raise 3,000 Irish troops, while also attempting to use his political friends to put pressure on the president to accept his offer. Mayor Opdyke of New York, in an unfortunate turn of phrase, and clearly oblivious to the brewing battle which was about to erupt in his own city, wrote to Lincoln on July 6. "It is very desirable," wrote Opdyke, "that action in the matter be prompt that the General may take advantage of the present auspicious moment when the war spirit is again thoroughly aroused." When no favorable reply had been received by October, Meagher wrote the secretary of state, William Seward. In what his biographer called a "pathetic, coaxing letter from a down-and-out applicant," this time Meagher promised that before New Year's Day he could organize a corps of veteran soldiers from 5,000 to 7,000 strong. No immediate reply was received from the War Department.[16]

In one of the final and characteristic twists in Meagher's particular saga, in December he was invited to visit his old companion in arms, Michael Corcoran. It was not until August 1862 that Corcoran was eventually released from a Confederate jail following his capture at Bull Run. On his release he was feted as a hero, and after much pressure was applied to the War Department, found himself made a brigadier general. Corcoran, in a last hurrah for the days when a much-hyped ethnic leader was able to raise new troops, then proceeded to recruit four new Irish regiments in New York, although many of the recruits were of dubious quality. The regiments became known as "Corcoran's Irish Legion." In December 1863 they were camped near Fairfax, Virginia, when Meagher came calling. He and Corcoran "resolved to celebrate the Christmas holidays of 1863 in splendid style." On the afternoon of December 22, when Meagher was subsequently returning to Washington,

17. Fire in the Rear

> **Office of U. S. Military Telegraph,**
> No 20   WAR DEPARTMENT.
> The following Telegram received at Washington, 5.30 P.M. June 16 1863,
> From   N York   M.
> Dated, June 16   1863.
>
> His Ex.
>   The Prest of the United States
>   If called upon
> and authorized by the Govt I shall
> proceed at once to raise three thousand
> (3000) Irish Soldiers in this city to act
> as Cavalry & Infantry wherever they
> may be ordered.
>   Thos Francis Meagher
>   No 129 Fifth ave
>
> 33 Coll

Meagher's telegram to Lincoln of June 16, 1863: After he had resigned his command, Meagher, rather forlornly, offered to raise 3,000 troops. Leaving aside his increasingly tarnished reputation, the previous autumn, following Sharpsburg, he had managed to recruit fewer than 200 for the Irish Brigade (Abraham Lincoln Papers, Library of Congress).

Corcoran, reportedly the worse for the wear from drink, decided to ride Meagher's horse back to camp, even though the horse had a reputation for being an unruly and "a very spirited animal." Soon after setting off, Corcoran galloping ahead of his staff, "and going rather hard at the time," was apparently thrown from the horse. He never regained consciousness. Since the horse had not stumbled, it was concluded that the general had fallen off "in a fit."[17]

Meagher learned of his friend's demise the following day. But in a bizarre turn of events, the Army of the Potomac had no sooner lost one Irish general than it recovered another. On the same day, Meagher received word from the War Department that his resignation had been revoked. He was once more a brigadier general in the Volunteers, although as yet he was not assigned any specific command. Meagher's reinstatement was probably not unrelated to the forthcoming presidential campaign of 1864, a campaign that Lincoln believed he would find it difficult to win. The reinstated general then proceeded to give an oration in support of Lincoln and his vice-presidential candidate, Andrew Johnson. Meagher's support for Lincoln completed his estrangement from much of the Irish community, especially in New York, where the slaughters at Sharpsburg, Fredericksburg and Gettysburg had taken their toll on Irish support for the war. In less than two years, Meagher's dreams and ambitions, to be built on the foundations of ethnic leadership, had crumbled. Reacting to criticism of his position, in October Meagher wrote a bitter letter to Michael Guiney of the 9th Massachusetts, which was widely published in ethnic periodicals. "As for the great bulk of Irishmen in this country," wrote Meagher, "I frankly confess to an utter disregard, if not a thorough contempt, of what they think or say of me in my relations to the questions and movements that are supported or designed to affect the fortunes of this nation, or actually do so.... I have discarded with the haughtiest insensibility and disdain the 'Irish opinion' of this country, having come to the conclusion that it was passed redemption, and, therefore, passed consideration or respect."[18] Criticizing his "uncalled for and unwarranted attack upon our countrymen," the *Irish American* wrote of Meagher, "It is not an enviable position for one for whom a better fate might have been hoped; but it is of his own choosing.... [B]etween him and the people who loved and trusted him once he has opened a gulf he never can bridge over ... our indignation at his unprovoked attack upon our people has long since subsided into contempt, and we have no desire to add a deeper tint to an act that has gone so far to darken the record of a life, of which the promise was once so fair."[19]

Chapter 18

"What There Is Left of It"

The Furloughs

One of Meagher's most repeated requests to the War Department during the latter part of his tenure as commander of the Irish Brigade was that the regiments be allowed to return to their hometowns to try to recruit new members. This had always been refused. By late 1863, however, with huge numbers of the original three-year enlistments due to expire, the War Department was anxious to try to retain the services of as many of the veterans as possible. It was thus allowed that if three-quarters of any unit reenlisted, then the unit could return home as a body to rest and recruit. All the New York regiments easily fulfilled this requirement and were able to return home after Christmas, the 63rd and 69th arriving in New York on January 2, 1864, while the 88th New York arrived the following month.[1]

The estrangement between soldiers and civilians was almost complete. Gone were the days of cheering in the streets or even a dignified welcome for returning heroes. Instead, "a brief paragraph in the morning papers announced ... a few hundred veterans were returning to their homes for a short period." On the day of their arrival, "the sparse and grimy columns were escorted by a company or two of the Sixty-ninth militia, and the immediate relatives of the members." Some of the brigade officers, as well as Meagher, later met to discuss a more appropriate welcome for the returning men, and sure enough it was unanimously proposed that a "grand banquet" be given in their honor, to take place on January 16.

At noon on the appointed day, the men, no more than 300 all told, formed at City Hall. Headed by a marching band, they made their way down Broadway to the venue of the banquet, Irving Hall. Inside, the walls were covered with the remnants of the old banners of the brigade alongside the new ones that had been presented by the civilian committee. Around the galleries, where many of the womenfolk were wearing mourning clothes, hung shields with the names of the different engagements in which the brigade had taken part, a catalogue of names already becoming part of the folk memory of the United States and the killing grounds for over 1,300 men from the New York regiments alone.

After the men had eaten, Meagher and other invited guests went onto the floor of the hall. The officers saluted the enlisted men. As described by the *Irish American*, it was a characteristic Irish gesture "of the blood and brotherhood that united the chieftains of old to his clansmen." Then the speechmaking began. Meagher, addressing what he called "the rank and file, the bone and sinew, the stout hearts and the iron arms of the Armies of the Republic," told the assembled veterans that, "history has no power to bestow upon me any higher distinction than that I have been the general in command of the Irish Brigade." Before finishing he felt he had to fight some personal battles. Addressing his audience like a political gathering, he repeatedly asked whether "charges that had been privately circulated regarding him" were true. Had he recklessly exposed the lives of the officers and men of his command? Had he ever brought them into danger except when he had been ordered there? Was he not always at the head of the column when danger was encountered? Nobody spoiled Meagher's party, but maybe someone noticed the irony that Meagher was followed by Barney Williams, a noted Irish comedian and ballad singer of the day. Williams proceeded to sing "The Bould Soldier Boy." Looking around at the handful of men and widows in the hall, it was left to one of the guests, Colonel Brewster of New York's Excelsior Brigade, to provide the grimmest and most appropriate toast of the evening. "The Irish Brigade," he said raising his glass, "what there is left of it."[2]

New recruitment to the ranks of the New York regiments would owe much to the cajoling of the veterans on the furloughs. It also perhaps owed not a little to the role played by Nugent, who remained in New York until August 1864 in his assistant provost marshal's role, supervising the draft, and chief unofficial recruiting officer for the 63rd, 69th, and 88th regiments. In Pennsylvania, members of the 116th Regiment sent its recruiting parties trawling far upstate in search of recruits. "Fayette, Allegheny, Chester and Schuykill Counties of Pennsylvania State," wrote one officer of the regiment, "had emptied their school houses to furnish recruits." In Massachusetts, the only requirement Colonel Byrnes of the 28th Regiment had for renewing his regiment was for able-bodied men.[3] If the *Pilot* was a reflection of Irish opinion it was just as well. "We are an emigrant race," editor Patrick Donahoe wrote at the end of May. "We did not cause this war; vast numbers of our people have perished in it.... But the Irish spirit for the war is dead! ... Our fighters are dead." Donahoe advised his readers to withdraw whatever allegiance they had for President Lincoln: "It is now every man's duty to disagree with him."[4] Ethnicity, in effect, had no longer mattered since the regiment had taken its first major losses in front of the stone wall at Fredericksburg, and there had subsequently been disquiet in the regiment. One occasion in the summer of 1863 had led to court-martials over the "strangers," particularly officers, that had been brought into the regiment. "I think that great injustice is being done to the regiment," wrote one member of the 28th Massachusetts, "the Irish have won the right to have their own officers to lead them." The following April, another enlisted Irishman in the

18. "What There Is Left of It"

28th was writing to his wife complaining that, "That mean scoundrel of a Colonel of ours ... has been selling commissions in Boston," while "some of them are men who were dismissed from the service in other regiments."[5]

Nevertheless, "what was left" of the Irish Brigade, plus a sufficiently continuous trickle of new recruits from whatever sources, was just about adequate to reprieve the brigade from being disbanded. Veterans and rookies made their way back to the camps of the Army of the Potomac in Virginia, to train and wait for word of the next big push against the rebels. This time the army was under the leadership of U. S. or "Unconditional Surrender" Grant, who had been called by Lincoln from the west to take command of all the Union armies. Grant was once described as having the look of someone who had "determined to drive his head through a brick wall, and was just about to do it."[6] Lincoln had at last found someone who not only would use to the full the Union's greater resources, especially manpower, but someone who was unafraid of what Lincoln called the "arithmetic" of death and destruction necessary to win the war. It was going to be a fight to the finish, and a very bloody affair indeed.

Consolidation and Demoralization

It is not really possible to circle a date on a calendar when the story of Thomas Francis Meagher and the Irish Brigade, and the story of the Irish Brigade itself, draws to a conclusion. Meagher himself kept in touch with the brigade through to the end of the war. Except for a brief period in the autumn of 1864, there was a recognizable unit styled the Irish Brigade, which was the Second Brigade of the First Division of the Second Corps of the Army of the Potomac, and which was present at Appomattox for Lee's eventual surrender in May 1865. Yet it was not the same outfit. The playwright Denis Johnston, writing in the 1950s, compared Dublin's Abbey Theatre to a "knife that having 4 new blades and 5 new handles, still insisted that it was the same implement. What remains as a continuum is not the building, merely the architect's drawings." Arguably this applied to the Irish Brigade. This was partly due to the absence of Meagher, and partly as we have seen, for the type of recruit the survivors of the "original" brigade were able to muster up during the winter and spring of 1864. Just as the brigade became something different in 1864, so did the army, as did the war itself, becoming something so overwhelming that neither individual brigades, nor for that matter corps, nor generals, mattered that much.

In terms of those recruits that did join the brigade in early 1864, not all were necessarily of poor quality. The verdict of the Army of the Potomac's historian on some of the initial batch of recruits to the brigade was that "it got fighters," as indeed would be demonstrated in the battles of May and June — the Wilderness, Spotsylvania, and

Cold Harbor.[7] The problem was the scale of the slaughter initiated by Grant's campaign of attrition that began on May 1. Looking back to Bull Run, that first major battle of the war cost the Union less than 3,000 casualties. In the battle of the Wilderness alone between May 4 and May 7, Grant lost approximately 17,660 men. Within four weeks nearly 1,000 men of the replenished Irish Brigade, men that had been enlisted largely through a last heroic effort by the veterans in the brigade during that spring, were gone.[8] On June 24, one of the surviving recruits surveyed what was left. "I went along the line of our old Irish Brigade," wrote Daniel Chisholm of the 116th Pennsylvania, "It made me sad to see how she had been cut to pieces, her thinned ranks tell the tale of her battles and hardships.... The Glorious old 88th N.Y. and the gallant old 69th N.Y. the always ready 28th Massachusetts and the spoiling for a fight 63rd N.Y. and our own gallant 116th Pennsylvania comprise the Brigade. They all now present the appearance of Companies instead of regiments."[9]

They had begun the campaign with 10 officers ranking as major or above. Within six weeks, six of them, including two brigade commanders—Byrnes and Kelly—were dead of wounds or killed in action. The other four were in military hospitals badly wounded, leaving the senior captain as acting brigade commander. As the Army of the Potomac settled down into a protracted siege of Petersburg, south of the Confederate capital, what the brigade had been able to stave off since the previous year. eventually happened. On June 20, the order had already come through transferring the 28th Massachusetts from the Irish Brigade to the first brigade of the division. Then on June 26, Special Order 165 was issued. The second and third brigades of the First Division, the Irish Brigade and Colonel Nelson Miles' brigade respectively "will at once be consolidated." The Irish Brigade, it was stated with chilling brevity, was to be "discontinued."[10] With the 116th Pennsylvania and the 28th Massachusetts transferred out, the three New York regiments — by this stage the 63rd and 69th mustered six companies apiece, and the 88th only four — would form a battalion under Captain Richard Moroney in a new Consolidated Brigade, alongside seven other New York regiments.[11]

Given the demoralization of the men subsequent to the bruising campaign in which they had fought since May, it was hardly surprising that their time in the Consolidated Brigade would be the nadir of the New York regiments' service during the war. During August, after one particularly disheartening encounter at a place called Deep Bottom on the James River, their new division commander, Francis Barlow, who had witnessed firsthand the bravery of the brigade in front of the Bloody Lane at Sharpsburg, was bitter in his derision about the New York regiments. "I am compelled to say," wrote Barlow, "that these troops behaved disgracefully and failed to execute my orders. They crowded off to our right into the shelter of some woods, and there became shattered and broken to pieces."[12]

18. "What There Is Left of It"

Barlow was not alone in his poor opinion of the fighting qualities of the new Consolidated Brigade. Less than two weeks later, at a place called Reams' Station, their poor conduct greatly contributed to the worst disaster to befall the Second Corps, with a distraught Hancock seeing his command lose more than 2,000 prisoners, nine guns and 12 stands of colors. Clearly, something was badly amiss and not just with the Consolidated Brigade, but with the entire Second Corps. "Concerning the reported ill behavior of the troops," wrote Francis Walker, "it is enough to say that the two brigades referred to had been long the chief glories of the Second Corps." The chief of staff of the corps believed that "nothing could so clearly show the disorganization brought about by the terrible losses of this campaign as that such language could be truthfully used about these troops. The Irish brigade left its dead, with their sprigs of green in their caps, close under the stone wall at Fredericksburg; and had shown in every field the most determined bravery ... now according to General Barlow was loath to look at the enemy. It is evident that assaults 'all along the line' had left very little of the old material there."[13]

If the "old material" could no longer be trusted, then it could be kept out of harm's way, and following Reams' Station the Second Corps returned to the Petersburg lines, with the men soon engaged almost continuously in building entrenchments, laying out roads, and picket duty. So much so that Hancock eventually was led to protest that enough was enough. "The men have, in fact, become day laborers," he wrote, "and suffer in their proper character as soldiers."[14] For the men of the Irish Brigade who had survived from the start of the war, the wheel had almost come full circle. Their military duty had begun with the building of Fort Corcoran, and now they appeared resigned to ending the war as "day laborers."

Fall and redemption

Things, however, began to look up during September. On September 4, Meagher was in camp to join in the celebration of the third anniversary of the formation of the brigade. He had been visiting Hancock the previous month during which time Provost Marshal General Marsena Patrick's diary entry for August 18, 1864, noted that "Genl. Meagher is lying in the tent of the chaplain of the 20th as drunk as a beast, and has been so since Monday, sending out his servant for liquor and keeping his bed wet and filthy! I have directed Col Gates to ship him tomorrow if he does not clear out."[15] Colonel Gates himself recorded that Meagher had been drunk for a week until Gates had to inform him that he "could not furnish him quarters any longer and he left."[16] When he visited the brigade the following month, he was, ironically enough, on his way to a post in Georgia where he would once again find himself under the command of the old "envenomed martinet," Sherman. Maybe the visit helped waylay, at least temporarily, some of the demons in Meagher's head. The Irish were certainly keen to show that they could still put on a show despite all their trials and vicissitudes. Corby and Ouellet celebrated a high mass in "a beautiful chapel tent," specially constructed for the occasion, along with "a grand avenue lined with evergreens [which] led to the front entrance." Following the mass, the guests, which included a number of generals, "were conducted to the banquet hall ... ornamented with banners, flags, guidons and other military insignia." Following the meal, Meagher made the inevitable speech amid "a scene of gaiety and general enjoyment, distinctively characteristic of Irish gatherings." It was by all accounts a successful day. "When all the rest of the army were more or less dormant or bewailing the situation," Father Corby later wrote rather wistfully in his memoirs, "the Irish Brigade was making fun and cheer for itself and all the friends it could accommodate."[17]

On October 22, Brigadier General Miles made an official request that the Irish Brigade be allowed to reform, with Colonel Burke of the 88th New York to command.[18] Nine days later permission was granted, but with command of the brigade falling to Colonel Robert Nugent. Conscious of the disrepute into which some regiments had recently fallen, in his first official orders to the reconstituted brigade Nugent made a stirring appeal to the pride of the men. "In assuming command of the old Irish Brigade," he wrote, "it gives me much satisfaction to know that although fearfully decimated by the casualties of a campaign, they still maintain their old reputation for bravery and patriotism. The record of the Brigade has been a bright one; it has proved its fidelity to the Union by its courage and sacrifices on many a battlefield.... Let the spirit that animates the officers and men of the present be that which will strive to emulate the deeds of the old brigade." The following week the 28th Massachusetts was reassigned to the Brigade, although this was not the case with the 116th Pennsylvania, with its place being taken by the 7th New York Heavy Artillery.[19] Although Nugent led the reconstituted brigade like a man with a mission, it was not an easy task. Desertions from the trenches around Petersburg were hard to stem, and those units most suspect would be placed on duty in confined places such as forts where they could be easily watched. On one such occasion, in transferring the 69th and 88th New York regiments to such a place, their division commander wrote that both "regiments [were] mainly composed of substitutes who have recently joined and the frequency of desertions among this class of men renders it necessary that they be placed where they can be easily watched and guarded."[20] It is perhaps no coincidence that three times alone in the month of December the brigade was paraded to witness the executions of deserters.[21]

On March 17, 1865, the brigade held the by-now traditional St. Patrick's Day celebration with the usual races and "a spacious refreshment room, in which the officers of the Brigade dispensed sandwiches and whiskey-punch to the invited guests." It appears the search for recruits also went on among the celebrations, with

18. "What There Is Left of It"

some members of the brigade claiming that one of the generals present, the Frenchman, Regis de Trobriand, was really an Irishman, his name being D. T. O'Brian. Events would show it to have been the farewell party for the brigade.[22] Only the Virginia winter had prevented Grant from delivering the *coup de grace* to Lee. With the latter's army melting away, and the roads drying up with the onset of spring, victory could only be a matter of sooner rather than later. After a series of clashes, on April 1 Confederate resistance collapsed. When news of this reached Grant, he lost no time in ordering an all-out assault along the entire line for next morning, April 2. This time the whole army sensed the end was in sight, and when the attack came at dawn, it came "with more élan and power than the Army of the Potomac had shown for a long time."[23] The final decisive act of the Civil War in the east had begun.

Petersburg fell on April 3, with the Army of Northern Virginia in full retreat toward the south. In the vanguard of the pursuit was the old Irish Brigade. The regimental reports convey the breathlessness and the exhilaration of the final

"In assuming command of the old Irish Brigade," wrote Colonel Robert Nugent in October 1864, in his first official orders as commander of the Irish Brigade, "it gives me much satisfaction to know that although fearfully decimated by the casualties of a campaign, they still maintain their old reputation for bravery and patriotism" (Library of Congress).

chase as the old foe, Lee's invincibles, were for the first time during the war in full retreat.[24] The Army of Northern Virginia was brought to bay at Appomattox Court

177

House on Sunday, April 9. Almost as a final gesture, Lee had a notion to try to break through the Federal line blocking their way. "For the last time," wrote one historian, "rebel yells shattered the Palm Sunday stillness as the gray scarecrows drove back Union horsemen — only to reveal two Yankee infantry corps were closing in on Lee's rear. Almost outnumbered by five or six to one in effective troops, Lee faced up to the inevitable." Out of the Confederate lines came a lone rider, holding a staff in his hand with a white flag on the end. It was over.[25]

The following morning some wounds began to heal. "We have stacked arms a few yards apart," Daniel Chisholm wrote in his diary, "The boys in the Blue and in the gray are trading everything that is tradable.... The late hostile armies seem to have forgotten they were enemies yesterday morning, and are mixing and chatting the hours away in a very friendly manner."[26] The following month, the remaining veterans of the Irish Brigade were in Washington to take part in the Grand Review of the Army of the Potomac and Sherman's Army of Georgia. As they marched down Pennsylvania Avenue, every man's coat bore a sprig of green.[27] On Independence Day, two months later, just before being finally mustered out of the service, they took part in a monster procession down Fifth Avenue in New York. On July 22, the *Irish American* reported that the three New York regiments of the Irish Brigade "were mustered out of the U.S. service and fully paid off. Henceforth, by the historian alone must the name and fame of that gallant command be preserved."[28]

Accompanying the New York procession was the forlorn figure of Thomas Francis Meagher, "a solidly built man of forty-one, now greying slightly ... [but] inside the solid frame was a vacuum ... as he humbly moved down the avenue, on foot, in citizen's clothes."[29] By this time Meagher had again resigned his commission and his request to parade in uniform with the remnants of the Irish Brigade had been refused. Controversy had continued to accompany Meagher following his appointment out West. After pestering Sherman for a command, saying that he was "unwilling to remain unemployed at a time when the service of every soldier seems needed," he was eventually assigned two "provisional Brigades" comprising convalescents, stragglers and replacements.[30] It was not a happy experience. When bringing his command to join Sherman in January 1865, they somehow managed to get "lost" along the way. "If he [Meagher] has lost his men," wrote U.S. Grant in early February, "it will afford a favorable pretext for doing what the service would have lost nothing by having done long ago — dismissing him."[31] When they did eventually reach Sherman, they were described as having "no complete organization of any kind ... the whole command is but a mob of men in uniform."[32] On February 26, Meagher was relieved of command.[33] The following May with the war almost at an end, he again resigned his commission. Later that year, Lincoln's successor, Andrew Johnson, for whom Meagher had campaigned, appointed him as territorial secretary to Montana. He later became acting governor. On July 1, 1867, reportedly

18. "What There Is Left of It"

during a drinking bout aboard a steamboat at Fort Benton on the Missouri River, he fell overboard and was drowned. His body was never recovered.

The following year, David Powers Conyngham would publish his *Campaigns of the Irish Brigade*; in 1870 and 1892 there were the accounts of Meagher by Lyons and Cavanagh, followed in 1893 by Corby's memoirs and then St. Clair Mulholland's in 1903. These encomiums — Conyngham's, Corby's and St. Clair Mulholland's in particular — as described by one critic "forged a body of literature remarkable for its propensity to mythologize Irish participation in the Civil War, North and South."[34] Perhaps this was true in terms of their lionizing of Meagher and their avoidance of the hostility toward the war among the broad swath of Irish opinion in America and Ireland. But for the men who actually fought and died in the Irish Brigade, their story needed little mythologizing. They left their native and adopted countries with a series of indelible and noble images to grace the pages of any history.

Notes

Preface

1. *The Man Who Shot Liberty Valance*, directed by John Ford, (Hollywood, CA: Paramount Pictures, 1963).
2. D. P. Conyngham, *The Irish Brigade and Its Campaigns* (New York: William McSorley, 1867).
3. W. Corby, *Memoirs of Chaplain Life* (Chicago: La Monte, O'Donnell, 1893).
4. St. Clair Mulholland, *The Story of the 116th Regiment, Pennsylvania Volunteers* (Philadelphia: F. McManus & Company Printers, 1903). In his critique of the myth making aspects of these accounts, Craig Warren takes some well aimed shots, albeit at a relatively easy target. C. Warren (2001) "'Oh, God, What a Pity!" The Irish Brigade at Fredericksburg and the Creation of Myth.' *Civil War History*, Vol. 47, Issue 3.
5. Typical of this is Paul Jones' enjoyable account of the brigade published in 1969. P. Jones, *The Irish Brigade* (Washington, D.C.: Robert Luce, 1969).
6. L. Kohl and M. Richard, eds., *Irish Green and Union Blue: The Civil War Letters of Peter Walsh, Color Sergeant, 28th Massachusetts Volunteers* (New York: Fordham University, 1986); K. O'Brien, ed., *My Life in the Irish Brigade: the Civil War Memoirs of Private William McCarter, 116th Pennsylvania Infantry* (Mason City, CA: Savas, 1996). Two other accounts have also been published. S. Barnard, ed., *Campaigning with the Irish Brigade: Pvt. John Ryan, 28th Massachusetts* (Terre Haute: AST, 2001), while interesting in parts, is best filed under "unreliable memoirs" for much of Ryan's time with the Irish Brigade. W. S. Menge and J. August Shimrak, eds., *The Civil War Notebook of Daniel Chisholm. A Chronicle of Daily Life in the Union Army, 1864–1865* (New York: Ballantine, 1989), comprises the combined diaries and letters of three members of the 116th Pennsylvania who joined up in 1864. It is equally interesting but focuses more on their everyday experiences as soldiers rather than on the Irish Brigade as such, something that is apparent in the subtitle of the book.
7. W. Fox, *Regimental Losses in the American Civil War, 1861–1865* (Albany: Brandow, 1898), 118.
8. W. Burton, *Melting Pot Soldiers: The Union's Ethnic Regiments* (Ames: Iowa University, 1988), ix-x.
9. K. O'Grady, *Clear the Confederate Way! The Irish in the Army of Northern Virginia* (Mason City: Savas, 2000).
10. J. M. Hernon, Jr., *Celts, Catholics and Copperheads: Ireland Views the American Civil War* (Columbus: Ohio State University, 1968); and O'Grady, *Clear the Confederate Way!* v-vi.
11. Randle quoted in C. Reardon, *Pickett's Charge in History and Memory* (Chapel Hill: University of North Carolina, 1997), 3.
12. R. Athearn, *Thomas Francis Meagher. An Irish Revolutionary in America* (Boulder: University of Colorado, 1949).
13. A recent biography by Gary Forney, while informative about his earlier and later years, does not dwell on Meagher's Civil War exploits and makes no mention of any of the criticisms contained in the accounts by Burton and O'Grady. G. F. Forney, *Thomas Francis Meagher: Irish Patriot, American Yankee, Montana Pioneer* (Philadelphia: Xlibris, 2003).
14. "Ireland had given birth to many a gifted child of genius" was how Conyngham began the biographical sketch of Meagher in his *Campaigns*, 532.
15. W.F. Lyons, *Brigadier Thomas Francis Meagher: His Political and Military Career; With Selections From His Speeches and Writings* (New York: D. & J. Sadler, 1870); M. Cavanagh, *Memoirs of Gen. Thomas Francis Meagher* (Worcester, MA: Messenger, 1892).
16. J. Bilby, *Remember Fontenoy! The 69th New York and the Irish Brigade in the Civil War* (Hightstown, NJ: Longstreet House, 1995). Bilby also contributes an essay, "Thomas Francis Meagher, The Man who made the Irish Brigade" in J. G. Bilby and S. D. O'Neill, eds., *"My Sons Were Faithful and They Fought": The Irish Brigade at Antietam: An Anthology* (New Jersey: Longstreet House, 1997), which is equally exculpatory and almost tends to suggest that stories about Meagher were somehow got up and maintained by subliminal anti-Irish prejudices. Rory Cornish nods approvingly at Bilby's suggestion in his contribution to the most recent episodic study of Meagher's life. R. T. Cor-

Notes — Chapter 1

nish, "An Irish Republican Abroad: Thomas Francis Meagher in the United States, 1852–65," in J. M. Hearne, and R. T. Cornish (eds.) *Thomas Francis Meagher. The Making of an Irish American* (Dublin: Irish Academic Press, 2006), 150.

17. K. O'Brien, "Sprig of Green: The Union Irish Brigade," in P. S. Seagrave, ed., *The History of the Irish Brigade. A Collection of Historical Essays* (Fredericksburg, VA: Sergeant Kirkland's, 1997).

18. F. Boyle, *A Party of Mad Fellows. The Story of the Irish Regiments in the Army of the Potomac* (Dayton, OH: Morningside House, 1996).

19. O'Grady, *Clear the Confederate Way!* 129.

20. A. Guelzo, *Abraham Lincoln: Redeemer President* (Grand Rapids, MI: Wm. B. Eerdmans, 1999), 469.

21. The painting is "Sons of Erin." Some battles were known by different names with the Federals tending to use the name of the nearest river, while the Confederates tended to use the nearest town. Examples of this are Bull Run / Manassas, Stones River / Murfreesboro and Antietam / Sharpsburg. In some accounts, such as Shelby Foote's trilogy, which name the author chose to use was a good indicator of where his sympathies lay. Sharpsburg is used in this account more for its lyricism alongside the names of Fredericksburg and Gettysburg rather than any indication of sectional sympathies.

22. O'Brien, ed., *McCarter*, 167. In a most extraordinary turn of events, the bottle referred to by McCarter was discovered in 1999. Its identity was confirmed by the handwriting on the label, which matched that of McCarter's original handwritten memoirs, held by the National Park Service. The bottle is now owned by a Civil War memorabilia shop, located, fittingly enough, in Fredericksburg. M. J. O'Donnell, "The Sprig of Green." *North-South Trader's Civil War* magazine 26, no. 3 (July 1999).

Chapter 1 — Saved by Sumter

1. Details of Corcoran in Burton, *Melting Pot Soldiers*, 9–10, and P. O'Flaherty, *The History of the 69th Regiment of the New York State Militia, 1852 to 1861* (Ph.D. dissertation, New York: Fordham University, 1963), 200–201. The phrase "beardless youth" was originally that of Meagher, who described Corcoran as having acted "lawfully, as a citizen, courageously as a soldier, indignantly as an Irishman." Cavanagh, *Meagher*, 353.

2. The identity of who fired the first shot at Sumter is a matter of dispute. In the green corner, competing for this honor, is one P. O. Donlan. See E. Lonn, *Foreigners in the Confederacy* (Chapel Hill: University of North Carolina, 1940), 208.

3. Lincoln quoted in J. McPherson, *Battle Cry of Freedom* (New York: Oxford University, 1988), 274.

4. Bowen and Weed quoted in Burton, *Melting Pot Soldiers*, 113.

5. Corcoran in O'Flaherty, *69th Regiment*, 229.

6. M. Daly, *Diary of a Union Lady, 1861–1865*, by H.E. Hammond (New York: Funk and Wagnalls, 1962), 15.

7. Newspaper quoted in B. I. Wiley, *The Life of Billy Yank* (Baton Rouge: Louisiana State University, 1952), 18.

8. Ibid, 31.

9. Departure of Washington Artillery in B. I. Wiley, *The Life of Johnny Reb* (Baton Rouge: Louisiana State University, 1943), 22.

10. Departure of the 69th described in *Irish American*, May 4, 1861; Conyngham, *Campaigns*, 12; and Lyons, *Meagher*, 77–78.

11. Captain James Butler quoted in C-M Garcia, "The 'Fighting' 69th New York State Militia at Bull Run," in Seagrave, ed., *Irish Brigade*, 38.

12. Figures for numbers of Irish who served in the Civil War from C. Wittke, *The Irish in America* (New York: Russell & Russell, 1956), 135–136. For examples of predominantly Irish regiments see E. Lonn, *Foreigners in the Union Army and Navy* (Baton Rouge: Louisiana State University, 1951), 672–674.

13. Description of Irish in C. Wittke, *We Who Built America* (Cleveland: Western Reserve University, 1940), 133.

14. A. Nevins and M. Thomas, eds. *The Diary of George Templeton Strong*, Vol. 2 (New York: Macmillan, 1952), 348.

15. Immigrant letter quoted in K. Miller, *Emigrants and Exiles: Ireland and the Irish Exodus to North America* (New York: Oxford University, 1985), 326.

16. Diarist and newspaper quoted in W. Shannon, *The American Irish* (New York: Macmillan, 1963), 29.

17. Description of Irish itinerant laborers by Thomas D'Arcy McGee quoted in Wittke, *Irish in America*, 26.

18. Immigration figures, and quote by W. F. Adams quoted in Wittke, *We Who Built America*, 130–31.

19. Descriptions of immigrant Irish in Miller, *Emigrants and Exiles*, 326, and Wittke, *We Who Built America*, 40, 43.

20. Shannon, *American Irish*, 47.

21. Farmer quoted in Wittke, *We Who Built America*, 147–148.

22. J. F. Maguire, *The Irish in America* (New York: Arno, 1968 reprint), 251.

23. Health commissioner quoted in H. R. Diner, "'The Most Irish City in the Union.' The Era of the Great Migration, 1844–1877," in R. H.

Bayor and T.J. Meagher, eds. *The New York Irish* (Baltimore: Johns Hopkins University, 1996), 99.

24. Foster quoted in A. Cook, *The Armies of the Streets: The New York City Draft Riots of 1863.* (Lexington: University Press of Kentucky, 1974), 10.

25. Health inspector and details of living conditions in A. P. Man, "The Irish in New York in the early eighteen sixties." *Irish Historical Studies* 7, no. 26 (September 1950), 92.

26. *Irish News* quoted in Miller, *Immigrant and Exiles*, 326.

27. Archbishop Hughes quoted in K. Mulroy, "Wearing of the Blue: The Irish in the U.S. Army, 1776–1876," in, J. Langellier, ed., *Miles Keogh* (New York: Upton, 1991), 34.

28. Formed as secret societies, membership was restricted to native-born Protestants, and these were pledged to vote for no one except other native-born Protestants for public office. If asked by outsiders about the society, members were to respond, "I know nothing." Hence the name. McPherson, *Battle Cry of Freedom*, 135.

29. Description of Know-Nothingism in M. Holt, "The Politics of Impatience: The Origins of Know-Nothingism." *Journal of American History*, 60, September 1973, 329.

30. Incident with Cardinal Bedini told in McPherson, *Battle Cry of Freedom*, 132–133.

31. Russell in M. Crawford, ed., *William Howard Russell's Civil War: Private Diary and Letters 1861–1862* (Athens; University of Georgia, 1992), 7, 10.

32. Lincoln quoted in M. Neely Jr., *The Last Best Hope of Earth: Abraham Lincoln and the Promise of America* (Massachusetts: Harvard University, 1993), 52–54.

33. "Western wilds" quote in Holt, "The Politics of Impatience," 324.

34. R. M. Miller, "Catholic Religion, Irish Ethnicity, and the Civil War," in R. Miller, H. Stoute and C. Wilson, eds., *Religion and the American Civil War* (New York: Oxford University, 1999), 263.

35. *New York Tribune* quoted in Wittke, *Irish in America*, 125.

36. Douglass quoted in Man, "The Irish in New York," 97–98.

37. B. Catton, *Never Call Retreat* (New York: Doubleday, 1965), 216.

38. Douglass quoted in Man, "The Irish in New York," 95.

39. Slave quoted in Wittke, *Irish in America*, 125.

40. Chargehand in Crawford, *Russell's Civil War*, 71.

41. Description of Irish workers and unloading of cotton in Lonn, *Foreigners in the Confederacy*, 28.

42. Mike Walsh quoted in Shannon, *American Irish*, 52–53.

43. *Irish American*, January 21, 1860.

Chapter 2—"You Are All Green Alike"

1. Camp at Georgetown in Jones, *Irish Brigade*, 52.

2. Description of Corcoran in *Boston Pilot*, January 4, 1862.

3. Meagher's advertisement quoted in Athearn, *Meagher*, 93. The name "Zouave" was given to any unit which attempted to adopt the colorful dress and precision drill of the French Zouaves, so named as they were originally composed of Algerians, the word Zouave originally being based on the name of an Algerian tribe. Their uniforms were often of a mixed variety but could include red or blue baggy pants, and short-waisted tasseled jackets.

4. *Irish American*, May 18, 1861.

5. For officer's comment, see *War of the Rebellion: A Compilation of the Official Records of the Union and Confederate Armies* (hereafter *OR*; all quotes from Series 1 unless otherwise indicated), 128 vols. (Washington, D.C.: Government Printing Office, 1880–1902), Vol. 2, 653.

6. Letter in *Irish American*, June 29, 1861.

7. "Northern shovelry" quotation from L. Lewis, *Sherman: Fighting Prophet* (New York: Harcourt Brace, 1932), 168.

8. Irate letter in *Irish American*, June 22, 1861. O'Flaherty writes that the fort itself was originally named Fort Seward, in honor of the New York politician who was currently the state secretary, but quotes another source claiming that Colonel Hunter, the brigade commander, "promptly renamed it Fort Corcoran, in tribute to the great work of building it in so short a time." O'Flaherty, *69th Regiment*, 255–256.

9. Incident over pay described in Jones, *Irish Brigade*, 54–55.

10. Mustering out incident in W. T. Sherman, *Memoirs of General William Tecumseh Sherman By Himself* (Bloomington: Indiana University, 1957 reprint), 180; and O'Flaherty, *69th Regiment*, 269–70.

11. Preparations of men for march in T.F. Meagher, *The Last Days of the 69th in Virginia* (New York: Irish American, 1861), 4. This highly melodramatic account was printed serially in the *Irish American* during August 1861. See also O'Flaherty, *69th Regiment*, 261–2.

12. Soldier quoted in M. H. MacNamara, *The Irish Ninth in Bivouac and Battle* (Boston: Lee and Shepherd, 1867), 192.

13. Sherman in Sherman, *Memoirs*, 180.

14. Incident over ambulance told in Lewis, *Sherman*, 172. It clearly rankled the Irishmen so badly that it is also referred to in the official report of the 69th made after the battle by Captain Kelly following Corcoran's capture. *OR*, Vol. 2, 371–72.

15. Lincoln quoted in T. Harry Williams, *Lincoln and His Generals* (New York: Alfred Knopf, 1952), 21.

16. Patterson was born in Tyrone in 1792, the son of a rebel whose family had been forced to emigrate to Pennsylvania after the rebellion of 1798; this was apparently the first time in warfare that a railroad had been used to shift troops from one theater to another. Description of Patterson's "maneuver" in McPherson, *Battle Cry of Freedom*, 339.

17. Although the structure of the Federal army would frequently change during the course of the war, the basic building block remained the company, commanded by a captain or lieutenant, and consisting of around 100 men; companies were then organized into regiments, nominally consisting of 1,000 men, and commanded by colonels; a number of regiments would then combined to form brigades, commanded by brigadier generals; brigades would be combined to form divisions, a number of which might then form an army corps.

18. Soldier quoted in W. C. Davis, *Battle at Bull Run* (Baton Rouge: Louisiana State University, 1977), 92.

19. Sherman, *Memoirs*, 186.

20. Davis, *Bull Run*, 96.

21. Soldiers' remarks regarding Sherman quoted in Lewis, *Sherman*, 170.

22. For skirmish at Blackburn's Ford see ibid.

23. Davis, *Bull Run*, 124.

24. Description of 69th the night before Bull Run in Lewis, *Sherman*, 172; and Meagher, *Last Days of the 69th*.

25. Davis, *Bull Run*, 158.

Chapter 3 — The Fighting 69th

1. Start of Union advance described in S. Foote, *The Civil War: A Narrative*, 3 vols. (London: Bodley Head, reprint, 1991), 1, 75. Ironically, Beauregard had planned to attack McDowell that very morning, and there was much confusion in the initial changeover from the orders to attack across Bull Run to the sudden change to double quick to the north.

2. Sherman's report in *OR*, Vol. 2, 369.

3. For officer in 4th Alabama see Davis, *Bull Run*, 185–187.

4. Sherman's report in *OR*, Vol. 2, 369.

5. Burnside's report, *OR*, Vol. 2, 398.

6. McDowell in Davis, *Bull Run*, 187.

7. Description of Jackson in H. Kyd Douglas, *I Rode with Stonewall* (Chapel Hill: University of North Carolina, 1940), 10.

8. Most accounts carry a version of the "stonewall" story. See e.g. Davis, *Bull Run*, 196–97, McPherson, *Battle Cry of Freedom*, 342, Kyd Douglas, *Stonewall*, 10. For an account of the less-flattering interpretation of Bee's remarks, see, D. S. Freeman, *Lee's Lieutenants: A Study in Command*, 3 vols. (New York: Charles Scribner's Sons, 1943–44), 1, 733–34.

9. The superior Confederate artillery fire which they were able to bring to bear on the attacking Union forces was a significant factor in turning the tide of battle. Meagher's not entirely objective view was that, "We beat their men — their batteries beat us." *The Last Days of the 69th*. Sherman's brigade originally had its own battery attached to it, but was unable to find a suitable crossing over Bull Run near the Stone Bridge where the infantry had crossed.

10. Criticism of handling of Union infantry in G. F. R. Henderson, *Stonewall Jackson and the American Civil War* (New York: Grosset and Dunlap, 1943), 112.

11. "Medieval moment" described in Lewis, *Sherman*, 176.

12. Incident with flag bearer described in Conyngham, *Campaigns*, 21.

13. Soldier's description in *Irish American*, August 8, 1861.

14. Colonel Porter's report in *OR*, Vol. 2, 384.

15. Kelly's report in *OR*, Vol. 2, 371.

16. Description of charge in Conyngham, *Campaigns*, 19.

17. Jackson quoted in Henderson, *Stonewall Jackson*, 114.

18. Retreat of Union troops in Foote, *Civil War*, I, 80–81.

19. Kelly's report *OR*, Vol. 2, 371.

20. Sherman's report in *OR*, Vol. 2, 370.

21. For capture of Corcoran see report of Colonel Radford, 13th Virginia Cavalry in *OR*, Vol. 2, 522.

22. Rorty's letter in *Irish American*, October 26, 1861.

23. Meagher's case for the defense was essentially *The Last Days of the 69th*.

24. Russell quoted in Athearn, *Meagher*, 97.

25. Villiard quoted in R. Beatie, *Army of the Potomac. Birth of Command. November 1860-September 1861.* (Cambridge, MA: Da Capo, 2002), 257. "Villiard," as described by Burton in his *Melting Pot Soldiers*, "like many other German immigrants, regarded the soldiers of the New York Irish regiments as riffraff," 120.

26. Daly, *Diary of a Union Lady*, 100.

27. Quotes from Confederates in Conyngham, *Campaigns*, 22.

28. Soldier in *Irish American*, August 8, 1861.

29. Sherman in *Memoirs*, 188.

30. Highlanders historian quoted in Athearn, *Meagher*, 98.

31. Story of captain told in Sherman, *Memoirs*, 190. "Of course I didn't know anything about it," Lincoln afterward told Sherman, "but I thought you knew your own business best." Ibid., 191.

32. Return of 69th described in Lyons, *Meagher*, 78.

Chapter 4 — Standing by the Union

1. Remark about Irish antipathy toward blacks quoted in Man, *Irish Historical Studies*, 106.

2. Letter to Jefferson Davis in OR, Series 4, Vol. 3, 4.

3. *Irish American*, December 22, 1860.

4. Mulholland, *116th Regiment*, 4.

5. Rorty quoted in Dungan, *Distant Drums: Irish Soldiers in Foreign Armies* (Belfast: Appletree, 1993), 20.

6. *Boston Pilot* quoted in F. Walsh, "The Boston *Pilot* Reports the Civil War." *Historical Journal of Massachusetts*, June 1981, no. 9, 7. The image of northern Irish enlisting in the Union army should be balanced by a similar phenomenon of southern Irish enlisting with equal fervor in the Confederate army. John Mitchell, like Meagher, had been a Young Irelander, and had three sons who fought for the Confederacy. One was killed in Fort Sumter in 1864, reportedly professing that "I die willingly for South Carolina, but oh! That it had been for Ireland." Another son was killed at Gettysburg, while the third lost an arm in one of the battles near Richmond. Lonn, *Foreigners in the Confederacy*, 151.

7. Maguire, *Irish in America*, 552.

8. Motivation of immigrant groups in Burton, "Title Deed to America: Union Ethnic regiments in the Civil War." *Proceedings of the American Philosophical Society* 124 (December 1980), 462.

9. Private Casey in Burton, *Melting Pot Soldiers*, 69.

10. Walsh, "Boston *Pilot*," 5.

11. Newspapers in Man, "Irish in New York," 106.

12. Archbishop Hughes in Mulroy, *Myles Keogh*, 36.

13. Father Creedon in Lonn, *Foreigners in the Union Army and Navy*, 550.

14. Hernon, *Celts, Catholics and Copperheads*, 8.

15. *Irish American*, June 15, 1861.

16. War correspondent in B. Brown, "The Blue, The Gray and the Green." *Army*, March 1980, 38.

17. Corcoran in Burton, *Melting Pot Soldiers*, 53. This belief was nearly borne out in November 1861 with the Trent affair when a Union ship stopped a Royal Mail steamer and removed two Confederate commissioners bound for Europe. Threats were exchanged but the crisis ended when Lincoln quietly authorized the return of the commissioners. See McPherson, *Battle Cry of Freedom*, 389–91.

18. Frenchman quoted in Burton, *Melting Pot Soldiers*, 55.

19. Economic background given in Man, "Irish in New York," 106.

20. Immigrants letters in Miller, *Emigrants and Exiles*, 359.

21. *New York Herald* in Man, "Irish in New York," 105–6. An interesting piece of data unearthed by Lawrence Kohl in a survey of 500 Irish Brigade enlistment records from New York indicated that "the great majority of the men of the brigade were married, older men who had already taken out American citizenship." If, according to Kohl, "These were hardly the type who would have been most likely to have rushed back to Ireland to fight against the British," what exactly was the motivation for the majority of men who joined the brigade and how this would have changed over time? Kohl in Bilby, *Remember Fontenoy!* 29.

22. Quote regarding tour of South in S. P. Bellor, *Never Were Men So Brave. The Irish Brigade during the Civil War* (New York: Margaret K. McElderry, 1998), 20.

23. Cavanagh, *Meagher*, 368–369.

24. O'Flaherty, *69th Regiment*, 29.

25. Biographical details of Meagher from Athearn, *Meagher*. The accounts written by his fellow contemporaries involved with the Irish Brigade, such as Cavanagh, Lyons and Conyngham — the former two in particular who were his friends and supporters — are unquestioningly loyal and suitably gushing. The only full-length biography is that by Athearn and while it is at least skeptical, it does not delve too deeply into the controversies surrounding his time with the Irish Brigade other than reporting them. Most of the standard historical accounts of or about the war such as Catton and Lonn are almost as unquestioningly admiring as the most filiopiestic accounts. The only sustained criticism is the more recent study of ethnic regiments by Burton, who has little time for Meagher or indeed any of the other "professional ethnic" officers as he describes them, from other nationalities.

26. "Professional ethnic" in Burton, "Title Deed," 458. Burton expands on this issue in his subsequent *Melting Pot Soldiers*.

27. Conyngham, *Campaigns*, iii.

28. Maguire, *Irish in America*, 546

29. Kohl, ed., *Irish Green and Union Blue*, 100–101.

30. Description of recruiting office in Lyons, *Memoirs*, 86.

Chapter 5 — Commissioning a Brigade

1. *Tipperary Advocate* and the *Nation* in Hernon, *Celts, Catholics and Copperheads*, 14–15.
2. Soldier's letter quoted in Lonn, *Foreigners in the Union Army and Navy*, 401.
3. *The Phoenix* in O'Flaherty, *69th Regiment*, 232. Some accounts claim that the prediction of *The Phoenix* was realized at Bull Run with the 69th encountering the Louisiana Zouaves, a Confederate regiment which contained a good many Irish longshoremen from New Orleans, soon after crossing the river to enter the fight. Although the Zouaves were part of the Confederate force on Henry House Hill later in the day, it was the 4th Alabama Regiment which the 69th first engaged.
4. Meagher in Cavanagh, *Meagher*, 371.
5. Comment regarding recruitment in Catton, *Mr. Lincoln's Army* (New York: Doubleday, 1951), 185.
6. Details of initial outline of brigade in Garland, "The Formation of Meagher's Irish Brigade," *Irish Sword*, 1968, 162.
7. Daly, *Diary of a Union Lady*, 93,105.
8. "Acting brigadier" Meagher in Athearn, *Meagher*, 106.
9. Corcoran remained in prison for almost a year before returning to recruit the Irish Legion. While in prison he had refused parole, which at that time meant that he would be released on condition that he would not bear arms again. He was also held as a hostage to guarantee the safety of some captured Confederate privateers who had been sentenced to death as pirates. It was later held that the southern privateers were legitimate men-of-war rather than pirates. Details of Corcoran's imprisonment in Burton, *Melting Pot Soldiers*, 115, and Lonn, *Foreigners in the Union Army and Navy*, 200–01.
10. Description of Meagher in Burton, *Melting Pot Soldiers*, 119.
11. For the return of the 69th Militia see O'Flaherty, *69th Regiment*, 300–1.
12. Motion quoted in Lonn, *Foreigners in the Union Army and Navy*, 119–20.
13. Exchange between Meagher and Bagley in Athearn, *Meagher*, 104.
14. Meagher's remarks in Daly, *Diary of a Union Lady*, 63.
15. Nugent and Meagher in Lonn, *Foreigners in the Union Army and Navy*, 120.
16. Captain Lyons in Lyons, *Meagher*, 85.
17. Other details of "maneuverings" in Athearn, *Meagher*, 99–104. Meagher's offer to Cameron in *OR*, Series 3, Vol. 1, 491. Captain Meagher's letter to Cameron, secretary of war, is extraordinarily brusque. "Authorize positively to organize an Irish Brigade of 5,000," he demands of the minister, and continues, "Please reply at once by telegraph, afterward by official letter. Expedition in the matter is of vital importance."
18. Details of festival in Jones Wood in *Irish American*, September 7, 1861.
19. Meagher's speech in Boston reproduced in Lyons, *Meagher*, 91–121. As regards the fear that Irish would end up killing Irish, Meagher dismissed this as "foolish cant ... it is not the first time they have done so ... there is nothing at all new in that feature of the case."
20. For designations of regiments see Garland, *Irish Sword*, 162–5.
21. Lorenzo Thomas to Meagher in *OR*, Series 3, Vol. 1, 895.
22. Description on 88th in Lonn, *Foreigners in the Union Army and Navy*, 120.
23. The account of the formation of the Boston and Philadelphia regiments is taken from Burton, *Melting Pot Soldiers*, 127–131 and *passim*. Also by the same author, "Irish Regiments in the Union Army: The Massachusetts Experience." *Historical Journal of Massachusetts*, June 11, 1983, 104 -19.
24. Curtin to Cameron in *OR*, Series 3, Vol. 1, 526–7.
25. Sympathizer in *OR*, Series 4, Vol. 3, 5.
26. For Pennsylvania regiment see Mulholland, *116th Regiment*, 7.
27. Corcoran was released under the system of exchange, whereby a Confederate prisoner of equivalent rank was released from a Federal prison.
28. Numbers in 116th in *OR*, Series 3, Vol. 3, 759.
29. "Alma mater" in Conyngham, *Campaigns*, 28.
30. Life at Fort Schuyler in *Irish American*, November 16 and 19, 1861, and Lyons, *Meagher*, 122–23.
31. Exchange between Cameron and Meagher in Athearn, *Meagher*, 107.
32. Details of conflicts between Archbishop Hughes and Meagher in O'Flaherty, *69th Regiment*, 105, 123. Hughes' opinion on ethnic regiments in Burton, *Melting Pot Soldiers*, 120.
33. Presentation of flags in Conyngham, *Campaigns*, 29–33.
34. *New York Daily Tribune* and departure of regiments in Athearn, *Meagher*, 108.

Chapter 6 — Frolics and Frustrations

1. Members of the brigade and life in camp described in Jones, *Irish Brigade*, 75, and Conyngham, *Campaigns*, 36.

Notes — Chapter 7

2. Fondness of Irish for drink in Wiley, *The Life of Billy Yank*, 309. With both author and subjects showing admirable consistency, Wiley wrote of the Irish soldiers in the Confederate rank and file that "they were rough, quarrelsome, plunderous and impervious to discipline." Wiley, *The Life of Johnny Reb*, 324.

3. Chaplain quoted in Wittke, *The Irish in America*, 137. The regiment was the 37th New York.

4. Fitz-John Porter quoted in Burton, *Melting Pot Soldiers*, 153. One of the most amusing of the many stories regarding the Irish and drink concerns a reported incident in the Confederate army. An officer had invited a guest into his tent for a drink of whiskey from a barrel that he stored in a corner. On finding the barrel mysteriously empty, a brief investigation revealed a hole drilled into the said barrel from the outside of the tent and a long straw lying on the ground nearby. A short distance away, two Irish companies were said to be literally rolling drunk on the ground. Brown, "The Blue, The Gray and the Green." *Army*, March 1980, 41.

5. Description of Meagher in William C. Davis, *The American Civil War* (London: Salamander, 1995), 302.

6. O'Brien, ed., *McCarter*, 16.

7. *The Times* quoted in Bellor, *Never Were Men So Brave*, 14.

8. Corby, *Memoirs of Chaplain Life*, 75.

9. Mulholland, *116th Regiment*, 31–33. For accounts of this ghoulish "feast" see Ch. 14.

10. Barnard, *Ryan*, 53.

11. Details of chaplains in Lonn, *Foreigners in the Union Army and Navy*, 312. Father Dillon in Corby, *Memoirs of Chaplain Life*, 286–92. Other descriptions were provided by Colonel Denis Burke for an article in the *New York Tablet*, which is reproduced in Corby, op. cit. 299–303. Archbishop Hughes had relieved a Father Thomas H. Mooney from duty with the 69th New York in 1862, "after learning that the militant Mooney had baptized with holy water the one cannon mounted in Fort Corcoran and had strongly urged the men to flail the enemy." Miller, "Catholic Religion," 269.

12. "Parish of army" in Jones, *Irish Brigade*, 81.

13. Maria Daly in Daly, *Diary of a Union Lady*, 75.

14. Mass in Conyngham, *Campaigns*. Letter to Judge Daly in Athearn, *Meagher*, 108–109.

15. Meagher taking command described in *Irish American*, February 22, 1862.

16. Corby, *Memoirs of Chaplain Life*, 23.

17. McClellan described in Williams, *Lincoln and his Generals*, 26–7.

18. Senator Ben Wade quoted in Catton, *Terrible Swift Sword* (New York: Doubleday, 1963), 176–77.

19. Seward in Catton, *Mr. Lincoln's Army*, 92–93.

20. Confederate withdrawal in Foote, *Civil War*, 1, 264.

21. Weather described in Corby, *Memoirs of Chaplain Life*, 32.

22. Description of men in ranks in Conyngham, *Campaigns*, 52.

23. Meagher in Lyons, *Meagher*, 128.

24. "Dead men's bones" in Corby, *Memoirs of Chaplain Life*, 32, and McDowell in Foote, *Civil War*, 1, 265.

25. Journey to and departure of Irish Brigade from Alexandria in Conyngham, *Campaigns*, 52, 56.

Chapter 7 — Fort Monroe to Fair Oaks

1. Details of Richardson and Sumner in F. A. Walker, *History of the Second Army Corps in the Army of the Potomac* (New York: Charles Scribner's Sons, 1886), 5, 9–11.

2. Story about Richardson in Conyngham, *Campaigns*, 54.

3. Disembarkation at Fort Monroe, ibid., 57.

4. McClellan to wife in Sears, *The Young Napoleon*, 180.

5. Johnston quoted in Sears, *To The Gates of Richmond: The Peninsula Campaign* (New York: Ticknor and Fields, 1992), 65.

6. The brigade employed outside Yorktown in *OR*, Vol. 11, 332, and Jones, *Irish Brigade*, 85–86.

7. Details of camp and chapel in Corby, *Memoirs of Chaplain Life*, 40.

8. Discussion of diet and disease in the army in McPherson, *Battle Cry of Freedom*, 485–488.

9. Death of Patrick Casey in Conyngham, *Campaigns*, 63.

10. Soldier's description of march to Yorktown in letter to *Boston Pilot*, May 9, 1862.

11. Reaction of Meagher described in Athearn, *Meagher*, 110–11.

12. Changing camp to Tyler's Farm described in Conyngham, *Campaigns*, 64–67, and Meagher's report in *OR*, Vol. 11, 775.

13. For a description of the races, see Mulholland, "The Irish Brigade in the War for the Union," published in Corby, *Memoirs of Chaplain Life*, 350–391, and Conyngham, *Campaigns*, 73.

14. Johnston, fearing that the three Federal corps north of the river were about to receive reinforcements from Washington under Irwin McDowell, had originally intended to attack these. When he received word that McDowell had been recalled, he switched tactics to attack the lesser numbers south of the river. McDowell had been recalled because of the actions of Stonewall Jackson, one of the

heroes of Bull Run. Jackson and his command were about to march and fight their way into legend as well as military textbooks, with the famous Shenandoah Valley campaign, during which they outmarched and outfought three chasing Federal armies, one of which was led by General James Shields.

15. Battle characterized in Foote, *Civil War*, 1, 445.

16. There is a good description of the battle in H. Bridges, *Lee's Maverick General: Daniel Harvey Hill* (New York: McGraw-Hill, 1961), 37–58 and Sears, *To the Gates of Richmond*, 117–145.

17. Sumner described by Sears, *To the Gates of Richmond*, 129.

18. Corby, *Memoirs of Chaplain Life*, 61.

19. Richardson's report in *OR*, Vol. 11, 764.

20. Description of march to Fair Oaks in Corby, *Memoirs of Chaplain Life*, 61, and Conyngham, *Campaigns*, 72.

21. Description of nighttime and the scene the following morning in Meagher's report, *OR*, Vol. 11, 786, and Lyons, *Meagher*, 134–5.

22. Sumner's talk to Irish Brigade in Meagher's report, *OR*, Vol. 11, 776-7. Conyngham's version of the exchange can be found in his *Campaigns*, 154 — "Boys, I am your general. I know the Irish Brigade will not retreat. I stake my position on you." "We've never run yet and we're not going to do it now," came the reply from a Sergeant McCabe. "I know it, I know it," replied Sumner, riding off. Corby has a slightly different version, see *Memoirs of Chaplain Life*, 359.

23. Nugent's report in *OR*, Vol. 11, 780.

24. Kelly's report, ibid. 781.

25. Conyngham, *Campaigns*, 76. One of the reasons why the fire of the brigade was often "so telling" was the type of muskets which they used. Most of the army was equipped with the relatively new rifled musket, which fired a hollow-based bullet that could kill at half a mile and was highly accurate up to 250 yards. These had, in effect, made the traditional bayonet charge obsolete as, armed with rifled muskets, the attackers could rarely get near enough to use a bayonet. The Irish Brigade, however, at Meagher's insistence, were equipped with "old-fashioned" smoothbore muskets. These were known as "buck and balls," and fired a cartridge that contained a ball and three buckshot. Its effect at close range was not dissimilar to that of a shotgun, but its extreme range was about 200 yards and "accuracy was almost nil at any range." See W. Goble, "Irish Brigade Ordnance at Antietam," in Bilby and O'Neill, *My Sons Were Faithful*, 61–66, and Catton, *Mr. Lincoln's Army*, 186–8.

26. Joel Cook, a reporter for the *Philadelphia Inquirer* in 1862, quoted in C. Dowdey, *The Seven Days: The Emergence of Lee* (Boston: Little Brown, 1964), 6.

27. Soldier's letter in *Irish American*, June 14, 1862.

28. Casualties given in R. U. Johnson and C. C. Buel, eds., *Battles and Leaders of the Civil War. Vol. 3, The Struggle Intensifies* (New York: Century, 1887–88), 218.

29. Conyngham, *Campaigns*, 77.

30. Criticism of Meagher in O'Grady, *Clear the Confederate Way!* 127.

31. Meagher's report in *OR*, Vol. 11, 778. Despite Meagher's own admission of his lack of knowledge of the actions of the 88th and 69th at Fair Oaks, Cornish describes how "Meagher personally brought the 88th up to the firing line and was indefatigable in riding along the line cheering his men on." Cornish, "An Irish Republican Abroad," 151.

32. Ibid.

33. Nugent's and Kelly's reports, ibid., 780, 781.

34. W. Holden, W. Ross and E. Slomba, eds., *Stand Firm and Fire Low: The Civil War Writings of Colonel Edward E Cross* (New Hampshire: University of New Hampshire, 2002), 113.

35. Ibid., 29.

36. French's report in *OR*, Vol. 11, 783.

37. Brooke quoted in O'Grady, *Clear the Confederate Way!* 318.

38. Visit of General Prim described in Lyons, *Meagher*, 149–50.

Chapter 8 — "Column of Generous Friends"

1. Aftermath of battle of Fair Oaks in Sears, *To The Gates of Richmond*, 148, and Lyons, *Meagher*, 145–6.

2. A. P. Hill's attack at Mechanicsville described in J. Robertson Jr., *General A. P. Hill: The Story of a Confederate Warrior* (New York: Random House, 1987), 67–74.

3. Confederate officer in Johnson and Buel, *Battles and Leaders*, 2, 352.

4. Soldier of 9th Massachusetts quoted in Sears, *To The Gates of Richmond*, 230.

5. Porter's dispatches in ibid., 233.

6. Richardson's report in *OR*, Vol. 13, 54.

7. Meagher's report in ibid., 70–71.

8. French's report in ibid., 75–6.

9. French observer quoted by Mulholland in Corby, *Memoirs of Chaplain Life*, 365.

10. Arrival of French and Meagher described in Colonel Warren's report in *OR*, Vol. 13, 379.

11. "Generous friends" in report of Brigadier General George McCall, in ibid., 388.

12. Finish of action described in Lyons, *Meagher*, 156.

Notes — Chapter 9

13. Porter's report in *OR*, Vol. 13, 226.
14. Confederate quoted in Athearn, *Meagher*, 111–12.
15. McClellan's report in *OR*, Vol. 13, 57.
16. 29th Massachusetts described in Jones, *Irish Brigade*, 90.
17. Reporter quoted in J. McCormack, "Never Were Men So Brave," *Civil War Times Illustrated*, April 1969, 36.
18. Officer describing "Yankee warfare" in Catton, *Glory Road*, 38.
19. Dr. Ellis in Conyngham, *Campaigns*, 77.
20. Correspondent quoted in Boyle, *Mad Fellows*, 15.
21. French's report in *OR*, Vol. 13, 76.
22. Description of Meagher is from Walker, *Second Army Corps*, 62.
23. Meagher's demeanor at Gaines Mill and quote from soldier in Sears, *To the Gates of Richmond*, 248.
24. There is no record of any charges against Meagher and he himself refers fleetingly to the incident in his report. See *OR*, Vol. 13, 71. Boyle has suggested that Meagher had fouled up the movement of some supply trains and Richardson got angry enough to place him under arrest. Boyle, *Mad Fellows*, 136.

Chapter 9 — To Malvern Hill

1. Position of Irish Brigade in French's report, *OR*, Vol. 11, 76.
2. D. H. Hill's account can be found in Johnson and Buel, *Battles and Leaders*, 2, 358. In the same source there is also a subsequent letter written by William Osborne of the 29th Massachusetts who was one of the soldiers Hill passed that night, and who remembered the incident. "We should all have esteemed it a great honor if we had made your [Hill's] acquaintance that night," wrote Osborne.
3. Incident with flag and matches described in Athearn, *Meagher*, 112.
4. McClellan's meeting with subordinates in Catton, *Mr. Lincoln's Army*, 135–6.
5. Loss of sermons in Corby, *Memoirs of Chaplain Life*, 87.
6. For Franklin's and Burns' accounts of the action around Savage Station, see Johnson and Buel, *Battles and Leaders*, 2, 372–74. Heintzelman's later explanation for withdrawing was that, "The whole space near Savage Station was crowded with troops — more than I supposed could be brought into action judiciously." So, without a word to his colleagues, he left. Sumner was so disgusted with Heintzelman's actions that he subsequently refused to speak to him. *Battles and Leaders*, 2, 371n.
7. Franklin in ibid. 378–9.
8. Irish Brigade at White Oak Swamp described by Lieutenant Turner in Conyngham, *Campaigns*, 99–100. "Hell seemed" in T. L. Livermore, *Days and Events, 1860–1865*. (Boston: Houghton Mifflin, 1920), 86.
9. Confederate soldier quoted in Sears, *To the Gates of Richmond*, 288.
10. Description of Meagher at White Oak Swamp in Athearn, *Meagher*, 112–13.
11. Meagher's offer to go for ammunition in report of Lieutenant Rufus King, *OR*, Vol. 11, 59.
12. March to Glendale in Livermore, *Days and Events*, 91.
13. Officer quoted in Conyngham, *Campaigns*, 207.
14. Sumner quoted by Mulholland in Corby, *Memoirs of Chaplain Life*, 367.
15. Arrival of Irish Brigade described by Josiah Sypher in Boyle, *Mad Fellows*, 142.
16. Private A. W. Stillwell in Sears, *To the Gates of Richmond*, 309.
17. Arrival at Malvern Hill in Livermore, *Days and Events*, 94.
18. D. H. Hill in Bridges, *Lee's Maverick General*, 77.
19. Charge described in Catton, *Terrible Swift Sword*, 320.
20. D. H. Hill in Johnson and Buel, *Battles and Leaders*, 2, 393, 394.
21. Hunt in Sears, *To the Gates of Richmond*, 330.
22. Heintzelman quoted by Porter in Johnson and Buel, *Battles and Leaders*, 2, 416.
23. Story of Captain O'Donoghue by Mulholland in Corby, *Memoirs of Chaplain Life*, 368.
24. Richard Auchmuty quoted in H. S. Commager, *The Blue and the Gray* (Indianapolis: Bobbs Merrill, 1950), 147.
25. Porter's account in Johnson and Buel, *Battles and Leaders*, 2, 421–427.
26. Description of Walker in Boyle, *Mad Fellows*, 155.
27. Walker, *Second Army Corps*, 83.
28. Porter in Johnson and Buel, *Battles and Leaders*, 2, 421.
29. Description of Irish Brigade at Malvern Hill in Conyngham, *Campaigns*, 104–5, and Mulholland in Corby, *Memoirs of Chaplain Life*, 368–70.
30. Remark of Confederate officer in Corby, *Memoirs of Chaplain Life*, 369.
31. Porter in Johnson and Buel, *Battles and Leaders*, 2, 421.
32. Paul Semmes in *OR*, Vol. 11, 724.
33. Use of guns explained to Sumner in Lonn, *Foreigners in the Union Army and Navy*, 503. Corby has this exchange taking place after Fair Oaks although Malvern Hill was the more likely scene. Corby, *Memoirs of Chaplain Life*, 361.

34. Confederate officer quoted in Sears, *To the Gates of Richmond*, 334.
35. Scene the morning after described in Catton, *Mr. Lincoln's Army*, 140.
36. Jubal Early quoted in Dowdey, *Seven Days*, 348.
37. Sergeant Haggerty in Meagher's report, *OR*, Vol. 11, 75.
38. Donovan's account in Daly, *Diary of a Union Lady*, 175.
39. Couch and Kearny quoted after the battle in Sears, *To the Gates of Richmond*, 336, 338.
40. Final description of battlefield in ibid., 335.

Chapter 10— Rebels Resurgent

1. The description of the incident with Ouellet is taken from Corby, *Memoirs of Chaplain Life*, 302-3.
2. The account of the incident with Lieutenant Colonel Fowler and Meagher is told by Major John Dwyer of the 63rd, and reproduced in ibid., 287-90. Meagher's version is in *OR*, Vol. 11, 73-4.
3. Remarks quoted in Conyngham, *Campaigns*, 102.
4. Sumner's remark in Lonn, *Foreigners in the Union Army and Navy*, 503.
5. Description of brigade and casualties in Jones, *Irish Brigade*, 93, 101.
6. Adjutant general in *OR*, Vol. 14, 325.
7. Governor Andrew in Catton, *Terrible Swift Sword*, 324.
8. *Galway Vindicator*, quoted in *Boston Pilot*, June 14, 1862.
9. *Irish American*, July 19, 1862.
10. Account of meeting in *Irish American*, August 2, 1862.
11. *Boston Pilot*, August 17, 1986.
12. Soldier's letter quoted in C. O'Danachair, ed., "A Soldier's letters home, 1863-74," *Irish Sword* 3. Summer 1957, 57.
13. Meagher in Jones, *Irish Brigade*.
14. Letters of Lieutenant Andrew Birmingham of the 69th in Jones, *Irish Brigade*, 99-100, 95-96.
15. Federal officers quoted in Catton, *Terrible Swift Sword*, 329.
16. Meagher quoted in Athearn, *Meagher*, 115; *Boston Pilot*, August 16, 1862; and *Irish American*, September 20, 1862. The only person able to raise substantial numbers of Irish for new regiments was Corcoran, who was released that August from prison after his capture at Bull Run. His reputation untarnished, he toured the North to great acclaim and managed to recruit four new regiments who became known as "Corcoran's Irish Legion," which included a large number of his fellow Fenians who had not previously signed up, on Corcoran's own advice. The quality of these new recruits was questionable, with ambitious young officers, largely American, employing "whiskey and money" as the principal attractions to enlist new recruits. In one regiment, the 155th New York, one enterprising officer "toured New York's jails and prisons, offering bribes to criminals to entice them into his company." Burton, *Melting Pot Soldiers*, 117.
17. The story of the Second Battle of Bull Run is wonderfully told in the first chapter of Catton, *Mr. Lincoln's Army*, 1-52. A more comprehensive account can be found in J. Hennessy, *Return to Bull Run: The Campaign and Battle of Second Manassas* (Norman: University of Oklahoma Press, 1993).
18. Description of Lee's men in Foote, *Civil War*, 2, 663.
19. Return of Irish Brigade from Peninsula in Conyngham, *Campaigns*, 135-138.
20. Return to Arlington Heights described in Corby, *Memoirs of Chaplain Life*, 110-11.
21. McClellan on Pope in Williams, *Lincoln and His Generals*, 157 and *OR*, Vol. 11, 98.
22. "Tattered flags" in Boyle, *Mad Fellows*, 177.
23. Soldier's description of Maryland in Catton, *Mr. Lincoln's Army*, 164.
24. Incident between Gossen and Richardson in Conyngham, *Campaigns*, 143.
25. "Free and easy" quote in Boyle, *Mad Fellows*, 183.
26. Irish Brigade at Frederick and advancing to Sharpsburg in Corby, *Memoirs of Chaplain Life*, 111-12.
27. Meagher in *OR*, Vol. 19, 293.
28. "Steeplechase" between Gossen and Reynolds described in R. Bailey, *Antietam, The Bloodiest Day* (New York: Time Life, 1984), 63.
29. Officer quoted in Catton, *Mr. Lincoln's Army*, 254.
30. Position of Irish Brigade described in J. Priest, *Antietam: The Soldier's Battle* (New York: Oxford University, 1989), 9.

Chapter 11— "The Longest Saddest Day"

1. Description of September 17 by Captain Henry King in Bridges, *Lee's Maverick General*, 124.
2. McClellan's instructions to Sumner in Sears, *Landscape Turned Red*, 218.
3. Description of Sumner's advance and repulse in F. W. Palfrey, *The Antietam and Fredericksburg* (New York: Charles Scribner's Sons, 1889), 84, 87.
4. Criticism of Sumner's direction of troops in Walker, *Second Army Corps*, 101.
5. Advance of French's men in Priest, *Antietam*, 139-41.

Notes — Chapter 12

6. Soldier's letter in *Irish American*, September 27, 1862.

7. Description of Sunken Road in Catton, *Mr. Lincoln's Army*, 292.

8. Confederate description of Federal advance in J. B. Gordon, *Reminiscences of the Civil War* (New York: Charles Scribner's Sons, 1904), 85.

9. Bullets in grass described in T. Galwey, *The Valiant Hours* (Harrisburg: Stackpole, 1961), 40–42.

10. *Irish American*, September 27, 1862.

11. Sergeant Hart's encounter with the unexploded shell told in Priest, *Antietam*, 9–10.

12. Soldier from 88th described in ibid., 159.

13. Meagher's report in *OR*, Vol. 19, 293. Mulholland has a slightly different version about Meagher's attention to uniform. In his version, Gosson, seeing Meagher's uniform was "all over dirt" suggested he brush it off. "Yaas," Meagher responded, "we shall all have a brush before long." Mulholland in Corby, *Memoirs of Chaplain Life*, 371.

14. Soldier's description in *Irish American*, October 11, 1862.

15. Meagher in *OR*, Vol. 19, 293.

16. Pulling down of fence described in Priest, *Antietam*, 159.

17. Soldier in 29th Massachusetts quoted in Bilby, *Remember Fontenoy!* 54–5.

18. Giving of absolution described in Corby, *Memoirs of Chaplain Life*, 112. This is the scene depicted by Don Troiani in "Sons of Erin."

19. Soldiers' descriptions in *Irish American*, October 11, 1862.

20. Fowler's report in *OR*, Vol. 19, 295.

21. McGee described in Major Cavanagh's report, ibid., 296.

22. Kelly's report in ibid., 298. A member of the brigade wrote to his wife describing how, "A Col. in our brigade I saw lying under a hill while his Regt. was fighting nearly half a mile in front of him. He is now being tried for misbehavior before the enemy... ." Letter quoted in S. O'Neill, "My Sons Were Faithful and They Fought. The Irish Brigade at Antietam," in Bilby & O'Neill, *"My Sons Were Faithful,"* 114. Lieutenant Colonel Fowler, who wrote the official report for the 63rd, makes no mention of Burke by name, referring only to "the colonel not being present." *OR*, Vol. 19, 295.

23. Description of Caldwell's advance and quotes from Meagher and Richardson in Priest, *Antietam*, 180–2.

24. Barlow's report in *OR*, Vol. 19, 289.

25. Richardson to 88th quoted in report of Colonel Kelly, ibid.

26. Officer in Conyngham, *Campaigns*, 150.

27. McClellan in *OR*, Vol. 19, 58.

28. Bodies in sunken road described in Livermore, *Days and Events*, 140.

29. Story of "bloody lane" in J. Murfin, *The Gleam of Bayonets. The Battle of Antietam and Robert E. Lee's Maryland Campaign, September 1862* (Baton Rouge: Louisiana State University, 1965), 262. Miller, "Catholic Religion," 261.

30. E. P. Alexander, *Military Memoirs of a Confederate* (New York: Charles Scribner's Sons, 1907), 262.

31. Close of battle described in W. C. Davis, *The American Civil War. A Historical Account of America's War of Secession.* (London: Salamander, 1996), 73.

Chapter 12 — To Fredericksburg

1. Lincoln's description of the Army of the Potomac in Williams, *Lincoln and His Generals*, 173.

2. Lincoln's dismissal of McClellan in McPherson, *Battle Cry of Freedom*, 569–70.

3. Mood in Irish Brigade in O'Brien, ed., *McCarter*, 67. Mulholland, somewhat melodramatically, described McClellan's departure as "the saddest hour that the Army of the Potomac ever knew. Every heart beat with a subdued throb, every eye was moist and tears wet alike the cheek of the white haired Sumner and the youngest drummer boy." Mulholland, *116th Regiment*, 43.

4. Meagher on McClellan's departure in Athearn, *Meagher*, 119.

5. Meagher's letter to Samuel Barlow in Sears, *Landscape Turned Red*, 343.

6. Report of Meagher's "death" in *Boston Pilot*, September 27, 1862.

7. Colonel Strother in Sears, *Landscape Turned Red*, 244.

8. Adjutant quoted in Boyle, *Mad Fellows*, 189–90.

9. McClellan's report in *OR*, Vol. 19, 59.

10. Hancock's report in ibid., 279.

11. Whitelaw Reid quoted in Burton, *Melting Pot Soldiers*, 123. "Miserable scribbler," in *Irish American*, October 11, 1862.

12. Corby on Meagher in Corby, *Memoirs of Chaplain Life*, 28–30.

13. O'Brien, ed., *McCarter*, 70–1.

14. Haverty's letter quoted in Boyle, *Mad Fellows*, 200–1.

15. Meagher's report in *OR*, Vol. 19, 294. At Sharpsburg, the 29th Massachusetts did carry rifled muskets, but by chance, a hollow in the ground offered them some protection and they suffered relatively fewer casualties. See Goble, "Irish Brigade Ordnance at Antietam," 64–66.

16. Description of Burnside in Palfrey, *The Antietam and Fredericksburg*, 54.

17. Burnside's advance to Fredericksburg in E. Stackpole, *The Fredericksburg Campaign; Drama on the Rappahannock* (Harrisburg: Stackpole Books, 1951), 79.
18. Meagher's letter to wife quoted in T. Keneally, *The Great Shame. A Story of the Irish in the Old World and the New.* (London: Chatto & Windus, 1998), 374.
19. Official to Governor Morgan in Burton, *Melting Pot Soldiers*, 123.
20. *Irish American*, October 11, 1862.
21. Daly, *Diary of a Union Lady*, 185.
22. *Boston Pilot*, September 27, 1862.
23. Report of proposal for new division in *Boston Pilot*, October 18, 1862.
24. *Irish American*, September 20, 1862.
25. Details of 116th Regiment and Meagher's welcome in Mulholland, *116th Regiment*, 24–33.
26. Irish Brigade at Harper's Ferry in Conyngham, *Campaigns*, 156.
27. Arrival of 28th Massachusetts in Barnard, *Ryan*, 71.
28. "Warning" about 28th Massachusetts in ibid., 73–4.
29. Exit of 29th Massachusetts in Jones, *Irish Brigade*, 111.
30. Pierce in Boyle, *Mad Fellows*, 162–4.
31. Descriptions of Hancock quoted in D. Jordan, *Winfield Scott Hancock, A Soldier's Life* (Bloomington: Indiana University, 1988), 57.
32. Story about sheep stealers in Walker, *Second Army Corps*, 135.
33. Skirmish with Confederate battery in Conyngham, *Campaigns*, 160.
34. Peter Walsh to wife in Kohl, ed., *Irish Green and Union Blue*, 35.
35. For details regarding the new battle flags, see Conyngham, *Campaigns*, 161–164.
36. Soldier to Corby in Corby, *Memoirs of Chaplain Life*, 130–131.
37. Daly, *Diary of a Union Lady*, 201–2.
38. Soldier's comment in Catton, *Glory Road*, 41.

Chapter 13 — Visions of Hell

1. Ammunition in O'Brien, ed., *McCarter*, 138, 140.
2. Description of bombardment in Mulholland, *116th Regiment*, 49–54.
3. Prisoners in O'Brien, ed., *McCarter*, 146.
4. Ibid., 156.
5. Crossing of the river in McCormack, "Never Were Men So Brave," 42.
6. Soldier quoted in Thomas Rice, "Desperate Courage" *Civil War Times Illustrated*. November/December 1990, 58.

7. Description of looting in Galwey, *Valiant Hours*, 58; Catton, *Glory Road*, 65; and Walker, *Second Army Corps*, 153.
8. Couch, *Battles and Leaders*, 3, 108.
9. Citizen quoted in O. Eisenschiml and R. Newman, *The Civil War, An American Iliad* (New York: Bobbs-Merrill, 1947), 344.
10. Description of night in Mulholland, *The 116th Regiment*, 55.
11. "Boards" in Kohl, ed., *Irish Green and Union Blue*, 42.
12. "Branches" in O'Brien, ed., *McCarter*, 153.
13. Freezing Confederates in Freeman, *Lee*, 2, 451.
14. Captain quoted in Rice, "Desperate Courage," 62.
15. Confederate officer in P. Walsh, "The Irish in South Carolina, Georgia, Alabama, Louisiana and Tennessee," *American-Irish Historical Society*, 103.
16. For Couch and Burnside on canal see Walker, *Second Army Corps*, 155.
17. "Crop of corn" in O'Grady, *Clear the Confederate Way!* 123.
18. Cobb quoted in Freeman, *Lee's Lieutenants*, Vol. 2, 330.
19. James Longstreet, "The Battle of Fredericksburg," in Johnson and Buel, *Battles and Leaders*, Vol. 3, 79.
20. For accounts of Kimball's attack, see Catton, *Glory Road*, 51–52.
21. Tobacco in Galwey, *Valiant Hours*, 59–64.
22. William Owen, "A Hot Day on Marye's Heights," in Johnson and Buel, *Battles and Leaders*, Vol. 3, 98.
23. Longstreet in Johnson and Buel, *Battles and Leaders*, Vol. 3, 79.
24. Walker, *Second Army Corps*, 164–169.
25. Kershaw quoted in Freeman, *Lee's Lieutenants*, Vol. 2, 364.
26. Federal soldier quoted in A. Nevins, *The War for the Union: War Becomes Revolution* (New York: Macmillan, 1960), 348.
27. Hancock's meeting described in Rice, "Desperate Courage," 62.
28. Morning and "fall in" described in Kohl, ed., *Irish Green in Union Blue*, 42; and O'Brien, ed., *McCarter*, 164.
29. "Burning powder" and "cheers" in ibid., 165.
30. Description of wounded German in Mulholland, *116th Regiment*, 60.
31. Quotes from Zook's men in Jordan, *Hancock*, 63.
32. Walker, *Second Army Corps*, 171.
33. Longstreet in Johnson and Buel, *Battles and Leaders*, Vol. 3, 81.
34. Conyngham, *Campaigns*, 167.
35. O'Brien, ed., *McCarter*, 167.

36. Mulholland, *116th Regiment*, 61.
37. Exchange between Nugent and Ouellet in Rice, "Desperate Courage," 63.
38. Meagher's report, *OR*, Vol. 21, 241.
39. Mulholland, *116th Regiment*, 62.
40. Condon's report, *OR*, Vol. 21, 249.
41. William McCarter quoted in K. O'Brien, "Sprig of Green: The Irish Brigade," in Seagrave, ed., *Irish Brigade*, 64.
42. O'Brien, ed., *McCarter*, 175.
43. Mulholland, *116th Regiment*, 64–65.
44. Galwey, *Valiant Hours*, 62.
45. Mulholland, *116th Regiment*, 64–65.
46. Kohl, ed., *Irish Green in Union Blue*, 43.
47. Confederate and reporter in Rice, "Desperate Courage," 66.
48. Quote from Mississippian in Daniel E. Sutherland, *Fredericksburg and Chancellorsville: The Dare Mark Campaign* (Lincoln: University of Nebraska, 1998), 55.
49. O'Brien, ed., *McCarter*, 178.
50. Walker, *Second Army Corps*, 172.
51. *Irish American*, January 10, 1863.
52. Walker, *Second Army Corps*, 172.
53. *Irish American*, January 3, 1863.
54. O'Brien, ed., *McCarter*, 183.
55. Nugent in Rice, "Desperate Courage," 66.
56. Kelly's report in *OR*, Vol. 21, 252.
57. Condon's report in ibid., 249.
58. Corby, *Memoirs of Chaplain Life*, 133.
59. Howard quoted in Couch in Johnson and Buel, *Battles and Leaders*, Vol. 3, 113.
60. Couch quoted in Walker, *Second Army Corps*, 175.
61. In front of the stone wall described in Mulholland, *116th Regiment*, 67.
62. William McCarter in Rice, "Desperate Courage," 69.
63. Mulholland, *116th Regiment*, 66.

Chapter 14 — "Our Noble Little Brigade Has Almost Disappeared"

1. Couch in Johnson and Buel, *Battles and Leaders*, Vol. 3, 115–116.
2. Burnside quoted in William Farrar Smith, "Franklin's 'Left Grand Division,'" in Johnson and Buel, *Battles and Leaders*, 3, 138.
3. Description of burial party in Barnard, *Ryan*, 83.
4. Correspondent quoted in Catton, *Glory Road*, 62.
5. Hancock's report in *OR*, Vol. 21, 228.
6. For a version of the story regarding Hancock and the parade following Fredericksburg, see Conyngham, *Campaigns*, 178.
7. Captain Nagle of the 88th in *Irish American*, December 27, 1862.
8. Kelly's report in *OR*, Vol. 21, 252.
9. Pickett, Longstreet and *Times* quoted in Athearn, *Meagher*, 121.
10. Meagher's explanation is in *OR*, Vol. 21, 243.
11. Cross in Holden et al., *Stand Firm and Fire Low*, 57. Perhaps also reflecting the difference between the "unemotional" New England and the "poetic" Irish temperaments, Cross described Meagher's oration to the brigade before the battle as a "frothy, meaningless speech, peculiar to the man." Ibid., 56–57.
12. Villiard quoted in Burton, *Melting Pot Soldiers*, 123–124.
13. Hancock's report in *OR*, Vol. 21, 228–229.
14. Medical certificate quoted in Keneally, *Great Shame*, 386.
15. Walker, *Second Army Corps*, 171–172.
16. D. Gwynn, *Young Ireland and 1848* (Cork: Cork University, 1948), 140–1.
17. Daly, *Diary of a Union Lady*, 190.
18. For descriptions of the "death feast" see Mulholland, *116th Regiment*, 75–76; Cavanagh, *Memoirs*, 71–73; and Conyngham, *Campaigns*, 354.
19. "Three cheers" in Barnard, *Ryan*, 82. Ryan describes the presentation as taking place outside a church rather than a theater as in most accounts.
20. Daly, *Diary of a Union Lady*, xxix, 271.
21. Corby, *Memoirs of Chaplain Life*, 134, 305.
22. Private quoted in Rice, "Desperate Courage," 70.
23. Officer quoted in Conyngham, *Campaigns*, 171.
24. Medical inspector in Catton, *Glory Road*, 108.
25. Description of Mud March in Conyngham, *Campaigns*, 174.
26. Couch in Johnson and Buel, *Battles and Leaders*, Vol. 3, 110.
27. Hooker quoted in Williams, *Lincoln and His Generals*, 234.
28. Lincoln and others on Hooker in Foote, *Civil War*, Vol. 2, 233–236.
29. Meetings of Fenians described in Galwey, *Valiant Hours*, 74–75.
30. St. Patrick's Day described in Conyngham, *Campaigns*, 183–188; Galwey, *Valiant Hours*, 76–79; Corby, *Memoirs of Chaplain Life*, 138–145; and Walsh in Kohl, ed., *Irish Green and Union Blue*, 79.
31. *Irish American*, April 18, 1863.
32. Consolidation of 116th in Mulholland, *116th Regiment*, 84.
33. Meagher and Dr. Reynolds in Athearn, *Meagher*, 122.

34. *Irish American*, December 27, 1862.
35. Ibid., January 17, 1863.
36. Ibid., January 31, 1863.
37. Peter Walsh in Kohl, ed., *Irish Green and Union Blue*, 62.
38. Letters from soldiers in *Irish American*, December 27, 1862.
39. Quotes from Ireland and ballad in Miller, *Emigrants and Exiles*, 359.
40. Corby, *Memoirs of Chaplain Life*, 146–151.
41. *Boston Pilot*, January 24, 1863.
42. Description of mass in Conyngham, *Campaigns*, 175.
43. Correspondent quoted in Rice, "Desperate Courage," 70.
44. Meagher to adjutant general in Athearn, *Meagher*, 123.
45. Meeting of Lincoln and Meagher in Conyngham, *Campaigns*, 177.
46. Letter to Stanton reproduced in ibid., 178–9.
47. For letters to and from Meagher regarding recruitment see Athearn, *Meagher*, 123–5.

Chapter 15 — A Sideshow of the Big Show

1. General Order 47 in Catton, *Glory Road*, 167.
2. Couch on Hooker in D. Couch, "The Chancellorsville Campaign." in Johnson and Buel, *Battles and Leaders*, 3, 161.
3. For deployment of Irish Brigade at the Rappahannock fords see Hancock's report, *OR*, Vol. 25, 311.
4. Peter Walsh to his wife in Kohl, ed., *Irish Green and Union Blue*, 89.
5. Confederate pickets in Mulholland, *116th Pennsylvania*, 105.
6. Move to Scott's Mills, ibid., 106–7.
7. Stampede from the woods, ibid., 107.
8. Gathering up members of the Eleventh Corps in Conyngham, *Campaigns*, 184.
9. Advance to Chancellorsville House and rescue of battery in Mulholland, *OR*, Vol. 39, 328.
10. Whiteford in *OR*, Vol. 39, 327.
11. Meagher's resignation letter to the assistant adjutant general reproduced in Lyons, *Meagher*, 180–83.
12. Frank Henry letter to Lincoln in the *Abraham Lincoln Papers at the Library of Congress*, http://memory.loc.gov/ammem/alhtml/malhome.html.
13. Holden, et al., eds., *Stand Firm and Aim Low*, 88.
14. Letter from War Department and description of Meagher's departure in Conyngham, *Campaigns*, 189.

Chapter 16 — Gettysburg — The "Terifick Battle"

1. Lee quoted in Foote, *Civil War*, Vol. 2, 345.
2. Lincoln and Hooker communications in Williams, *Lincoln and His Generals*, 252–254, 258, 259.
3. Captain Nagle quoted in Lyons, *Meagher*, 184.
4. Details of brigade in *OR*, Vol. 27, 157.
5. "Communicable disease" description in Athearn, *Meagher*, 133.
6. Description of march in Mulholland, *116th Pennsylvania*, 126–130, Walsh in Kohl, ed., *Irish Green and Union Blue*, 64–65 and Corby, *Memoirs of Chaplain Life*, 169–178.
7. Catton, *Glory Road*, 251.
8. Ibid., 261.
9. Corby, *Memoirs of Chaplain Life*, 178.
10. Description of Gettysburg in Foote, *Civil War*, Vol. 2, 446.
11. Departure of Hancock for battlefield in Jordan, *Hancock*, 81.
12. Description of battlefield in C. Champ, *Gettysburg: The Confederate High Tide* (Alexandria: Time-Life, 1985), 75–76.
13. Movement of Irish Brigade on July 1–2 in Kelly's report, *OR*, Vol. 27, 386.
14. Exchange between Meade and Sickles in Champ, *Gettysburg*, 78.
15. "Terifick battle" from Walsh in Kohl, ed., *Irish Green and Union Blue*, 107.
16. Hancock in Foote, *Civil War*, Vol. 2, 496.
17. Blessing of Irish Brigade in Corby, *Memoirs of Chaplain Life*, 181–184 and K. O'Brien, "The Irish Brigade in the Wheatfield" in Seagrave, ed., *Irish Brigade*, 103. Watching was the scene was the Lutheran chaplain of the 145th Pennsylvania, John Stuckenberg, whose regiment was in line to the right of the Irish Brigade. "Seeing the Irish brigade bowed in prayer and feeling deeply impressed with the idea that many might enter the battle never to return," Stuckenberg, in turn, sought and was given permission to hold worship among his own regiment. Stuckenberg's diary suggests the time of the absolution was earlier in the morning of July 2. Stuckenberg, J. H. W. *I'm Surrounded by Methodists ... Diary of John H. W. Stuckenberg Chaplain of the 145th Pennsylvania Volunteer Infantry* D. T. Hedrick and G. B. Davis Jr. (eds.) (Gettysburg, PA: Thomas Publications, 1995), 77. For a good discussion of the timing and possible location of Corby's blessing, see Murphy, T. L. *Kelly's Heroes. The Irish Brigade at Gettysburg* (Gettysburg, PA: Farnworth House Military Impressions, 1997), 20–26.
18. Meagher's critic, Cross, was mortally wounded in the Wheatfield. Cross, who had proved

his worth both as a leader and fierce fighter on many previous occasions, was, in the minds of many of his colleagues, overdue for promotion. But he was not feeling very good about this scrape. A little earlier, as the Second Corps had started to make its way off Cemetery Ridge, Hancock had called over to Cross, "This is the last time you'll fight without a [general's] star." "Too late General," replied Cross without emotion, "This is my last battle." As his men drove the Confederates back across the Wheatfield, Cross was wounded, dying in a field hospital later that night. "I think the boys will miss me," were his last words. Catton, *Glory Road*, 305.

19. Confederate officer in J. Jorgenson, *Gettysburg's Bloody Wheatfield* (Shippensburg, PA: White Mane, 2002), 98.

20. Kershaw quoted in Murphy, *Kelly's Heroes*, 32.

21. Caldwell's account and description of Kelly in *OR*, Vol. 27, 380.

22. Kelly's report in *OR*, Vol. 27, 386.

23. Smith's report in *OR*, Vol. 27, 389. Smith refers to a "cornfield" rather than a wheatfield.

24. St. Clair Mulholland's report in *OR*, Vol. 27, 392. Retreat from Wheatfield also described in Mulholland, *116th Regiment*, 134–139.

25. Byrnes' report in *OR*, Vol. 27, 387.

26. Longstreet to Lee in Foote, *Civil War*, Vol. 3, 529–30.

27. Advance of Pickett's men described by Mulholland in *OR*, Vol. 27, 392–3.

28. *Irish American*, July 30, 1863.

29. Description of brigade by Walsh in Kohl, ed., *Irish Green and Union Blue*, 109.

Chapter 17 — Fire in the Rear

1. For pursuit of Lee and camp at Morrisville see Mulholland, *116th Pennsylvania*, 149–152.

2. Story with General Hays described in Conyngham, *Campaigns*, 421.

3. Description of Irish in McPherson, *Battle Cry of Freedom*, 609.

4. For background to and a description of the riots, see Jones, *Irish Brigade*, 150–154; McPherson, *Battle Cry of Freedom*, 600–611; and A. Nevins, *Ordeal of the Union. Vol. 4. The Organized War* (New York: Scribner, 1971), 119–125. For a detailed account and broader interpretation, see I. Bernstein, *The New York City Draft Riots: Their Significance for American Society and Politics in the Age of the Civil War* (New York: Oxford University, 1990).

5. Story of Nugent's sword in Jones, *Irish Brigade*, 152.

6. Meagher to O'Mahony in J. Bilby, "Thomas Francis Meagher. The Man who made the Irish Brigade," in Bilby and O'Neill, "My Sons Were Faithful," 71.

7. Peter Walsh in Kohl, ed., *Irish Green and Union Blue*, 110.

8. Galwey, *Valiant Hours*, 137.

9. "Quaker Irish" referred to in Burton, "Title Deed to America," 458.

10. *Chicago Morning Post* in Nevins, *Organized War*, 129.

11. For recruitment figures see McPherson, *Battle Cry of Freedom*, 605.

12. Emigrant letters quoted in Miller, *Emigrants and Exiles*, 359–361.

13. Consul quoted in Hernon, *Celts, Catholics, and Copperheads*, 25–26.

14. For description of "brokers" see B. Catton, *A Stillness at Appomattox* (New York: Doubleday, 1953), 24–36.

15. Ibid., 29–30.

16. Details of Meagher's attempts to get his commission back given in Athearn, *Meagher*, 126–133.

17. Description of Corcoran's demise in Conyngham, *Campaigns*, 540.

18. Meagher's letter to Guiney in P. Guiney, *Commanding Boston's Irish Ninth: The Civil War Letters of Colonel Patrick R. Guiney, Ninth Massachusetts Volunteer Infantry*, ed. C.G. Samito (New York: Fordham University, 1998), 226.

19. *Irish American*, ibid., xxxii.

Chapter 18 — "What There Is Left of It"

1. For furlough of troops, see *OR*, Vol. 33, 358, 624.

2. Brigade arrival in New York and gathering in the Irving Hall, see Conyngham, *Campaigns*, 424–437; Corby, *Memoirs of Chaplain Life*, 213; and *Irish American*, January 23, 1864.

3. For recruitment see Mulholland, *116th Regiment*, 167–173; and Burton, *Melting Pot Soldiers*, 134.

4. *Boston Pilot*, 30 May 1863.

5. For disquiet in the 28th Massachusetts, see *Boston Pilot*, May 2, 1863; and Peter Walsh to his wife in Kohl, ed., *Irish Green and Union Blue*, 95, 150–151.

6. Grant described by Theodore Lyman in A. Nevins, *Ordeal of the Union: The Organized War to Victory, 1864–1865* (New York: Scribner's, 1971), 13.

7. Description of recruits in Catton, *Stillness at Appomattox*, 35.

8. Description of losses in Jones, *Irish Brigade*, 172, 176.

9. Chisholm in Menge and Shimrak, *Daniel Chisholm*, 26.

Notes — Chapter 18

10. Special Order 165 in *OR*, Vol. 40, 444.
11. Transfer of 28th Massachusetts in ibid., 220. Details of Consolidated Brigade in ibid., 241.
12. Barlow's report in *OR*, Vol. 42, 247–8.
13. For criticism of the Consolidated Brigade at Reams Station, see Walker, *Second Army Corps*, 573; and Brigadier General Nelson Miles' report in *OR*, Vol. 42, 252–3.
14. Hancock quoted in Jordan, *Hancock*, 164.
15. D. Sparks, ed., *Inside Lincoln's Army: The Diary of Marsena Rudolph Patrick, Provost Marshal General, Army of the Potomac* (New York: Thomas Yoseloff, 1964), 414–15.
16. Gates quoted in J. G. Bilby, "Thomas Francis Meagher. The Man who made the Irish Brigade," in Bilby and O'Neill, eds., *"My Sons Were Faithful,"* 72.
17. Description of celebration in Corby, *Memoirs of Chaplain Life*, 264–268; and Conyngham, *Campaigns*, 482–89.
18. Miles' request in *OR*, Vol. 42, Part 2, 306.
19. Nugent's address in ibid., 476–7. Conyngham states that the 116th "was not again added to the brigade, because Colonel Mulholland, then commanding, would rank Colonel Nugent." *Campaigns*, 505.
20. Miles in *OR*, Vol. 42, 160.
21. For executions of deserters see Nugent's report in *OR*, Vol. 40, 47.
22. Description of St. Patrick's Day in Conyngham, *Campaigns*, 514–5.
23. Grant's counterattack described in McPherson, *Battle Cry of Freedom*, 844–5.
24. Reports of pursuit of Lee in *OR*, Vol. 46, 92, 795, 710, 724–5.
25. McPherson, *Battle Cry of Freedom*, 848.
26. Menge and Shimrak, *Daniel Chisholm*, 79.
27. *Irish American*, June 3, 1865.
28. Ibid., July 22, 1865.
29. Description of Meagher in Athearn, *Meagher*, 142.
30. Communication to Sherman in *OR*, Vol. 39, 640.
31. Grant in ibid., 318.
32. Description of Meagher's command in *OR*, Vol. 47, 416.
33. Meagher relieved of command in ibid., 561.
34. Warren, "Oh, God, What a Pity!" 1.

Bibliography

Alexander, E. P. *Military Memoirs of a Confederate.* New York: Charles Scribner's Sons, 1907.
Athearn, R. *Thomas Francis Meagher. An Irish Revolutionary in America.* Boulder: University of Colorado, 1949.
Bailey, R. *Antietam, The Bloodiest Day.* New York: Time-Life, 1984.
Barnard, S., ed. *Campaigning with the Irish Brigade: Pvt. John Ryan, 28th Massachusetts.* Terre Haute, IN: AST, 2001.
Bayor, R. H., and T. J. Meagher, eds. *The New York Irish.* Baltimore: Johns Hopkins University, 1996.
Beatie, R. *Army of the Potomac. Birth of Command. November 1860-September 1861.* Cambridge, MA: Da Capo, 2002.
Bellor S. P. *Never Were Men So Brave: The Irish Brigade during the Civil War.* New York: Margaret K. McElderry, 1998.
Bernstein, I. *The New York City Draft Riots: Their Significance for American Society and Politics in the Age of the Civil War.* New York: Oxford University, 1990.
Bilby, J. *Remember Fontenoy! The 69th New York and the Irish Brigade in the Civil War.* Hightstown, NJ: Longstreet House, 1995.
Bilby, J. G., and S. D. O'Neill, eds. *"My Sons Were Faithful and They Fought": The Irish Brigade at Antietam: An Anthology.* New Jersey: Longstreet House, 1997.
Boyle, F. *A Party of Mad Fellows. The Story of the Irish Regiments in the Army of the Potomac.* Dayton, OH: Morningside House, 1996.
Bridges, H. *Lee's Maverick General: Daniel Harvey Hill.* New York: McGraw-Hill, 1961.
Brown, B. "The Blue, The Gray and the Green." *Army 30* (March 1980).
Burton, W. "Title Deed to America: Union Ethnic Regiments in the Civil War." *Proceedings of the American Philosophical Society* 124 (December 1980).
_____. *Melting Pot Soldiers: The Union's Ethnic Regiments.* Ames: Iowa University, 1988.
Catton, B. *Mr. Lincoln's Army.* New York: Doubleday, 1951.
_____. *Glory Road. The Bloody Road from Fredericksburg to Gettysburg.* New York: Doubleday, 1952.
_____. *A Stillness at Appomattox.* New York: Doubleday, 1953.
_____. *Never Call Retreat.* New York: Doubleday, 1965.
Cavanagh, M. *Memoirs of Gen. Thomas Francis Meagher.* Worcester, MA: Messenger Press, 1892.
Champ, C. *Gettysburg. The Confederate High Tide.* Alexandria, VA: Time-Life, 1985.
Commager, H. S. *The Blue and the Gray* Indianapolis: Bobbs Merrill, 1950.
Conyngham, D. P. *The Irish Brigade and Its Campaigns.* New York: William McSorley, 1867.
Cook, A. *The Armies of the Streets: The New York City Draft Riots of 1863.* Lexington: University Press of Kentucky, 1974.
Corby, W. *Memoirs of Chaplain Life.* Chicago: La Monte, O'Donnell, 1893.
Crawford, M., ed. *William Howard Russell's Civil War. Private Diary and Letters 1861–1862.* Athens: University of Georgia, 1992.
Daly, M. *Diary of a Union Lady, 1861–1865.* Edited by H.E. Hammond. New York: Funk and Wagnalls, 1962.

Bibliography

Davis, W. C. *Battle at Bull Run*. Baton Rouge: Louisiana State University, 1977.

_____. *The American Civil War: A Historical Account of America's War of Secession*. London: Salamander, 1996.

Dowdey, C. *The Seven Days: The Emergence of Lee*. Boston: Little, Brown, 1964.

Dungan, M. *Distant Drums: Irish Soldiers in Foreign Armies*. Belfast: Appletree, 1993.

Eisenschiml, O., and R. Newman. *The Civil War, An American Iliad*. New York: Bobbs-Merrill, 1947.

Foote, S. *The Civil War: A Narrative*. 3 Vols. London: Bodley Head, reprint, 1991.

Forney, G. F. *Thomas Francis Meagher: Irish Patriot, American Yankee, Montana Pioneer*. Philadelphia: Xlibris, 2003.

Fox, W. *Regimental Losses in the American Civil War, 1861–1865*. Albany: Brandow, 1898.

Freeman, D. S. *Lee's Lieutenants: A Study in Command*. 3 Vols. New York: Charles Scribner's Sons, 1943–44.

Galwey, T. *The Valiant Hours*. Harrisburg: Stackpole, 1961.

Gordon, J. B. *Reminiscences of the Civil War*. New York: Charles Scribner's Sons, 1904.

Guelzo, A. *Abraham Lincoln: Redeemer President*. Grand Rapids: Wm. B. Eerdmans, 1999.

Guiney, P. *Commanding Boston's Irish Ninth: The Civil War Letters of Colonel Patrick R. Guiney, Ninth Massachusetts Volunteer Infantry*. Edited by C.G. Samito. New York: Fordham University, 1998.

Gwynn, W. *Young Ireland and 1848*. Cork: Cork University, 1948.

Williams, T. Harry. *Lincoln and his Generals*. New York: Alfred Knopf, 1952.

Hearne, J. M. and Cornish, R. T. eds. *Thomas Francis Meagher. The Making of an Irish American*. Dublin: Irish Academic Press, 2006.

Henderson, G. F. R. *Stonewall Jackson and the American Civil War*. New York: Grosset and Dunlap, 1943.

Hennessy, J. *Return to Bull Run: The Campaign and Battle of Second Manassas* Norman: University of Oklahoma, 1993.

Hernon, J. M., Jr. *Celts, Catholics and Copperheads: Ireland Views the American Civil War*. Columbus: Ohio State University, 1968.

Holden, W., W. Ross, and E. Slomba, eds. *Stand Firm and Fire Low: The Civil War Writings of Colonel Edward E Cross*. Durham: University of New Hampshire, 2002.

Holt, M. "The Politics of Impatience: The Origins of Know-Nothingism." *Journal of American History* 60 (September 1973).

Johnson, R. U., and C. C. Buel, eds. *Battles and Leaders of the Civil War. Vol. 2, The Struggle Intensifies*. New York: Century, 1887–88.

Jones, P. *The Irish Brigade*. Washington, D.C.: Robert Luce, 1969.

Jordan, D. *Winfield Scott Hancock, A Soldier's Life*. Bloomington: Indiana University, 1988.

Jorgenson, J. *Gettysburg's Bloody Wheatfield*. Shippensburg, PA White Mane Books, 2002.

Keneally, T. *The Great Shame: A Story of the Irish in the Old World and the New*. London: Chatto & Windus, 1998.

Kohl, L., and M. Richard, eds. *Irish Green and Union Blue: The Civil War Letters of Peter Walsh, Color Sergeant, 28th Massachusetts Volunteers*. New York: Fordham University, 1986.

Kyd Douglas, H. *I Rode with Stonewall*. Chapel Hill: University of North Carolina, 1940.

Langellier, J. ed. *Miles Keogh*. New York: Upton, 1991.

Lewis, L. *Sherman: Fighting Prophet*. New York: Harcourt Brace, 1932.

Livermore, T. L. *Days and Events, 1860–1865*. Boston: Houghton Mifflin, 1920.

Lonn, E. *Foreigners in the Confederacy*. Chapel Hill: University of North Carolina Press, 1940.

_____. *Foreigners in the Union Army and Navy*. Baton Rouge: Louisiana State University, 1951.

Lyons, W. F. *Brigadier Thomas Francis Meagher: His Political and Military Career; With Selections From His Speeches and* Writings. New York: D. & J. Sadler, 1870.

McCormack, J. "Never Were Men So Brave," *Civil War Times Illustrated*, April 1969.

MacNamara, M. H. *The Irish Ninth in Bivouac and Battle*. Boston: Lee and Shepherd, 1867.

Bibliography

McPherson, J. *Battle Cry of Freedom.* New York: Oxford University, 1988.
Maguire, J. F. *The Irish in America.* New York: Arno, 1968 reprint,
Man, A. P. "The Irish in New York in the early eighteen sixties." *Irish Historical Studies* 7, no. 26 (September 1950).
Meagher, T. F. *The Last Days of the 69th in Virginia.* New York: Irish American, 1861.
Menge, W. S., and J. August Shimrak, eds. *The Civil War Notebook of Daniel Chisholm: A Chronicle of Daily Life in the Union Army, 1864–1865.* New York: Ballantine Books, 1989.
Miller, K. *Emigrants and Exiles: Ireland and the Irish Exodus to North America.* New York: Oxford University, 1985.
Miller, R., H. Stoute, and C. Wilson, eds. *Religion and the American Civil War.* New York: Oxford University, 1999.
Mulholland, St. Clair A. *The Story of the 116th Regiment, Pennsylvania Volunteers.* Philadelphia: F. McManus, 1903.
Murfin, J. *The Gleam of Bayonets: The Battle of Antietam and Robert E. Lee's Maryland Campaign, September 1862.* Baton Rouge: Louisiana State University, 1965.
Murphy, T. L. *Kelly's Heroes. The Irish Brigade at Gettysburg.* Gettysburg, PA: Farnworth House Military Impressions, 1997.
Neely, M., Jr. *The Last Best Hope of Earth: Abraham Lincoln and the Promise of America.* Massachusetts: Harvard University, 1993.
Nevins, A., and M. Thomas, eds. *The Diary of George Templeton Strong.* Vol. 2. New York: Macmillan, 1952.
Nevins, A. *The War for the Union: War Becomes Revolution* New York: Macmillan, 1960.
_____. *Ordeal of the Union: The Organized War* New York: Scribner, 1971
O'Brien, K. *My Life in the Irish Brigade: the Civil War Memoirs of Private William McCarter, 116th Pennsylvania Infantry.* Mason, CA: Savas Publishing, 1996.
O'Donnell, M. J. "The Sprig of Green." *North-South Trader's Civil War* magazine 26, no. 3 (July 1999).
O'Flaherty, P. *The History of the 69th Regiment of the New York State Militia, 1852 to 1861.* Ph.D. dissertation, New York: Fordham University, 1963.
O'Grady, K. *Clear the Confederate Way! The Irish in the Army of Northern Virginia.* Mason City, CA: Savas Publishing, 2000.
Palfrey, F. W. *The Antietam and Fredericksburg.* New York: Charles Scribner's Sons, 1889.
Priest, J. *Antietam: The Soldier's Battle.* New York: Oxford University, 1989.
Reardon, C. *Pickett's Charge in History and Memory.* Chapel Hill: University of North Carolina, 1997.
Robertson, J., Jr. *General A. P. Hill: The Story of a Confederate Warrior.* New York: Random House, 1987.
Seagrave, P. S. *The History of the Irish Brigade. A Collection of Historical Essays.* Fredericksburg, VA: Sergeant Kirkland's, 1997.
Sears, S. *George B. McClellan. The Young Napoleon.* New York: Ticknor and Fields, 1988.
_____. *To The Gates of Richmond: The Peninsula Campaign.* New York: Ticknor and Fields, 1992.
_____. *Landscape Turned Red: The Battle of Antietam.* New York: Ticknor and Fields, 1983.
Shannon, W. *The American Irish.* New York: Macmillan, 1963.
Sherman, W. T. *Memoirs of General William Tecumseh Sherman By Himself.* Bloomington: Indiana University, 1957 reprint.
Sparks, D., ed. *Inside Lincoln's Army: The Diary of Marsena Rudolph Patrick, Provost Marshal General, Army of the Potomac.* New York: Thomas Yoseloff, 1964.
Stackpole, E. *The Fredericksburg Campaign: Drama on the Rappahannock.* Harrisburg: Stackpole Books, 1951.
Stuckenberg, J. H. W. *I'm Surrounded by Methodists . . . Dairy of John H. W. Stuckenberg Chaplain of the 145th Pennsylvania Volunteer Infantry.* Hedrick, D. T. and Davis Jr., G. B. eds. Gettysburg, PA: Thomas Publications, 1995.

Bibliography

Sutherland, D. E. *Fredericksburg and Chancellorsville: The Dare Mark Campaign*. Lincoln: University of Nebraska, 1998.

U. S. War Department. *The War of the Rebellion: A Compilation of the Official Records of the Union and Confederate Armies*. 128 Vols. Washington, D.C.: U.S. Government Printing Office, 1880–1901.

Walker, F. A. *History of the Second Army Corps in the Army of the Potomac*. New York: Charles Scribner's Sons, 1886.

Walsh, F. "The Boston *Pilot* Reports the Civil War." *Historical Journal of Massachusetts*, no. 9 (June 1981).

Walsh, P. "The Irish in South Carolina, Georgia, Alabama, Louisiana and Tennessee," *The Journal of the American-Irish Historical Society*, 3, (1900), 97–109.

Warren, C. "Oh, God, What a Pity!": The Irish Brigade at Fredericksburg and the Creation of Myth.' *Civil War History*, Vol. 47, Issue 3, 2001.

Wiley, B. I. *The Life of Johnny Reb*. Baton Rouge: Louisiana State University, 1943.

_____. *The Life of Billy Yank*. Baton Rouge: Louisiana State University, 1952.

Wittke, C. *We Who Built America*. Cleveland: Press of the Western Reserve University, 1940.

_____. *The Irish in America*. New York: Russell & Russell, 1956.

Index

Alexander, Porter 120–1
Andrew, Gov. John 49–50, 90, 112–3
Antietam Creek 95–8, 106, 111, 118
Appomattox Court House 177–8
Arlington Heights 18, 20, 94
Athearn, Robert 3

Bagley, James 45
Bank's Ford 149
Bardwell, George 127
Barlow, Francis 103–4, 107, 135, 174–5
Barlow, Samuel 108
Beauregard, P.G.T. 24, 27
Beaver Dam Creek 74
Bedini Cardinal 14
Bee, Barnard 29–30
Bilby, Joseph 3
Blackburn's Ford 26
Boatswain's Swamp 74
Boston Pilot 36, 37, 49, 86, 91, 143
Bowen, James 8
Boyle, Frank 4
Breslin, James 23
Brooke, John 70–1, 159
Bull Run (First) 23–7, 32–6, 38, 43–7, 51–2, 54, 58–9, 69, 75, 87, 90–1, 104, 134–5, 142, 154, 168, 174
Burke, Denis 176
Burke, John 67, 103
Burns, William 80–1
Burnside, Ambrose 27, 29, 93, 106–7, 110–11, 115, 119–21, 123, 131, 134, 137–8, 142
Burton, William 2, 4
Butler, Benjamin 49
Byrnes, Richard 112–3, 129, 160, 172, 174

Caldwell, John 61, 103–4, 123, 154, 158–9
Cameron, Simon 46, 49–50
Casey, Patrick 63
Cass, Thomas 49, 85
Cavanagh, Michael 3
Celts, Catholics and Copperheads 2
Chancellorsville 119, 147–54
Chickahominy River 63–4, 66–7, 70, 73–5, 78–80, 84, 91, 94, 111, 118
Chisholm, Daniel 174
Cincinnati Commercial 33, 131
Cincinnati Gazette 108
Clooney, Patrick 79
Cobb, Thomas 121–2
Cold Harbor 113, 174
Condon, Patrick 126
Conyngham, David Powers 1, 3
Corby, Fr. William 1, 56–9, 67–8, 88–9, 95, 102, 108, 115, 129, 137, 139, 143, 158, 176
Corcoran, Michael 7–9, 18, 21–3, 28, 31–2, 34–5, 37–8, 41, 44, 50, 112, 168, 170, 190n
Couch, Darius 87, 118, 120–7, 129, 131, 134–5, 137, 147, 154
Creedon, Father 37
Cross, Edward 71, 134, 152, 159
Curtin, Gov. Andrew 50
Custer, George Armstrong 75

Daly, Maria 9, 33, 44, 57, 87, 111, 115, 135–6
Daly, Judge Patrick 9, 44, 57, 108
Davis, Jefferson 35
Deep Bottom 174
Dillon, Fr. James 56–7, 60, 63, 89
Donahoe, Patrick 49, 172
Donovan, John 87
Douglass, Frederick 16
Duffy, Felix 75

Ellis, Doctor William 77
Emmet, Robert 44
Evans, Nathan G. "Shanks" 27

Fair Oaks 66–7, 69–74, 76–80, 83, 90, 135
Five Points 13
Fort Benton 179
Fort Corcoran 22, 45–6, 94, 174, 183n
Fort Munroe 59–63
Fort Schuyler 51
Fort Sumter 7, 24, 35, 39, 89
Foster, George 13
Fowler, Henry 88–9, 103
Fox, William 2

Franklin, William 80–2, 110, 116, 138
Fredericksburg 4–5, 50, 55, 71, 109–10, 114–21, 124, 128–38, 141–3, 147, 149, 151, 162, 165–6, 170, 172, 175
French, William 64, 69, 71, 75–7, 79, 97–9, 109, 129, 135
Funk, George 71

Galway Vindicator 90
Galwey, Thomas 122, 127, 166
Gates, Theodore 175
Georgetown College 18, 21
Gettysburg 57, 119, 153–7, 159, 161–2, 170
Gleason, John 54
Glendale 82–3
Gossen, John 54, 61, 64, 88, 94, 139
Grant, Ulysses 173–4, 177–8
Grapevine Bridge 66–8, 73, 75
Griffin, Charles 30
Guiney, Michael 170

Haggerty, Bryan 87
Haggerty, James 23, 29
Hancock, Winfield Scott 108, 113–4, 123, 126, 132–6, 146, 148, 150, 154–5, 158, 175
Harper's Weekly 69, 71
Harrison's Landing 56
Hart, Matthew 101
Haverty, Patrick 109
Hays, Alexander 163
Heenan, Denis 48, 50, 112, 126
Heintzelman, Samuel 80–1, 84–5
Hernon, Joseph 2
Hill, Ambrose Powell 74, 81
Hill, Daniel Harvey 66, 74, 79, 82, 84, 87, 98
Hood, John Bell 75, 97, 156, 158–9
Hooker, Joe 79, 97, 110, 138–40, 146–7, 149, 151, 153–4
Horgan, William 130
Howard, Otis 61, 69, 71, 129, 135, 145
Hughes, Archbishop 14, 37, 51, 143

Index

Irish American 17, 20, 36–7, 90, 99, 108, 111, 141–2, 162, 170–1, 178
Irish Patriot 49

Jackson, T.J. "Stonewall" 29–31, 74, 81–2, 114, 147–8, 150
Johnson, Andrew 170, 178
Johnston, Denis 173
Johnston, Joseph 24, 59, 62–4, 69

Kearny, Phil 60, 79–80, 87–8
Keeffe, John 31
Kelly, James 31, 45
Kelly, Patrick 48, 69, 71, 103, 128–9, 132, 135, 148, 152, 154, 159–60, 174
Kershaw, Joseph 122, 128, 159
Kimball, Nathan 122
Know-Nothing(s) 14–5, 37, 47

Lawton, Alexander 79
Lebroke, James 151
Lee, Robert E. 69, 73–4, 79–80, 83–4, 93–5, 107, 109–11, 124, 138, 146–7, 149, 151, 153, 161–3, 166, 177–8
Lincoln, Abraham 1, 4, 8, 15 18, 24, 33–4, 38, 41, 57–9, 61, 90, 93, 107, 138–9, 143, 145, 153, 168–70, 172–3
Longstreet, James 64, 66, 74, 82, 84, 121–2, 124, 131, 161
Lyons, W.F. 3, 45–6, 179

MacNamara, Michael 155
Malvern Hill 79, 83–6, 88–9
Marye's Heights 5, 71, 119, 121, 133–4
McCarter, William 2, 4–5, 182n, 55, 108–9, 129
McCleland, William 128
McClellan, George B. 58–9, 61–2, 64, 66, 72, 73–6, 79–80, 84, 87, 89–90, 92–5, 97–8, 104, 106–09, 113–15
McDowell, Irwin 23–7, 29, 58–9
McGee, James 103
McGuire, Bob 127
Meade, George 153, 155–6, 158, 166
Meagher, Thomas Francis 1–5, 20, 22–4, 26, 30–3, 38–52, 54–5, 57, 59, 61–4, 67, 69–72, 75–9, 82, 85, 88–96, 98–103, 107–115, 124, 126, 130, 132–37, 140–43, 145–6, 148–9, 152–54, 165–6, 168–75, 178–9
Mechanicsville 74, 81
Melting Pot Soldiers 2
Memoirs of Chaplain Life 1
Miles, Nelson 174
Monteith, William 49–50, 113

Morgan, Edwin 8, 47, 111
Moroney, Richard 174
Morrisville 163
Mulholland, St. Clair 1, 151, 160
Murphy, Matthew 49
Murphy, Thomas 49

Nagle, William 132
The Nation 43
New York Daily Tribune 16, 24, 34, 38, 45
New York Herald 36, 38, 71, 77
Nugent, Robert 45–7, 52, 68, 71, 85–6, 109, 126, 128–9, 134, 143, 165, 172, 176–7

O'Brien, Kevin 4
O'Donoghue, Joseph 85
O'Gorman, Richard 44
O'Grady, Kelly 2, 4
O'Mahony, John 165
O'Neill, John 127
O'Reilly, Fr. Bernard 23, 30
Ouellet, Fr. Thomas 57, 60, 88, 95, 126, 137, 176

Paez, Ramon 41
A Party of Mad Fellows 4
Patrick, Marsena 175
Patterson, Robert 24
the Peach Orchard 156, 158–60
Phelan, Michael 44
The Phoenix 43, 186n
Pickett, George 119, 162–3
Pierce, Ebenezer 76, 113
Pope, John 93–4
Porter, Alexander 31
Porter, Fitz-John 55, 74–6, 84–5, 87–9, 92

Quinlan, Francis 127, 130
Quinlan, James 81, 85

Rafferty, Peter 89
Randle, James 2
Rappahannock River 50, 58, 110, 114–6, 118, 129, 131, 136–7, 141, 145, 147–8, 150–1
Reams' Station 175
regiments, units: *Massachusetts* (9th Volunteer Infantry) 48, 75, 117, 154–5, 170; (28th Volunteer Infantry) 1–2, 5; (29th Volunteer Infantry) 1; *New York* (4th Heavy Artillery) 11; (7th Heavy Artillery) 11, 176; (63rd Volunteer Infantry) 1, 10, 46, 48, 52, 54, 56–7, 67, 85, 88–9, 101–4, 109, 129–30, 133, 148, 171–2, 174; (69th State Militia) 7–10, 18, 20–1, 25, 29–36, 39–40, 43–5, 142, 171; (69th Volunteer Infantry) 1, 3, 10, 45–7, 49, 51–2, 54, 57, 64, 68, 70, 75, 8–7, 89, 92, 102–4, 109, 119, 126, 128, 130, 133, 137, 142, 148, 160, 171–2, 174, 176; (88th Volunteer Infantry) 1, 10, 46, 48, 52–7, 68–70, 79–81, 85–6, 89, 98, 101–04, 109, 126, 128–30, 132, 137, 142, 148, 151–54, 171–2, 174, 176; *Pennsylvania* (69th Volunteer Infantry) 50; (116th Volunteer Infantry) 1, 2, 4, 11, 48, 50, 57, 112, 117–8, 124, 126–7, 129–30, 141, 148, 151, 153, 155, 159–60, 172, 174, 176
Reid, Whitelaw 108
Remember Fontenoy! 3
Richardson, Israel 61, 64, 67, 75, 82, 94, 101, 103–4, 106, 109, 113
Ricketts, James 30
Rorty, James McKay 32, 36
Russell, William Howard 15–6, 32
Ryan, John 112

St. Patrick's Day 60, 139–40, 146, 176
Sandberg, Carl 4
Schouler, William 49
Scott, Winfield 22
Scott's Mills 149
Second Bull Run 23, 93, 110
Sedgwick, John 61, 80, 97–8
Seven Days' battles 74, 82, 87–91, 109, 113–4, 129
Seward, William 50, 58, 90, 168
Sharpsburg 4, 71, 79, 89, 91, 95, 97, 104, 106–13, 118–9, 123, 127, 129, 134–5, 138, 142, 153, 162, 169–70, 174
Sherman, William T. 25–7, 30, 32–5, 175, 177
Shields, James 44, 47, 51, 57, 111
Sickles, Dan 85, 151, 156, 158
Smith, James 160
Smyth, Thomas 122
Stanton, Edwin 90, 144
Stuckenberg, John 159n
Sudley Springs 26–7, 29
Sullivan, Denis 129
Sumner, Edwin V. 56, 61, 66–8, 71, 75, 79–86, 89, 97–8, 109, 114, 137–8
sunken road 98–9, 101–6, 108–10, 113, 122–3, 162

Templeton Strong, George 11
Thomas, Lorenzo 48
Treanor, B.S. 49
Troiani, Don 4
Two Taverns 163
Tyler, Daniel 24–6
Tyler's Farm 63–4, 73

United States Ford 148

Index

Villiard, Henry 33, 134–5, 184n

Walker, Francis 85, 134, 175
Walsh, Mike 17
Warren, Craig 181n
Warren, G.K. 76
Weed, Thurlow 8

Welsh, Peter 2
the Wheatfield 156, 158–60
White Oak Bridge 81–2
White Oak Creek 80
White Oak Swamp 113
Whiteford, Edward 151
Williamsburg 62–3, 66, 69, 81

Yorktown 62–3, 93
Young, John 130

Zook, Samuel 123, 159
Zouaves (Meagher's) 20, 30, 38–9, 44, 141

www.ingramcontent.com/pod-product-compliance
Lightning Source LLC
Chambersburg PA
CBHW081557300426
44116CB00015B/2912